intercessory High Priestly ministry in our behalf in the heavenly sanctuary, and expositions of grace and truth within the rest of the New Testament Scriptures (the Books of Acts through Revelation).

In what follows in this treatise, I refer to the five different facets of what Jesus has done or is doing for us (as enumerated above) as the "*five facets of what Jesus has done or is doing for those who (choose to) believe in His name*".[1]

The first four facets of what Jesus has done or is doing for us are "*once for all facets*"; nothing can be added, nothing can be taken away. The only facet that is ongoing is Jesus' role as our great High Priest in the Heavenly Sanctuary - a work that continues until Jesus puts on His kingly robes and sits on the great white throne of judgment at the end of time.[2]

Since *anyone, whosoever,* or *everyone* can make the choice to believe in the name of Jesus, the five facets of what Jesus has done or is doing for those who believe in His name apply to every person in this world within which we live, breathe, move, and have our being.[3]

If the Christian Church takes the message in John 1:17 to heart, every Christian doctrine must have its basis or foundation in the New Testament and must relate to the five facets of what Jesus has done or is doing for those who believe in His name.

Does this imply then that the Old Testament is redundant and of no use whatsoever? Clearly

---

[1] *Sinless Life* - John 1:1; Hebrews 4:14-16
Death on the Cross - Acts 2:22-23; Galatians 3:13-14
Resurrection - Acts 2:24-37; Acts 10:40
Ascension - Acts 1:9; 1 Timothy 3:16
Intercessory Ministry - Hebrews 4:14-16; 1 John 2:1-2
[2] Revelation 20:11-15
[3] John 3:16.

not. First of all, the Apostle Paul states clearly in 1Corinthians chapter 10, verse 11:

> *These things* (recorded in the Old Testament) *happened to them as examples and were written down as warnings for us, on whom the fulfillment of the ages has come.*[4],[5]

Given we are supposed to learn from God's interactions with people in the Old Testament, there must be principles outlined in the Old Testament, which interpreted within the context of the five facets of what Jesus has done or is doing for us, have value for managing relationships, goals or objectives, and interactions within either of spiritual or civil contexts. I have discussed some of these principles in my book titled, *"Truths that Create or Enhance Loving Relationships: The Christian Perspective"*.

In this book, I explore the meaning of John 1:17 and implications of that meaning for practical daily Christian living. In doing so, I need to make clear that in so far as the context of John 1:17 is concerned, grace is *"unmerited favor from God"* and truth is *"a proper understanding of the character of God"*. Romans 5:8 discusses unmerited favor with these words,

---

[4]Words in brackets mine.

[5]Unless stated otherwise, all scripture quotations are from the *New King James Version* (*NKJV*) or *New International Version* (*NIV*) of the Bible. I have switched between these versions to provide renditions of verses that I believe best suit the context of discussions. In all cases, I have ensured the original meaning of verses in question is not sacrificed in achievement of a simpler rendition. I have achieved this by comparing all renditions with the original text as translated in *Young's Literal Translation* (*YLT*) of the Bible. Wherever stated, the acronym *YLT* stands for Young's Literal Translation.

But God demonstrates His own love toward us, in that **while we were still sin-
ners, Christ died for us**.

1John 4:17 states the goal of the Christian life
as follows:

Love has been perfected among us in this:
that we may have boldness in the day of
judgment; because **as He is, so are we
in this world**.

In so far as John 1:17 is concerned, truth and
grace refer to two different aspects of Jesus' ministry in our behalf. In Jesus' sacrifice on the cross,
resurrection from the dead, ascension to heaven,
and High Priestly ministry in our behalf, the unmerited favor of God has been consummated for
man's salvation.

In Jesus' life, God has demonstrated His character - truth - so we have a better understanding
of who He is, and as such can be as He is in this
world. In this regard, Jesus told His disciples in
John 14:9,

Jesus said to him, "Have I been with you
so long, and yet you have not known Me,
Philip? **He who has seen Me has seen
the Father**; so how can you say, 'Show
us the Father'?"

In so far as a proper understanding of what it
means to have faith in the name of Jesus is concerned:

*A proper understanding of grace enables
knowledge of benefits that accrue to us
from Jesus' death, resurrection on the third*

day, ascension to the Father, and inter-cessory ministry in our behalf.

A proper understanding of grace en-ables an appropriate response from us to Jesus' death, resurrection on the third day, ascension to the Father, and inter-cessory ministry in our behalf.

A proper understanding of the character of God as demonstrated in the life or teach-ings of Jesus Christ enables us under-stand who God expects us to be in this world.

In the first two sections of this treatise, I dis-cuss the "*grace*" and "*truth* aspects of the person of Jesus Christ, which we shall see are insepara-ble, within the context of *a practical understanding of the concepts of reconciliation, love, the work of the Holy Spirit, and Victorious Christian Living.* In the third section, I discuss some specific truths that have relevance to this age in which we find ourselves - an age in which there has been an at-tempt to decouple reason from faith. In the final section, I provide eight study guides that illustrate the new commandment from Jesus, which in John 13:34-35 is stated as follows,

A new commandment I give to you, that you love one another, as I have loved you, that you also love one another. By this all will know that you are My disci-ples, if you have love for one another.

Let us go on to know Jesus, God, the Father of our Lord Jesus Christ, and the Holy Spirit. In Jesus Name. Amen.

Oghenovo A. Obrimah, Ph.D.

Part I

Grace, Reconciliation, Love, and the Holy Spirit

CHAPTER 1

The Gift of God

Just about every Christian knows John 3:16 by ~~heart. Many persons who have come in contact~~ with Christianity, but are not Christians know of John 3:16, which says:

> For God so loved the world that He gave
> His only begotten Son that whosoever
> believes in Him should not perish but
> have everlasting life.

A cursory reading of John 3:16 infers that since God gave His Son, His Son is the gift to the world. Throughout the New Testament, however, Jesus is never referred to as God's gift to the world. Rather, it is the grace of God, eternal life, or the Holy Spirit that are referred to as God's gift to the world.

Consider the following passages:

♡ Then Peter said to them, Repent, and let every one of you be baptized in the name of Jesus Christ for the remission of sins; and you shall receive the gift of the Holy Spirit - Acts 2:38

♡ For the wages of sin is death, but the gift of God is eternal life in Christ Jesus our Lord - Romans 6:23

♡ But to each one of us grace was given according to the measure of Christ's gift - Ephesians 4:7

All of the passages outlined above refer to eternal life, grace, or the Holy Spirit as the gift we receive from God or our Lord Jesus Christ.

Consider now Jesus' own words in John 4:10&14,

> Jesus answered and said to her, "If you knew the gift of God, and who it is who says to you, 'Give Me a drink,' you would have asked Him, and He would have given you living water. ...whoever drinks of the water that I shall give him will never thirst. But the water that I shall give him will become in him a fountain of water springing up into everlasting life."

What is this living water that Jesus refers to in the preceding passage from the Book of John? The answer can be found in John 7:37-39 which says:

> On the last day, that great day of the feast, Jesus stood and cried out, saying, "If anyone thirsts, let him come to Me and drink. He who believes in Me, as the Scripture has said, out of his heart

will flow rivers of living water." But this
He spoke concerning the Spirit, whom
those believing in Him would receive; for
the Holy Spirit was not yet given, because Jesus was not yet glorified.

In Jesus' own words, the outcome of belief in
Him is receipt of the gift of the Holy Spirit. When
we receive the Holy Spirit, we receive living water
and become sources of living water or eternal life
to the world.

So is Jesus the gift of God? If we believe Jesus is the gift of God, we have completed our spiritual journey once we acknowledge Him as Lord
and Savior. Jesus Himself says, however, that the
purpose of believing in Him is receipt of the gift of
the Holy Spirit. This means we do not complete our
spiritual journey from sin to God until we ask for
and receive the gift of the Holy Spirit. For practical
purposes then, we must focus on the Holy Spirit as
the gift of God, with Jesus the person who makes
it possible for us to have access to the gift.

In Acts 19:1-7 and Acts 8:14-17, the Apostles
made clear in their actions that until believers in
the name of Jesus Christ received the Holy Spirit,
their spiritual journey to God was incomplete. But
were the Apostles redefining the essence of a Christian's journey. Absolutely not; they simply were
obeying our Lord Jesus Christ who made it clear
the goal of faith in Him is fellowship with the Holy
Spirit; fellowship that produces life - rivers of living water - in this world filled with so much futility,
angst, strife, hatred, and death.

Remark 1 *We have access to the Holy Spirit because Jesus won every battle that man had lost
up until His birth. So the Holy Spirit is Jesus' to*

give through His Father, our Father to everyone and anyone who believes in His name.

Recommended Prayer 1 *Thank you Father of my Lord Jesus Christ for your indescribable and immeasurable gift made possible by the sinless life, death, resurrection on the third day, ascension to heaven, and intercessory ministry of my Lord Jesus Christ. In Jesus Name. Amen.*

CHAPTER 2

The Grace of God

The word "*Grace*" means "*Unmerited Favor*". Since unmerited favor makes possible what would not have been otherwise possible, grace or unmerited favor confers "*power*". When the Scriptures refer to the "grace of God" then, ultimately they are referring to the "power of God".

Romans 1:16 states:

> For I am not ashamed of the gospel of Christ, for it is the *power of God* to salvation for everyone who believes...

So "what" or more appropriately "who" is the power of God? Listen to Jesus' words in Acts 1:8,

> "But you shall receive power when the Holy Spirit has come upon you..."

Remark 2 *The gift of God, the Holy Spirit, brings to us the power of God within the context of the preaching of the gospel of Christ; that is, the preaching of the grace of God. The purpose of the gospel then is access to the Holy Spirit.*

Consider these words in Hebrews 4:14-16,

> Seeing then that we have a great High Priest who has passed through the heavens, Jesus the Son of God, let us hold fast our confession. For we do not have a High Priest who cannot sympathize with our weaknesses, but was in all points tempted as we are, yet without sin. Let us therefore come boldly to the throne of grace, that we may obtain mercy and find grace to help in time of need.

> *These words in the book of Hebrews make very clear grace is received from the throne of God, which is a throne of grace, meaning the foundation of God's character is grace. Praise the Lord!*

When we come boldly to the throne of grace we obtain mercy or forgiveness for our *shortcomings* and help for our time of need. Notice I have used the word *shortcomings* as opposed to the word "sins". Many moral people all over the world do not violate the spirit of the Ten Commandments in the sense that they honor their parents; *do not steal from others*; do not attempt to gain advantage over others by getting them into trouble with false witness; *do not cheat on their spouses*; do not commit murder; *and do not covet anything that belongs to their neighbors.*

But can moral people claim not to have any spiritual shortcomings; shortcomings that have been introduced into the world by sin?

In respect of shortcomings, Romans 3:23 states,

For all have sinned and fall short of the glory (character) of God.[1]

Suppose a man borrows US$1,000,000 with the stipulation or condition that the debt is to be repaid in its entirety with gold that has a value of *US$1,000,000*. Now assume that somehow gold goes out of supply at the time this man is expected to make payment on the debt. If this man brings *US$1,000,000* in silver to the lender as repayment for the debt, can he or she claim not to have any shortcomings in so far as the fulfillment of the debt is concerned? Clearly Not! If the lender accepts payment in silver, this is magnanimity or mercy on the part of the lender.

Attempting to please God with our morality is akin to attempts at repaying in silver - a lower worth metal - a debt that is to be repaid in gold. The beauty of the gospel lies in the fact that God, who alone has gold in abundant supply has paid the debt in our behalf; He demands, however, we ackowledge our inability to pay the debt as stipulated in order for the debt to be totally wiped from our record. When we reject God's offer, we insist He accept our morality (silver) as payment for a debt that requires His righteousness (gold), an offer God cannot accept. Upon acknowledgement of our inability to pay, God bids us buy the gold that

---

[1]Words in brackets mine.

we need from Him (Revelation 3:18) - who alone is the source and origin of true righteousness.

Remark 3 *When man sinned, we lost a quality that was conferred on Adam and Eve before they sinned. There is no amount of morality that can restore this righteous quality. Since the righteous quality is of God, restoration of what was lost is possible only in God. The Father says the path to restoration is by faith in the name of Jesus Christ; that is, faith in the five facets of what Jesus has done or is doing for those who believe in His name.*

In so far as "*help*" is concerned, Jesus promised us a helper who would be with us always. Who is this Helper promised us? John 14:26 states,

> But the Helper, the Holy Spirit, whom the Father will send in My name, He will teach you all things, and bring to your remembrance all things that I said to you.

In the Old Testament, God's throne is referred to as a "*throne of mercy*" or the "*mercy seat*".[2] Since grace is unmerited, clearly grace encompasses mercy. Mercy does not of itself, however, connote or confer power. Since grace brings to us the power of God - the Holy Spirit - grace transcends mercy. So has God been partial? Absolutely Not! Since the Holy Spirit could not be given to everyone until the first four facets of what Jesus has done for us were completed (John 7:37-39), people in the Old Testament only needed mercy; that is were not judged on the basis of their ability to obey; rather, they were judged on the basis of their willingness to

---

[2]Exodus 25:22

obey and willingness to repent of their sins. If the High Priest and supporting priests did not teach the people the word of God, however, since the people did not have access to the Scriptures or the Holy Spirit, spiritual decadence was the natural outcome of this dereliction of duty on the part of the High Priest (2 Chronicles 34:18-21).

Remark 4 *The New Covenant ratified with the blood of Jesus Christ removes man's dependence on other men for knowledge of God and gives us direct access to power that enables righteous living - the Holy Spirit. All of this is made possible by the five facets of what Jesus has done or is doing for those who believe in His name.*

Remark 5 *When we teach one another within the context of Church or commonality of faith in Jesus Christ, the goal always is to direct people's attention to Jesus Christ, the author and finisher of our faith. That is, the goal is to help each other arrive at a better understanding of how to relate with, get to understand or know, and receive power for righteous properous living from the Father of our Lord Jesus Christ.*

> *So how do we receive the Holy Spirit?* Acts 2:38 states:

> Then Peter said to them, Repent, and let every one of you be baptized in the name of Jesus Christ for the remission of sins; and you shall receive the gift of the Holy Spirit.

> In Luke 11:13, Jesus says,

> *If you then, being evil, know how to give good gifts to your children, how much more*

*will your heavenly Father give the Holy
Spirit to those who ask Him!*

In Galatians 3:13-14, we are given the following
promise,

> Christ has redeemed us from the curse
> of the law, having become a curse for
> us (for it is written, "Cursed is everyone
> who hangs on a tree") that the blessing
> of Abraham might come upon the Gen-
> tiles in Christ Jesus, that we might re-
> ceive the promise of the Spirit through
> faith.

Jesus makes very clear in Luke 11:13 that God
already has promised and desires us to have the
Holy Spirit, so all we have to do is ask in order to
receive.

Jesus' words are echoed in 1John 5:14, which
states:

> Now this is the confidence that we
> have in Him, that if we ask anything ac-
> cording to His will (*and He has said it is
> His will for us to have the Holy Spirit*), He
> hears us. And if we know that He hears
> us, whatever we ask, we know that we
> have the petitions that we have asked of
> Him.[3]

Remark 6 *In order to enter into the grace of God
and as a result, receive power from God, we need
to repent of our sins (be willing to live the way God
says is good for us), accept the sacrifice Jesus made
for us on the Cross of Calvary, then ask God for the*

---

[3]Words in brackets mine.

Holy Spirit and believe we have received according to His promise.

Recommended Prayer 2 *Father of my Lord Jesus Christ, I thank you for the blood of Jesus Christ shed on my behalf for forgiveness of my sins. I acknowledge that I am sinful and in need of your salvation, and receive Jesus Christ as my Lord and Savior. Having acknowledged and repented of my sin, and having received Jesus as my Lord and Savior, I ask for the infilling of the Holy Spirit and believe that I receive according to your word. Thank you Father that having received the Holy Spirit, I have power to live right to the praise of the glory of your Holy name. In Jesus Name. Amen.*

CHAPTER 3

Grace, the Holy Spirit, and Love

In Chapter One, we discussed Jesus' pronouncement that rivers of living water would flow out of those who believed in His name.

Jesus made this pronouncement to the crowds of people following Him (John 7:37-39) and also to an audience of one - "the woman by the well" (John 4:10,14). This "*rivers of living water*" concept was so important then, it was fitting for a sermon to a crowd, and fitting for private dialogue with a woman in search of meaning in life. In Chapters One and Two, we established from the Scriptures (Bible) that the phrase "*rivers of living water*" refers to the person of the Holy Spirit.

The question then is:

> What exactly are the rivers of living water that the Holy Spirit makes possible in the life of a Christian?

The answer to this question can be found in Romans 5:1,5 which says:

> Therefore, having been justified by faith, we have peace with God through our Lord Jesus Christ, through whom also we have access by faith into this grace in which we stand, and rejoice in hope of the glory of God. Now hope does not disappoint, because the love of God has been poured out in our hearts by the Holy Spirit who was given to us.

This text says our hope of participating or sharing in the glory of God is sure to be realized because the love of God has been made available to us through the Holy Spirit.

There are two complementary interpretations of "the *love of God*".

Interpretation One: God's Nature

In Romans 8:7-8 Paul states:

> The sinful mind is hostile to God. It does not submit to God's law nor can it do so. Those controlled by the sinful nature cannot please God (*NIV*).

When we receive the Holy Spirit of God, the Holy Spirit changes our hearts such that we have love for God, love for the commandments of God, and love for the things of God. Since the Holy Spirit brings to us the capacity to respond to and love God, the Holy Spirit provides us with power for practical daily Christian living. The grace of God is manifest then in regeneration of our hearts -

regeneration that we do not merit, but has been earned for us via the five facets of what Jesus has done or is doing for those who believe in His name.

This work of the Holy Spirit was foretold in the Old Testament in Ezekiel 36:26, which states:

> I will give you a new heart and put a new spirit within you; I will take the heart of stone out of your flesh and give you a heart of flesh. I will put my Spirit within you and cause you to walk in my statutes, and you will keep my commandments and do them.

Since God is love (1John 4:8), the love we receive through the Holy Spirit enables us to love God and participate in God's glory (become like God); that is, enables us to begin to walk in love.

Remark 7 *The first interpretation of "love of God" is "Capacity to love God and the things of God." It is this capacity that enables us share or participate in the glory of God because "God is love".*

Interpretation Two: Capacity to Love Like Jesus

In 1Corinthians 13:1-3, we cannot please God if we do not have the love of God. In 1John 4:8, *"he who does not love does not know God for God is love."* In Galatians 5:22-23, with the exception of peace and joy, which come from God because,

> the Kingdom of God...is righteousness and peace and joy in the Holy Spirit (Romans 14:17),

every virtue listed as fruit of the Spirit is, as enumerated in 1Corinthians 13:4-8, a characteristic of love.

The two passages in Galatians 5:22-23 (*Galatians*) and 1Corinthians 13:4-8 (*1Corinthians*) mention patience and kindness. Faithfulness in Galatians maps to "Love always protects, always trusts, always hopes, always perseveres" and "Love never fails" in 1Corinthians. Gentleness in Galatians maps to "love is not rude" in 1Corinthians. Self control in Galatians maps to "Love does not envy, does not boast, is not proud, is not easily angered in 1Corinthians. Love in Galatians refers to love of God, the first interpretation of love of God we discussed in this chapter. Given Paul is discussing evidence of love within the context of interactions between people in 1Corinthians, we should not expect the inclusion of love of God in the discussion of attributes of love in 1Corinthians.

In John 13:34-35 Jesus told His disciples,

A new commandment I give to you, that you love one another, as I have loved you, that you also love one another. By this all will know that you are My disciples, if you have love for one another.

In John 13:34-35, Jesus states clearly that He is giving His disciples a new commandment. In stating a new commandment, Jesus is making clear that the old commandment no longer applies.

*But is this new commandment better than
the old?*

The old commandment states in Leviticus 19:18:
"You shall love your neighbor as yourself". Under this commandment, the standard of love is a
flawed human standard. Under this standard, if
a man allows his wife to have sex with men other
than himself, it becomes okay for him to have sex
with another man's wife. Similarly, if a woman allows her husband to have sex with women other
than herself, it becomes okay for her to have sex
with another woman's husband. Why? She has
loved the other man or woman exactly as she has
loved herself. It was to forestall this sort of interpretations of the commandment, *"You shall love
your neighbor as yourself"* that God provided explicit interpretations of Leviticus 19:18 within the
context of the *"Ten Commandments"* listed in the
Old Testament Scriptures (Exodus Chapter 20). In
the Old Testament then, along with all other commandments, the seventh commandment - You shall
not commit adultery (Exodus 20:14) - prevented
perverse interpretations of the commandment, "You
shall love your neighbor as yourself".

Under the new commandment, the standard of
love is the love of God, for which we have the life
and teachings of Jesus and the Apostles as a demonstration. Since love does not envy, is not self seeking, does not delight in evil, and rejoices in the
truth, a Christian cannot make a case for adultery, stealing, false witness, or covetousness to be
permissible under the new covenant. Since love is
not rude and does not delight in evil, a Christian
cannot make a case for dishonoring of their parents.

Once we accept the love of God as the standard

for managing our relationships, all of the explicit commandments that relate to interactions between people in the Ten Commandments automatically come into play. When we come under the new commandment then, we automatically subscribe to the old commandment not because we are under the old commandment, but because the new commandment encompasses all of the character standards embodied in the old commandment.

> I note here that since God does not force Himself on those who choose not to enter into relationship with Him, staying away from those who do not want to develop a relationship with us is a valid Christian response to relationship management, even if these persons are family members. This is why Jesus said in Matthew 12:50, *"For whoever does the will of My Father in heaven is My brother and sister and mother."*

While the new commandment encompasses all of the character standards embodied in the old, it definitely, clearly, and most assuredly surpasses the old in glory. This is the case because in addition to constraining us as to what not to do, the new commandment requires us to be patient, kind, keep no record of wrongs, always protect, always trust, always hope, and always persevere. That is, while commandments five through ten of the Ten

Commandments principally tell us what not to do, the new commandment not only constrains us as to what not to do, it also tells us the things that are expected of us, virtues we attain to with the help of the Holy Spirit. It is because the new commandment surpasses the old in glory that we can be brought out from under the law and domiciled in the grace of God.

> The foregoing establishes the new commandment imposes a greater hurdle on relationships, objectives, goals, or motives of life, and interactions within civil or spiritual contexts. In introducing a new commandment, Jesus is not introducing lawless liberty; rather, He is drawing us closer to God's standard of love.

Remark 8 *The second interpretation of the "love of God" is "Capacity to love one another as Christ has loved us."*

Listen to these words in 2Corinthians 3:7-11,

> *Now if the ministry that brought death, which was engraved in letters of stone, came with glory, so that the Israelites could not look steadily at the face of Moses because of its glory, fading though it was, will not the ministry of the Spirit be even more glorious? If the ministry that condemns men is glorious, how much more glorious is the ministry that brings righteousness! For what was glorious has no glory now in comparison with the surpassing glory. And if what was fading away came with glory, how much greater is the glory of that which lasts! (NIV)*

This text states very clearly and unambiguously that we no longer look to the Ten Commandments for direction in life. Rather, we look for direction from the Holy Spirit, our Helper and Teacher. So far, however, we have only established that "*love of God*" satisfies requirements imposed in the Ten Commandments that relate to interactions between people.

The question then is:

> Is it possible for us to be brought out from under the law without satisfaction of commandments one through four of the Ten Commandments, which relate to our relationship with God?

In their essence, commandments one through four of the Ten Commandments tell us to honor God, the Creator of Heaven and Earth. Now the same God, the Creator of Heaven and Earth has directed that we honor Him by believing in the name of Jesus Christ, His only begotten Son. This means once a person confesses faith in Jesus Christ, he or she immediately and for all time (provided they continue to believe in the name of Jesus Christ) satisfies commandments one through four of the Ten Commandments.

As is the case with commandments that relate to interpersonal relationships, confessing Jesus as Lord and Savior brings us into compliance with commands one through four of the Ten Commandments, yet transcends these commands (as we shall see in later chapters). When we confess faith in the name of Jesus Christ, we declare we have no other God but the Father of our Lord Jesus Christ; we declare the name of Jesus Christ is precious to us; we declare the only image of God is our Lord Jesus Christ; we declare the God who set apart the seventh day for rest, who also is the Father of our Lord Jesus Christ is Creator of heaven and earth. In honor of Him as Creator and so far as it lies within our power, we set apart one day every week to rest from what we do for a living in order to develop our relationship with Him and develop family relationships or friendships. If we all make it our goal to spend one day each week celebrating family, friendship, and the goodness of God, we will have better relationships in this life.

In regard to the entire law given in the Ten Commandments, we see we have been set free so we can participate in the greater glory revealed in the new covenant that has been ratified in the blood of Jesus Christ, blood shed on our behalf for the remission of our sins so we can have fellowship with God through the Holy Spirit whom He has given to us.

Remark 9 *The Ten Commandments were given so man would not be able to find excuses for moral sin during an age within which knowledge of God had been almost totally lost. In the current age, knowledge abounds, particularly within the context of organized society, education, professional ethics, and civil authority, so no one can plead ignorance of requirements of morality - requirements embodied in the Ten Commandments. In the current age, God wants to take man beyond the boundaries of morality to experience the glory of God because **Love encapsulates, but transcends morality.** A man who risks his life to rescue a drowning child is not expressing morality. There is no moral code that demands such actions from such a man. Rather, such a man has expressed the love of God in his or her actions, love that transcends morality, love* that is consistent with the maxim, "You shall love your neighbor as yourself", but that is better reflected in the maxim, "Love one another as I (Christ) have loved you". Growth in love is the evolutionary process that enables man attain loftier heights physiologically, mentally, sociologically, and spiritually, without any degradations in the quality of interactions between men created by God male (man) and female (woman).

Recommended Prayer 3 I thank you Father that I am not under law, but under grace. I recognize Lord Jesus that since the Holy Spirit is a gift I receive from you because I have believed in your name, the love of God can continue to be poured into my heart only if I continue in your grace - the grace of God - and the righteousness that comes by faith. Thank you Father of my Lord Jesus Christ for righteousness, peace, and joy in the Holy Spirit and the Love that changes my heart and enables me love you and my fellow man. In Jesus Name. Amen.

CHAPTER 4

Grace, Reconciliation, & the Holy Spirit

An important conclusion that we arrive at based on discussions so far is:

Remark 10 *Jesus lived, died, resurrected, ascended to His Father, our Father, and intercedes for us so we can receive the gift of the Holy Spirit. When we understand this, we understand the importance of fellowship with the Holy Spirit for practical daily Christian living.*

Romans 8:9 states the importance of the Holy Spirit in this manner:

> *...If anyone does not have the Spirit of Christ, he does not belong to Christ.*

> So how do we know we have the Spirit of Christ?

Well, since the Holy Spirit pours God's love into our hearts such that we love God and our fellow man (male and female),

Remark 11 *The only sure evidence that we have the Spirit of Christ is our capacity or ability to walk in love, with love defined within the context of Jesus' life and teachings, and the life and teachings of the Apostles. The summary definitions of love in 1Corinthians 13:4-8, and fruit of the Spirit in Galatians 5:22-23, which in Chapter Three are shown to be equivalent, apply especially.*

The importance of the "*love of God*" in the life of a Christian is expressed eloquently in 1Corinthians 13:1-3, which says,

> Though I speak with the tongues of men and of angels, but have not love, I have become a sounding brass or a clanging symbal. And though I have the gift of prophecy, and understand all mysteries and all knowledge, and though I have all faith, so that I could remove mountains, but have not love, I am nothing. And though I bestow all my goods to feed the poor, and though I give my body to be burned, but have not love, it profits me nothing.

Within the context of the ministry of Jesus, it is often said Jesus was born so we can receive forgiveness for our sins. This is true and has been enunciated in preceding chapters. If we stop here, however, we miss an important objective of the five facets of what Jesus has done or is doing for those who believe in His name. For ease of recollection, these five facets comprise of what has been accomplished via:

> Jesus' sinless life on earth

> Jesus' death on the Cross

> Jesus' resurrection on the third day

> Jesus' ascension to His Father in Heaven

> Jesus' intercessory ministry on our behalf

In this chapter, I want to make clear that Jesus was not born just so our sins can be forgiven. In doing this, I will arrive at an alternative statement of why Jesus was born that is equivalent to saying:

Jesus lived, died, resurrected, ascended to His Father, our Father, and is interceding for us in the Heavenly sanctuary so we can receive the gift of the Holy Spirit and remain in fellowship with His Father, Himself (Jesus) and the Holy Spirit.

Jesus' life and death: a means to an end

Remark 12 *If Jesus was born just so our sins can be forgiven, only His life on earth and His death on the Cross would be necessary.*

By living a sinless life and paying the price for ours sins via His death on the Cross, Jesus would succeed where Adam failed, meaning His righteousness could be credited to our accounts. Since all that is required for our sins to be forgiven is the payment of our debt - death - and credits of the righteousness of God for our shortcomings, only Jesus' life on earth and death on the Cross are necessary to facilitate the remission or forgiveness of our sins. So while the forgiveness of ours sins is a critical component of our salvation, it is a means to an end, not an end in of itself.

Jesus' resurrection: a means to an end

Remark 13 *If Jesus was born just so He can save us from our sins, only His life on earth, His death on the Cross, and His resurrection on the third day would be necessary.*

Jesus via His resurrection on the third day demonstrated He has power to give life to whatever is dead within His creation. Listen to these words in Romans 6:1-4,

> *What shall we say then? Shall we continue in sin that grace may abound?*

*Certainly not! How shall we who died
to sin live any longer in it? Or do you
not know that as many of us as were
baptized into Christ Jesus were baptized
into His death? Therefore we were buried
with Him through baptism into death, that
just as Christ was raised from the dead
by the glory of the Father, even so we also
should walk in newness of life.*

The preceding text makes clear the resurrection
of Jesus Christ from the dead is the assurance God
has provided us that we can overcome sins and
weaknesses. So when a Christian believes He can
overcome sins and weaknesses, this faith is rooted
in what God has already done; that is, is rooted in
a definable event or demonstration of God's power
or deity, and cannot be regarded as mere philo-
sophical thought or positive Chrisitian thinking.
Since the objective of *"newness of life"* is demonstrated and made possible by the resurrection of
Jesus Christ from the dead, there must be additional reasons for Jesus' ascension to the Father
and His intercessory ministry in our behalf in the
heavenly sanctuary.

Remark 14 *Our faith in God that "we are a new
creation in Jesus Christ" is not a demonstration of
positive Christian thinking and is not mere philo-
sophical thought or aspiration. On the contrary, our
faith is rooted in a definable event, that is, the resurrection of our Lord Jesus Christ from the dead in
the power of the eternal Spirit of God. Yes, we walk
by faith, but it is not faith in abstract thought, philosophy, or visions, it is faith that is rooted in what
God has done or accomplished within the context of
the history of man on earth.*

Jesus' ascension: a means to an end

While Jesus' resurrection ensures we can walk in newness of life; that is, have power to overcome sin and weaknesses, it was not sufficient to acquire for us the gift of the Holy Spirit. Stated somewhat differently, while Jesus' resurrection brings power to overcome sin, since it was not sufficient to bring us into fellowship with the Holy Spirit, it was not sufficient to enable us know God.

How do we know this? In John 16:7, Jesus told His disciples plainly,

> Nevertheless I tell you the truth, it is to your advantage that I go away; for if I do not go away, the Helper will not come to you; but if I depart (to be with my Father), I will send Him to you.[1]

> *So why did Jesus have to ascend to heaven to be with His Father, our Father before we could receive the Holy Spirit?*

The first reason is a very simple administrative rationale, which is:

Order

Throughout the history recorded in the Old and New Testaments, only one of the Father, Son, and Holy Spirit takes the stage as our primary focus at any given point in time. In the Old Testament, man is primarily engaged in interactions with the

---

[1]Words in brackets mine.

Father of our Lord Jesus Christ, with supporting cameos from Jesus (the Son of God) and the Holy Spirit. In the Gospels (Matthew, Mark, Luke, and John), man is primarily engaged in interactions with Jesus Christ, with supporting cameos from the Father of our Lord Jesus Christ and the Holy Spirit. In the post-Gospels age, man is primarily engaged in interactions with the Holy Spirit, who brings to us the fellowship of the Father and the Son. Since in this age, the Holy Spirit brings us into fellowship with Jesus Christ and the Father of our Lord Jesus Christ, this age is blessed beyond every other age since creation. It is to this honor of fellowship with Father, Son, and Holy Spirit that the Apostle Paul alludes in the following statement recorded in Ephesians 2:17-18,

> And He (**Jesus**) came and preached peace to you who were afar off and to those who were near. For through Him we both have access by one **Spirit** to the **Father**.

Remark 15 *We need to believe in the name of Jesus Christ to receive the Holy Spirit, so we can have fellowship with our Father, the Father of our Lord Jesus Christ. In aggregate then, we have fellowship with Father, Son, and Holy Spirit. No other age since creation has had the opportunity to be in fellowship with Father, Son, and Holy Spirit at the same time. Truly, we are blessed with all spiritual blessings in heavenly places in Christ Jesus (Ephesians 1:3).*

The second rationale for Jesus' ascension to be with the Father is a profound spiritual rationale, which is:

Prevention of Idolatry

Jesus ascended to the Father so the Father could remain the focus of our worship. Since we cannot now see either of the Father or the Son in a physical sense, we are not inclined to substitute worship of the Son for worship of the Father. If Jesus had remained on earth, the fact that God essentially is with us in a physical sense would make us focus on worshipping Jesus to the exclusion of the Father. The command from God, however, is embodied in these words by Jesus in John 5:22-23,

> For the Father judges no one, but has committed all judgment to the Son, that all should honor the Son just as they honor the Father. He who does not honor the Son does not honor the Father who sent Him.

If Jesus had remained on earth after His resurrection, it would be difficult for us to look past Him to the Father, because it would be more comforting to take a trip to see Jesus than to pray to a Father whom we cannot see or touch in a physical sense. In order for our worship to be directed to both the Father and the Son and not the Son only, it was imperative that Jesus ascend to be with His Father, our Father. Since the Holy Spirit is Spirit, we cannot idolize the Holy Spirit in the place of Jesus Christ or the Father. God's wisdom is manifest, however, in that fellowship with the Holy Spirit brings us into fellowship with both the Father and the Son.

Since there will not be sin in the new heavens and new earth, there would not be any problems for which we need to journey to the throne of God in order to obtain solutions. When Jesus sets up His throne on the new earth, we are in fellowship with God and do not relate to God on the basis of needs or wants. Our entire focus is on our relationship with God. In the new earth, there is no incentive or room for idolatrous worship of Jesus to the detriment of God, the Father of our Lord Jesus Christ. In a world filled with sin and problems, however, it would be much easier to go to Jerusalem to ask Jesus for a miracle or solution to problems than to pray and have faith for the same miracle or solution.

Jesus' Intercessory Ministry

Finally, what is the relevance of Jesus' ministry in the heavenly sanctuary for those who believe in His name?

Listen to these words in Hebrews 10:19-23, and 9:13-14

Therefore, brethren having boldness to enter the Holiest by the blood of Jesus, by a new and living way which He consecrated for us, through the veil, His flesh, and having a High Priest over the house of God (who Himself is in the Holiest - Hebrews 9:11-12), let us draw near with a true heart in full assurance of faith, having our hearts sprinkled from an evil conscience and our bodies washed with pure water. Let us hold fast the confession of our hope without wavering, for He who promised is faithful.[2]

For if the blood of bulls and goats and the ashes of a heifer, sprinkling the unclean sanctifies for the purifying of the flesh, how much more shall the blood of Christ, who through the eternal Spirit offered Himself without spot to God, cleanse your conscience from dead works to serve the living God?

Remark 16 *In Jesus Christ, God bids us come into the Holiest (Most Holy Place) where He Himself and the Lord Jesus Christ are so we can be purified from our sins. This imagery is of extreme importance because it means absent fellowship with the Father and the Son, which is possible only through fellowship with the Spirit, Jesus is unable to apply His blood for the cleansing of our conscience; cleansing that enables us become more sensitive to what is right and what is wrong, and enables us develop a relationship with the living God.*

Now consider these words in 2Corinthians 5:16-18, and 1John 3:2-3,

So from now on we regard no one from a worldly point of view. Though we once

---

[2]Words in brackets mine.

regarded Christ in this way, we do so no longer. Therefore if anyone is in Christ, he is a new creation; the old has gone, the new has come! All this is from God, *who reconciled us to himself through Christ,* and gave us the ministry of reconciliation.

Beloved, now we are children of God; and it has not yet been revealed what we shall be, but we know that when He is revealed, we shall be like Him, for we shall see Him as He is. And everyone who has this hope in Him purifies himself, just as He is pure.

The preceding two texts from the Bible talk about what we will be and our spiritual nature; that is, demonstrate a Christian not only has power to overcome sins and weaknesses, but also has power to

| become | a new creation in a spiritual sense.

Remark 17 *While Jesus' resurrection brings the power to live right, only fellowship with the Holy Spirit brings to us the power that enables us "**become**".*[3] *Becoming requires reconciliation with God.*

Remark 18 *Jesus' ministry in the heavenly sanctuary completes the Father's purpose of reconciliation between man and God. Since no one can know the thoughts or the mind of God without the Spirit of God (1 Corinthians 2:9-12), we cannot be reconciled to God without His Spirit in us. In the cleansing of our sins and consciences, and body, God reconciles*

---

[3]For more on becoming and how it differs from overcoming, go to Chapter 6.

us to Himself, His thoughts, His ways, and His purposes.

> *Jesus lived, died, resurrected, ascended to His Father, our Father, and is interceding for us in the Heavenly sanctuary so we can be reconciled to the Father.*

Analogy

Suppose a man falls into a drug habit, gets convicted by civil authorities and serves time for drug possession. On release from prison, this man's father ensures he is fully rehabilitated, puts in motion processes that make it possible for his son's mistakes to be wiped out of his civil record, and provides his son with every resource needed in order for him to be able to live right. Suppose this son lives right; that is, takes advantage of all of the resources his father has placed at his disposal. Does this imply restoration of the relationship between this father and son? Absolutely Not! It is not the resources that enable reconciliation. It is the time spent together by father and son within the context of forgiveness of imperfections and desire for reconciliation that enables renewal of their relationship. The life, death, and resurrection of Jesus Christ provide us with the resources we need in order to live right. **If we do not, however, enter the Holiest in order to develop relationship with our Father, we will never experience reconciliation.** Since we cannot have any real communion with God without His Spirit, Jesus' ascension to the Father, which makes possible our receipt of the Holy Spirit is crucial for our reconciliation to

God. Without reconciliation we cannot become because we never are able to find out the heart of
God concerning our lives.

Our part in the reconciliation process

1John 3:2-3 says we need to purify ourselves.
Hebrews 10:19-23 bids us come into the Holiest
place by faith so Jesus can apply His blood and
thereby cleanse us from our sins so we can live a
life that pleases Him. Combined, both verses indi-
cate our part is to come into fellowship with God,
having faith in the life giving power demonstrated
in the resurrection of Jesus Christ from the dead.
God's part is the cleansing of our body, soul, and
spirit from sin so we can live right.

1John 1:5-7 corroborates as follows:

> This is the message which we have
> heard from Him and declare to you, that
> God is light and in Him is no darkness
> at all. If we say that we have fellow-
> ship with Him, and walk in darkness we
> lie and do not practice the truth. But
> if we walk in the light as He is in the
> light, we have fellowship with one an-
> other and the blood of Jesus Christ His
> Son cleanses us from all sin.

What is this light that John refers to:

> Your word is a lamp to my feet and a
> light to my path - Psalm 119:105.

We demonstrate faith in God by choosing deliberately to walk in the light; that is, by applying

the teachings of Jesus Christ, which have been ex-
pounded upon by the Apostles, to our lives and
desiring to make changes as necessary or implied
by the word of God. This means we devote some
of our time to fellowship with God (talking with or
to God, studying the Bible to know more of God,
and fellowship with other believers either in person, online, or via the reading of expository works
on the gospel that have been inspired by the Holy
Spirit) in order to experience the cleansing power
available to us in the blood of Jesus Christ. The
fellowship works so long as we have or maintain
faith in God's power to make us a new creation in
Jesus Christ.

The question is:

> Would God be just or impartial or non-
> hypocritical if He revealed Himself to peo-
> ple who profess faith in Jesus Christ but
> do not have any respect for the written
> word of God within the sense of obedi-
> ence to the written word? If Jesus is the
> Word of God personified (John 1:1), how
> can we expect to have fellowship with Him
> in a real sense if we have no desire or do
> not exercise any effort to obey the written
> word He personifies?

Concerning this, Jesus Himself declares the following in John 13:34-35; John 14:15; and John
14:21&23,

> A new commandment I give to you,
> that you love one another, as I have loved
> you, that you also love one another. By
> this all will know that you are My disci-
> ples, if you have love for one another.

If you love me, keep my commandments.

He who has my commandments and keeps them, it is he who loves Me. And he who loves Me will be loved by My Father, and I will love him and manifest Myself to him. Jesus answered and said to him, "If anyone loves Me, he will keep my word; and My Father will love him, and We will come to him and make Our home with him."

Remark 19 *If we have no desire to walk in love and do not exercise any effort to walk in love in the power of the Holy Spirit, Jesus makes it very clear we will never have personal revelations of Himself or of His Father. There is no middle ground here. There is only room for obedience and revelational knowledge or disobedience and continuation in revelational darkness.*

Remark 20 *When we receive Jesus Christ, we become eligible to receive the Holy Spirit who pours the love of God - ability or capacity to love God into our hearts. This same love of God translates into ability to love our fellow man (male and female). The ability or capacity to love God is the beginning of our reconciliation to God. Reconciliation does not actually occur, however, if we do not enter into fellowship with the Father, Son, and Holy Spirit so we can be cleansed of our sins and receive a nature that delights in fellowship with and service to God. In order to be reconciled, we must believe that what God says is good, is good. We must also believe that what God says is not good for us, ultimately is bad for us. We conclude then that Jesus was born so we can receive the Holy Spirit, or equivalently, so we can be reconciled to God.*

But do we fret over our fallen state (sins) or our weaknesses (imperfections that may not necessarily be sin)? Absolutely Not! We focus on our fellowship with the Holy Spirit, repenting of sins or weaknesses as the Holy Spirit brings them to our notice, overcoming in the power of the Holy Spirit by confession of who we are in Jesus Christ, declarations of the victory won for us via the shedding of the blood of Jesus, and receipt of grace appropriate to our needs. If we focus on our sins or weaknesses, instead of our lives revolving around our fellowship with Jesus Christ, our lives revolve around overcoming sins and weaknesses, in essence, a focus on ourselves instead of a focus on Jesus Christ.

Using the imagery of a race, Hebrews 12:1-2 summarizes the reconciliation process as follows:

> Therefore we also, since we are surrounded by so great a cloud of witnesses, let us lay aside every weight, and the sin which so easily ensnares us *(let us believe God as to what is good and what is evil)* and **let us run with endurance the race that is set before us, looking unto Jesus**, the author and finisher of our faith, who for the joy that was set before Him endured the cross, despising the shame, and has sat down at the right hand of the throne of God.[4]

Remark 21 *Belief or faith in the name of Jesus Christ means belief or faith in the five facets of what Jesus has done or is doing for those who receive Him.*

---

[4]Words in brackets mine.

Recommended Prayer 4 *Thank you Father of my Lord Jesus Christ that I am reconciled to you through the five facets of what Jesus has done or is doing for me, facets that make it possible for me to receive the baptism of the Holy Spirit. By your grace, I submit to the cleansing power in the blood of Jesus Christ and the word of God so I can be at every moment reconciled to you, walk in newness of life, and experience victory over lusts that are in the world to the glory of your Holy Name. Thank you for inviting me into the Holiest so I can be fully reconciled with and develop a new and living relationship with you, my Lord Jesus Christ and the Holy Spirit. Thank you for entrusting this ministry of reconciliation to all of us who have believed in the name of Jesus Christ and thank you for righteousness, peace, and joy in the Holy Spirit. In Jesus Name. Amen.*

CHAPTER 5

The "laver" and the Christian Race

I prefer the scripturally sound *reconciliation* terminology because it keeps our attention on our relationship with God. The reconciliation terminology embeds sanctification (2Peter 3:18), but keeps our focus on the objective of sanctification, which is deeper fellowship with Father, Son, and Holy Spirit.

In the preceding chapter, the *reconciliation process*, which also is commonly referred to as the *sanctification process* is depicted as a race in which Jesus Christ is the prize (Hebrews 12:1-2).

In a sprint race, such as the Olympic 100 metres, athletes pretty much try to run at their fastest speed from the beginning to the end of the race. In long distance races, such as the Olympic 5,000 metres, however, athletes alter their speed and their gait over the entire course of the race because having reserves of energy for a short sprint towards the end of the race is significantly important for winning the race.

Jesus' words in John 17:1-3 are consistent with the depiction of the reconciliation process as a race.

Jesus spoke these words, lifted up
His eyes to heaven, and said, "Father,

43

the hour has come. Glorify Your Son, that Your Son also may glorify You, as You have given Him authority over all flesh, that He should give eternal life to as many as You have given Him. *And this is eternal life, that they may know You, the only true God, and Jesus Christ whom You have sent.*

So why is the analogy of a race appropriate?

Because it takes time to get to know a person.

In order to get to know a person, we first

get acquainted with the person | then we

endeavor to spend time with the person.

Using knowledge acquired within the course of interactions with that person, we next

attempt to understand the person.

When our attempts at understanding the person prove successful, we begin to feel we

know the person

Given there are at least four stages in the "*getting to know*" process, clearly the *getting to know* process is more like a long distance race than a sprint. In so far as Jesus and the Father are concerned, the getting to know process is a reconciliation process because our relationship with God was broken when man sinned in the Garden of Eden (Genesis Chapter 3). Within the context of our discussions, what is most important about man's sin is that it was rooted in lack of faith that whatever God says is good for us is good, and whatever God says is bad for us is to be avoided.

So why should we trust God concerning His boundaries? In so far as historical reasons are concerned,

For more on historical reasons for trusting God, see Chapter 17.

○ We should trust God because Jesus' life is a fact of history that is evident in dating nomenclature, with time before the birth of Christ denoted *BC*, and time after the birth of Christ denoted *AD*.

○ We should trust God because the beauty of Jesus' character as depicted in the Bible is not contested.

○ We should trust God because all historians (e.g. Josephus, the most trusted historian of Jewish Antiquities) agree Jesus did many supernatural works of healing while He was on earth.

○ We should trust God because as implied in the Bible Israel is regarded by reputable historians as one of the ancient civilizations, with mention of Hebrews or Israel first appearing in third party (extra biblical) sources during the period, 1550 to 1400 BC.[1]

---

[1]Source: Hallo, W.W., 2015, "Ancient Near East," in *The*

With respect to spiritual or relationship based
reasons,

✠ We should trust God because in Jesus Christ
He stooped down from heaven to share our
pain, pain we caused ourselves via disobedience in the Garden of Eden.

✠ We should trust God because He not only shared
our pain, He provided a solution to our pain -
reconciliation through Jesus Christ, and access to the Holy Spirit.

✠ We should trust God because the boundaries
He has set demonstrate He desires societies
within which people do not infringe on other
people's rights or privileges, and societies within
which gains accumulated from legitimate productive activities are protected.

✠ We should trust God because in this world,
we have more than enough evidence that while
love always builds up, hatred always tears
down the fabric of society. Since God's objective is to fill us with love, we should trust
God.

✠ We should trust God because disappointments
experienced in interactions with those who
claim to believe in God are not evidence that
God is not true; rather, they are evidence that
not everyone who claims to believe in Jesus
Christ fully understands what that means, or
sincerely believes in the grace of God. I have
written this treatise to help Christians and

History of The World: Earliest Times to The Present Day, John
Whitney Hall (ed.), World Publications Group, Bridegewater MA
USA.

seekers of truth who are not Christians better understand what it means to believe in the
name of Jesus Christ.

The Laver of Water and the Christian Race

In the Old Testament (Exodus 40:6-15, 30-32),
priests ministering to God in behalf of the people
had to wash themselves with water from a laver before they could enter into the presence of God. In
John 13:10, Jesus told His disciples that a person
who is already clean need only wash their feet. In
the washing of the feet then, the priests proclaimed
that while they were already clean, they were still
in need of some washing. The washing off of dirt
from the priests' hands signified the requirement
that the hands being lifted up to God in the service of the sanctuary were "holy hands" (1 Timothy
2:8).

Remark 22 *Only Christians who regard themselves
as already clean, yet still in need of cleansing in the
sense that there likely are things in their lives that
require cleansing of which they are not yet aware,
can be fully reconciled to God.*

So what does this water for cleansing signify?
Consider these words in Ephesians 5:25-26,

Husbands love your wives, just as Christ
loved the church and gave himself up for
her to make her holy, cleansing her by
the washing of water through the word.

The preceding text makes very clear it is the word of God that we utilize in the washing of our hands - what we do - and our feet - the direction of our lives. This is made very clear in Hebrews 4:12, which states:

> For the word of God is living and powerful, and sharper than any two-edged sword piercing even to the division of soul and spirit, and of joints and marrow, and is a discerner of the thoughts and intents of the heart.

Remark 23 *If we are to enter into the Most Holy or Holiest place as discussed in the preceding chapter, we must be willing to allow God wash us with His word. Our part is the willingness to be washed and to do whatever God requires of us so the effects of the washing can be actualized in our lives. If we do not study or come into contact with the word of God, we cannot be washed with the word by God.*

My Experience with the word of God

Sometime between the completion of High School (Secondary School) education in 1989 and commencement of college education in 1990, I received Jesus Christ as Lord and Savior. Immediately, I experienced the joy of the Lord and the love of God and began to study and teach from the Bible.[2]

---

[2] Looking back now at how much I did not know, it is a wonder God allows us as young Christians to be so filled with the Holy Spirit we feel confident sharing the little knowledge we have at a time when we are just beginning to get to know Jesus as Lord and Savior.

Over the course of the next 20 years, with the exception of the Book of Revelation, I read all of the New Testament Scriptures at least 6 times, and the Gospels (Matthew, Mark, Luke, and John) about 10 times. With the exception of the Book of Ezekiel, I have read the Old Testament scriptures through at least 4 times. While this amount of study may not seem much of an accomplishment to those who believe in reading the Bible through every year, I confess the Holy Spirit has never allowed me to approach the study of the word of God with the objective of yearly completion in mind.

Over the course of 20 years (commencing 1990), there were days I came away from the word of God with deep revelations. Those days were significantly outnumbered, however, by days on which I left the study of the word only with the satisfaction that I had done what God expected of me in order to be washed with the word.

Starting about 2010, all of a sudden the word began to come alive in my spirit. When I studied the word of God, it was as if the word in me was interacting with the written word. I was so filled with the word of God the Holy Spirit began telling me *"the word is in you now; at this point in time, I want you to focus on living out the word that is already in you."*

> Is this outcome of the study of the word of God biblical? Absolutely!

John 1:1 tells us Jesus is the Word of God personified. Now listen to these words in Colossians 1:27 and Galatians 2:20,

> *To them God willed to make known what are the riches of the glory of this mystery*

*among the Gentiles: which is Christ in
you, the hope of glory.*

I have been crucified with Christ; *it is
no longer I who live, but Christ who lives
in me;* and the life which I now live in
the flesh I live by faith in the Son of God,
who loved me and gave Himself for me.

Remark 24 *The word of God enables us get ac-
quainted with God. The study of the word of God
provides us the opportunity to spend time with God,
and generates insights that enable us begin to understand God. At the end of it all, we get to know
God and have fellowship with Father, Son, and Holy
Spirit (eternal life). Once we have fellowship with
Father, Son, and Holy Spirit, the study of the word
becomes part of our fellowship with God.*

Remark 25 *The word of God enables Christ, the
one to whom all of the word testifies, to be formed in
us (Galatians 4:19). Since Jesus is the Word of God,
the word in us that has become part of us interacts
with the written word.*

Why am I providing this revelation of myself?

*I have come to the realization that if
we would patiently continue in the word
of God, thanking God on days we receive
some deep revelation, and trusting Him
on days during which we only have the
comfort of obedience, the day will come
when we will be so filled with the word of
God, the word will come alive in us. Why
does the word come alive eventually? Because regardless of whether we receive*

> some deep revelation or not, whenever
> we study the word, the word is implanted
> in our spirit for the salvation of our souls.
> When the implanting becomes sufficient
> for its purpose, Christ is formed in us, the
> entire word comes alive in us, and we
> enter into the most **exhilarating, inde-**
> **scribable, unfathomable fellowship** with
> the Father, Son, and Holy Spirit.

My journey to this state of blessedness in Jesus Christ took about 20 years. Yours need not take that long. If you resist truths revealed to you by the Holy Spirit, however, this will lengthen your journey. I pray you will take to heart these words in James 1:21,

> Therefore lay aside all filthiness and over-
> flow of wickedness, and receive with meek-
> ness the implanted word, which is able
> to save your souls.

Recommended Prayer 5 *Father, I ask for the grace to come to your word with meekness, receiving the word with the goal of obeying the word. I believe that as I receive your word into my spirit, the day will come when your word will come alive in me and usher me into a more blessed state of fellow-ship with you, my Lord Jesus Christ and the Holy Spirit. In Jesus name. Amen.*

CHAPTER 6

The Purpose of Grace

In relation to our condition prior to receiving the "grace of God", "unmerited favor", or, equivalently, the "power of God", since Jesus came to save us from our sins, an important objective of the grace of God is

> "power to live right relative to what our Lord Jesus Christ defines to be right or righteous living".

This implies the grace of God affects our decisions, our actions, and our choices. But is this all there is to the grace of God? Thankfully not. John 1:12-13 states:

> But as many as received Him (Jesus Christ), to them He gave the right to become children of God, to those who believe in His

name: who were born, not of blood, nor
of the will of the flesh, nor of the will of
man, but of God.[1]

The King James Version (KJV) of the Bible translates the word right as "*power*". Since rights confer power in well functioning societies, the word
power is appropriate in John 1:12. Taken in context, John 1:12 says part of the purpose of grace is
to enable us "become" in a spiritual sense.

Consider these words in 1Corinthians 15:47-
49, & 2Corinthians 3:18:

> The first man (Adam) was of the earth,
> made from dust; the second Man is the
> Lord from heaven (Jesus Christ). As was
> the man of dust, so also are those who
> are made of dust; and as is the heavenly
> Man, so also are those who are heavenly.
> And as we have borne the image of the
> man of dust, we shall also bear the im-
> age of the heavenly man.[2]
>
> And we, who with unveiled faces all
> reflect the Lord's glory, are being trans-
> formed into his likeness with ever in-
> creasing glory, which comes from the Lord,
> who is the Spirit.

The preceding two verses make clear the Holy
Spirit not only empowers us as regards choices,
decisions, or actions, but in a spiritual sense also
transforms us into the likeness of Jesus Christ.
Since man was created in the image of God at the
beginning, and since Jesus Christ is the express
image of God, transformation into the likeness of

---

[1] Words in brackets mine.
[2] Ibid.

Jesus Christ restores the image of God in man (both male and female). Since restoration of the image of God enables us achieve our highest purposes on earth in so far as the things of this life are concerned - marriage, profession, fatherhood, motherhood etc. - it is to our advantage to allow the Holy Spirit transform us into the likeness of Jesus Christ.

So what is our part to play in this transformation process:

- ꙮ We need to keep our eyes focused on Jesus - Hebrews 12:1-2

- ꙮ We need to have our minds renewed - Romans 12:2

So how do we renew our minds? Colossians 3:10 and 2Peter 3:18 state:

> ...put on the new self (new person that you have become in Jesus Christ), *which is being renewed in knowledge* in the image of its Creator (*NIV*).[3]
> ...*grow in the grace and knowledge* of our Lord and Savior Jesus Christ.

The immediately preceding two texts show very clearly that knowledge is a critical component of our transformation into the likeness of Jesus Christ. Since knowledge without ability to actualize the knowledge is meaningless, we need to grow in grace or power or ability in order for the growth to be realized in our lives.

Remark 26 *For a young Christian, the most important sources of knowledge of Jesus Christ are the New Testament Scriptures.*

---

[3]Ibid.

The reason why it is recommended that Christians read the Bible everyday is because this is the primary medium, outside of revelations we receive via direct interaction with the Holy Spirit, through which we acquire knowledge of Jesus Christ, knowledge without which we cannot be transformed into the likeness of Jesus Christ. Combined with the power we have received through the Holy Spirit, knowledge of Jesus Christ enables us to grow and be transformed into the likeness of Christ.

A word of caution on growth in Jesus Christ is necessary to ensure we realize the pace of growth is entirely up to our Lord Jesus Christ, who understands best the appropriate timing of events in our spiritual lives. Using the analogy that Jesus is the Head of His Church, with the Church as His body (Colossians 1:18), Colossians 2:19 states:

> Let no one cheat you of your reward, taking delight in false humility and worship of angels, intruding into those things which he has not seen, vainly puffed up by his fleshly mind, and not holding fast to the Head, from whom all the body, nourished and knit together by joints and ligaments, **grows with the increase that is from God**.

In our fellowship with God, we must never forget our growth in Jesus Christ, equivalently, the pace of our transformation into the likeness of Jesus Christ comes from God. Yes, we need to acquire knowledge of Jesus Christ from the study of the Bible, the reading or study of good books on spirituality, participation in fellowship with other believers within the context of church services etc. Ultimately, however, the pace of growth and the timing of growth belong to God. Since He loves us, any delay in actualization of growth is for our benefit and the benefit of the Church.

God already demonstrated this principle in so far as the timing of the birth of Jesus Christ is concerned. Galatians 4:4-5 states:

> **But when the time had fully come**, God sent his Son, born of a woman, born under law, to redeem those under law, that we might receive the full rights of sons.

This text shows the Jews waited for the manifestation of the Son of God for many years before He actually arrived in the person of Jesus Christ. So why does growth not happen at the earliest possible time we think we are ready for it? Because God fits us into His purposes on earth as part of His church; that way the growth we achieve embeds purpose and is in step with whatever God is doing in His Church. Ephesians 2:19-22 states:

> Now therefore, you are no longer strangers and foreigners, but fellow citizens with the saints and members of the household of God, having been built on the foundation of the apostles and prophets, Jesus Christ Himself being the chief cornerstone, **in whom the whole building, being fitted together, grows into a holy temple in the Lord**, in whom you also are being built together for a dwelling place of God in the Spirit.

Since we all are fitted together, each believer's growth is not independent of the growth of other

believers. Note, however, that this growth is not a
church organization growth because the reality is
God relates to us as believers, not as denominational believers. Suppose, however, the lead pastor or archbishop of a denomination puts together
a spiritual plan for people in his denomination under the guidance of the Holy Spirit. Would God
bless and be part of such a plan? Absolutely! Ultimately, however, the church is a spiritual entity,
as opposed to a physical denominational entity.
The spiritual nature of the church is enunciated
in the immediately preceding verse, which states
categorically the church is a dwelling place of God
in the Spirit. Since each believer is expected to
be filled with the Holy Spirit, this imagery is consistent with the purpose of God as has been discussed in preceding chapters.

The spiritual nature of the Church

The spiritual nature of the church is perhaps
best enunciated in these words from Philippians
3:20 and Hebrews 12:22-24,

> For **our citizenship is in heaven**, from
> which we also eagerly wait for the Savior,
> the Lord Jesus Christ, who will trans-
> form our lowly body that it may be con-
> formed to His glorious body, according
> to the working by which He is able even
> to subdue all things to Himself.
> But you have come to Mount Zion and
> to the city of the living God, the heav-
> enly Jerusalem, to an innumerable com-
> pany of angels, to the general assembly

and church of the firstborn who are registered in heaven, to God the Judge of
all, to the spirits of just men made perfect, to Jesus the Mediator of the new
covenant, and to the blood of sprinkling
that speaks better things than that of
Abel.

The first text states clearly our citizenship is in
heaven. So why are we here on earth? We are here
on earth to demonstrate the love and wisdom of
God to the world so others also can come to believe
in Jesus Christ as Lord and Savior. We are here
to demonstrate to the world that God's thoughts
and ways, which have become our thoughts and
our ways are better than any alternative man can
conceive.
Ephesians 3:10 states,

...that now the manifold wisdom of
God might be made known by the church
to the principalities and powers in heavenly places, according to the eternal purpose which He accomplished in Christ
Jesus our Lord, in whom we have boldness and access with confidence through
faith in Him.

While we remain on earth physically until the
Second Coming of our Lord Jesus Christ, spiritually we are citizens of heaven and are in fellowship with every spiritual entity in the kingdom of
God, which of course includes our Father (the living God), angels, the general assembly and church
of the firstborn registered in heaven (every other
living believer whose name is written in the book
of life - Revelation 21:27), the spirits of just men

made perfect (believers that have died physically but whose spirits or life are in Jesus Christ - Colossians 3:1-4), Jesus Christ, and the blood of Jesus Christ without which we cannot be cleansed of our sins.

Remark 27 *God expects us to grow in the grace and knowledge of our Lord Jesus Christ by allowing our minds to be renewed such that we love God's thoughts, Gods' ways, and Gods' definitions of what constitutes righteous living. Since God seeks to sync our growth with those of other believers such that our contribution to His kingdom incorporates some uniqueness, the pace of our growth and the nature of our growth is of God.*

Recommended Prayer 6 *Lord Jesus Christ, thank you for preserving your inspired word - the Bible - to make it easier for me to get to know you and your Father, my Father, Creator of heaven and earth. I thank you for every work inspired by the Holy Spirit that enables me acquire a better understanding of you and for bringing me into fellowship with every other citizen of your Kingdom. I confess according to your promise that study of your word transforms me into your likeness for my edification and for the glory of your holy name. Thank you for the Holy Spirit who reveals you and the Father to me. I trust you for the pace and timing of my transformation even as I continue in your word. All of this I pray in the name that is above all other names, the name of my Lord Jesus Christ. In Jesus Name. Amen.*

CHAPTER 7

Something More

One of the secrets to happiness in life is always having something to look forward to in the future. If two people are in a happy marriage, anticipation of birthdays, anniversaries, special dates, holidays, vacations, celebrations of children's achievements etc. give meaning to life alongside professional or spiritual objectives yet to be achieved. This is one of the most important reasons for the institution of marriage, which is companionship that gives meaning to life. In the absence of a happy marriage or within the context of being single, life has meaning within the context of professional, social, or spiritual objectives yet to be attained.

In the preceding chapter, we discussed how as we grow in the grace and knowledge of Jesus Christ, we become like Jesus Christ in character. Since this is the ultimate spiritual achievement on this earth, in the absence of some other objective, we would not have anything to look forward to that gives additional meaning to our relationship with God the Father, Son, and Holy Spirit. The Father of our Lord Jesus Christ has rather very wisely ensured we do not have any such vacuum in our spiritual lives. This He has achieved by promising us two very special rewards for receiving Jesus Christ into our hearts.

New heavens and a New Earth

The first reward the Father has promised us is:

New heavens and a new earth within which there is no sin, within which we have glorious bodies and are in physical proximity to our Lord Jesus Christ.

In this regard, we have the following words in Revelation 21:1-7,

Now I saw a new heaven and a new earth, for the first heaven and the first earth had passed away. Also there was no more sea. Then I, John, saw the holy city, New Jerusalem, coming down out of heaven from God, prepared as a bride adorned for her husband. And I heard a loud voice from heaven saying, "Behold, the tabernacle of God is with men, and He will dwell with them, and they shall be His people. God Himself will be with them and be their God. And God will wipe away every tear from their eyes; there shall be no more death, nor sorrow, nor crying. There shall be no more pain, for the former things have passed away."

Then He who sat on the throne said, "Behold, I make all things new." And He said to me, "Write, for these words are true and faithful."

And He said to me, "It is done! I am Alpha and the Omega, the Beginning and the End. I will give of the fountain of the water of life freely to him who thirsts. He who overcomes shall inherit all things, and I will be his God and he shall be My son. "

If we have this hope of new heavens and a new earth, how is this expected to reflect on how we live in this world?

Consider the following words in Hebrews 9:27-28 and Philippians 3:20-21.

And as it is appointed for men to die once, but after this the judgment, so Christ was offered once to bear the sins of many. To those who eagerly wait for Him He will appear a second time, apart from sin, for salvation.

For our citizenship is in heaven, from which we also eagerly wait for the Savior, the Lord Jesus Christ who will transform our lowly body that it may be conformed to His glorious body, according to the working by which He is able even to subdue all things to Himself.

The word of God says Jesus is coming back to save those who *eagerly* wait for Him like a bride

waits for a bridegroom. How do we eagerly wait for
Him? 1John 3:1-3 and 2Peter 3:13-14 provide the
answer in the following fashion,

> Beloved, now we are children of God;
> and it has not yet been revealed what
> we shall be, but we know that when He
> is revealed, we shall be like Him, for we
> shall see Him as He is. And everyone
> who has this hope in Him purifies him-
> self, just as He is pure.

> But in keeping with his promise we are
> looking forward to a new heaven and a
> new earth the home of righteousness.
> So then, dear friends, since you are look-
> ing forward to this, make every effort to
> be found spotless, blameless and at peace
> with him.

Remark 28 *We reveal eagerness for the second coming of Jesus Christ in desire and efforts to purify
ourselves from sins and weaknesses, with full knowledge that it is the blood of Jesus Christ that enables
our cleansing. Our part is willingness and effort to
wash ourselves with the word of God via confession
of sins or weaknesses revealed to us in the word of
God and faith in the word of God that he who is
born of God receives power to overcome any sin or
weakness.*

Remark 29 *If we are in fellowship with the Father,
Son, and Holy Spirit in this world the thought of being in the presence of Jesus Christ in a physical
sense as opposed to a spiritual sense ought to fill
us with eager anticipation of the second coming of
our Lord Jesus Christ. If we are not eagerly waiting*

for Him, we do not yet know Him as we ought to know Him.

Reward for Overcoming

The second reward the Father has promised us is expressed by Jesus in Revelation 22:12-13:

> *And behold I am coming quickly, and My reward is with Me, to give to every one according to his work. I am the Alpha and the Omega, the Beginning and the End, the First and the Last.*

The devil stole man's dominion from Adam and Eve fairly and squarely. He offered advice contrary to our Father's commands, advice he knew would get Adam and Eve into trouble with God. Eve acted upon advice she knew was contrary to the word of God. It was the knowledge that she was acting contrary to God's commands that constituted her action as sin. As some men still do today, Adam decided to sink or swim with his wife. The good news of Jesus Christ is that God wants us to be able to overcome the devil and recover our dominion fairly and squarely. We overcome the devil not by recovering our dominion from him, but by receiving it back from our Lord Jesus Christ who already has recovered the dominion via the five facets of what He has done or is doing for those who believe in His name. The only reason we have sin in this world is because in their actions, some men and women still pledge allegiance to the devil, the god of this world. If we believe God and continue in faith, hope, and love, we overcome the devil, the world, and our flesh, and receive the promise in Revelation 21:7, which states,

> He who overcomes shall inherit all things, and I will be his God and he shall be My son.

All things means "All Things".

Recommended Prayer 7 *Father of my Lord Jesus Christ, thank you for thinking this all through and ensuring I always have something to look forward to in my relationship with You. I look forward to eternity with you in a world free of sin, pain, or death; in a world filled with Your Life and Love. I thank You Father for bestowing on me all things even as I persevere in overcoming to the praise of the glory of Your Holy name. In Jesus Name. Amen.*

Part II

Victorious Christian Living

In John 10:10, Jesus says,

> I have come that they might have life
> and have it more abundantly.

In Romans 5:17, we find the following words,

> For if by one man's offense death reigned
> through the one, much more those who
> receive abundance of grace and of the
> gift of righteousness will reign in life through
> the One, Jesus Christ.

Romans 8:35,37 states,

> Who shall separate us from the love of
> Christ? Shall tribulation, or distress, or
> persecution, or famine, or nakedness, or
> peril, or sword? Yet in all these things
> we are more than conquerors through
> Him who loved us.

All of the preceding verses state categorically that people who have faith in the name of Jesus Christ, whom now are referred to as Christians are supposed to have life abundantly, reign in life, and overcome any adverse circumstances that come their way.

Clearly, living without sin is an integral component of reigning in life in so far as Christians are concerned. In this regard, the cliché, "*prevention is better than cure*" is a well received advice that is more true than most other clichés. This cliché has a counterpart in Christian doctrine in 1John 2:1-2, which states:

> My little children, these things I write
> to you, so that you may not sin. And if

anyone sins, we have an Advocate with
the Father, Jesus Christ the righteous.
And He Himself is the propitiation for
our sins, and not for ours only but also
for the whole world.

If we believe in the name of Jesus, we are to
aspire not to sin, meaning a life of continual confession of sin and repentance from the same sins
is not supposed to be characteristic of a Christian. When we do not abide in Jesus Christ for
whatever reason - work, relationships, aspirations,
challenges - however, we are apt to make mistakes
or commit sin. The good news of course is that Jesus lives to intercede for us in those times when
we slip and fall. Better not to fall, however, than to
have to rise from a fall.

If we are to live without sinning, we must have
preventive strategies or defences that enable us
overcome the wiles of the devil - our adversary who
delights in seeing us fall short of the glory of God.

The question then is:

What are the preventive strategies or defences available to those who believe in
the name of Jesus that enable us live
without sinning?

Equivalently,

What are the keys to experiencing all of
the spiritual benefits that are supposed
to accrue to those who exercise faith in
the name of Jesus Christ?

In what follows, I refer to these keys as "*Keys to
Victorious Christian Living (VCL)*". These *Keys* are
the focus of the following eight chapters.

CHAPTER 8

Thanksgiving

> VCL Key 1: Thanksgiving

If a city does not want to be caught by surprise during conflict with enemies, it sets watches around the city so as to have advance warning of the massing of an attack. Because Jesus already has won the victory for those who believe in His name, we do not need to have advance warning of an impending attack by our ultimate self characterized enemy, the devil. Rather, we only need to know how to appropriate the victory that has been won for us already via the five facets of what Jesus has done or is doing for those who believe in His name.

Remark 30 *We experience Victorious Christian Liv-*

ing when we understand how to appropriate victo-
ries that have been won for us already via the five
facets of what Jesus has done or is doing for those
who believe in His name.

In Matthew 26:41, Jesus tells His disciples to,
"watch and pray, lest you enter into temptation...".
In these words, Jesus provides us with two of the
most important tools for Victorious Christian Living, which are *"watching* and *prayer"*.

Prayer is easy to define; it is communion with
God that involves talking to or talking with God.
An important point that many Christian teachers
overlook in teaching about prayer is:

Remark 31 *Since God is talking to us during our*
study of the Bible, study of the word of God, which
of necessity induces a response from us in what-
ever form: prayer (talking to God in response to
the word we have read), obedience, thanksgiving,
lessons learned etc. is an activity designed to in-
duce prayer.

Consider the following words in Romans 8:35,37:

> Who shall separate us from the love of
> Christ? Shall tribulation, or distress, or
> persecution, or famine, or nakedness, or
> peril, or sword? Yet in all these things
> we are more than conquerors through
> Him who loved us.

An appropriate prayer response to these words
is:

Recommended Prayer 8 *I thank you Father of my*
Lord Jesus Christ that nothing in this life can sepa-
rate me from the love you have demonstrated for me

in Jesus Christ. I thank you Father that I am more than a conqueror through Jesus Christ my Lord and Savior. I am more than a conqueror because I receive every victory that enables me reign in this life from you through my Lord Jesus Christ. In Jesus Name. Amen.

Remark 32 *When we pray the word of God we have assurance we are praying according to the will of God and as such are confident our prayers are answered. Why? 1John 5:14-15 states, "This is the confidence we have in approaching God: that if we ask anything according to his will, he hears us. And if we know that he hears us - whatever we ask - we know that we have what we asked of him."*

What it means to Watch

Contrary to the word "*pray*", the word "*watch*" does not have any direct interpretation, because we are dealing with a spiritual watch as opposed to watching for some physical enemy. The question then is,

"How exactly does a Christian watch?"

In 1Corinthians 6:13-14, the Holy Spirit commands,

"Watch, stand fast in the faith, be brave, be strong. Let all that you do be done with love.

1Corinthians 6:13 states a principle. In the verse following, verse 14, we are provided with a corresponding action. Put together, the Holy Spirit is telling us in 1Corinthians 6:13-14 that we watch, stand fast in the faith, are brave and strong when we have love as the foundation or motive of all of our actions. This means we satisfy the command to "watch" within the course of our daily activities, decisions, or actions. This also means any Christian can watch just as much as every other Christian. That is, no one is put at a disadvantage. Since the President or Prime Minister of a country watches within the course of his or her daily activities, he or she cannot watch so as not to enter into temptation any more than a soldier who serves to protect the life of the President or Prime Minister.

Remark 33 *Whenever we resist the temptation to depart from love as the motive or foundation of our actions, we are watching, standing fast in the faith, and exemplifying bravery or strength.*

Consider these words in 1Thessalonians 5:6-8,

> Therefore let us not sleep, as others do, but let us watch and be sober. For those who sleep, sleep at night, and those who get drunk are drunk at night. But let us who are of the day be sober, putting on the breastplate of faith and love, and as a helmet the hope of salvation.

The immediately preceding verse adds faith and hope to love in so far as what it means to "watch" is concerned. Since our "hope" is to become like God (Romans 5:2) and "God is love" (1John 4:8); and since we receive the love of God through the Holy Spirit whom we receive by faith (Romans 5:2,5),

Remark 34 *Christian doctrine makes it very clear* **faith** *in Jesus Christ implies desire to walk in* **love** *and* **hope** *of sharing in the glory (character or nature) of God.*

When we resist the temptation not to walk in **love**, we are confessing desire to be like God in love (**hope**) and thereby confessing **faith** in the name of Jesus Christ; so watching induces both faith and hope (desire to be like God) alongside love.

*If we bask in the audacity of our **hope**, our hope of sharing the glory of God is rooted in **faith** in the five facets of what Jesus has done or is doing for those who believe in His name, implying we desire to be filled with the **love** of God. Starting with hope then, we find both love and faith.*

If we exercise **faith** in the name of Jesus Christ, we receive power to become sons of God, meaning our **hope** is to become like God; since God is **love**, we desire to walk in love.

Remark 35 *In Christian doctrine, faith, love, and hope are inseparable. It is this inseparability of faith, love, and hope that is expressed in 1 Corinthians 13:13, which states, "And now abide faith, hope, and love, these three; but the greatest of these is love". Why is love the greatest? Because both faith and hope make it possible for us to receive and grow in the love of God. We obey the command to watch by walking in faith, hope, and love.*

So wherein does thanksgiving come in?

Listen to these words in Colossians 4:2,

Continue earnestly in prayer, being vigilant in it with thanksgiving.

This verse states very clearly the key to watching or being vigilant within the context of prayer is
thanksgiving. Do we have any other corroboration
for the importance of thanksgiving?

1Thessalonians 5:18 and Romans 8:28 state:

In everything give thanks, for this is the
will of God in Christ Jesus for you.

*And we know that in all things God works
for the good of those who love him, who
have been called according to his purpose.*

Combined, these two texts provide the key to
understanding the importance of thanksgiving for
watching within the context of Victorious Christian
Living. The texts ask us to acknowledge and give
thanks to God in all things. **Not for all things,
in all things.** That is, in whatever situation we
find ourselves, we continue to acknowledge God,
we continue to thank Him for saving us from our
sins and giving us His Spirit - the Holy Spirit -
while asking for wisdom to know His will.

Why focus on wisdom to know His will?

Now this is the confidence that we have
in Him, that if we ask anything according to His will, He hears us - 1John 5:14.

If we know God's will within the context of what
we are passing through, we know what to request
of Him and have confidence of receiving from Him.
If we do not know His will, we express faith that
He is working for our good within the context of a
situation we are not happy with by continuing in

thanksgiving and not allowing ourselves to begin to distrust His love for us.

How does thanksgiving protect us?

When we continue to give thanks regardless of our circumstances, with a focus on understanding of how God expects us to respond to our circumstances, we do not give in to anxiety, the temptation to distrust God, the temptation to murmur, or the temptation to adopt unrighteous motives and actions towards the resolution of our circumstances. When God reveals His will either via communication with us in whatever form or via the working out of circumstances in a particular manner, we know where to focus our energies for our good and the glory of God.

Philippians 4:6-7 states,

> Be anxious for nothing, but in everything by prayer and supplication, with thanksgiving, let your requests be made known to God, and the peace of God, which surpasses all understanding, will guard your hearts and minds through Christ Jesus.

Remark 36 *When we watch in our prayers with thanksgiving, God gives us His peace that surpasses all understanding to guard our hearts and minds from all of the negative emotions, desires, and motives that can be induced in our hearts or minds by undesirable circumstances. Since this peace from God surpasses understanding, it cannot be rationalized, it can only be received by faith; that is, it can only be received by believing in God that if we do what He has commanded us - give thanks in all things - we will receive His peace in return.*

Remark 37 *When we give thanks to God in the midst of all things, this is faith in action. Whenever we are unable to give thanks in all things, we already are doubtful in our minds that "God is love".*

At this point, we have established the importance of thanksgiving within the context of unfavorable circumstances. The question then is,

> *Does giving thanks in all things remain important within the context of favorable circumstances?*

Note this question is not about whether we should give thanks for favorable circumstances or gifts we receive from God. Clearly, it is good to appreciate God whenever He blesses us with "all good things to enjoy" (1Timothy 6:17). In this regard, Colossians 3:15,17 states,

> And let the peace of God rule in your hearts, to which also you were called in one body; and be thankful. And whatever you do in word or deed, do all in the name of the Lord Jesus, giving thanks to God the Father through Him.

In Luke 10:17-20, we have the following words,

> Then the seventy returned with joy, saying, "Lord, even the demons are subject to us in Your name." And He (Jesus) said to them, "I saw Satan fall like lightning from heaven. Behold, I give you the authority to trample on serpents and scorpions and over all the power of the enemy, and nothing shall by any means hurt you. Nevertheless do not rejoice in

this, that the spirits are subject to you,
but rather rejoice because your names
are written in heaven."

In these words of Jesus are encoded the secret
to not falling flat on our face during times within
which God is accomplishing great things in our
lives. Jesus tells us not to rejoice in the great
things that He accomplishes in us. Rather, we are
to rejoice in our salvation, our fellowship with God,
the gift of eternal life that we have from God and
that becomes part of us via our knowledge of God
(John 17:3).
Why is this important?

Remark 38 *When we rejoice in what God is accomplishing in us, we eventually begin to focus on what God is doing as opposed to our relationship with God. God wants us to regard the great things He accomplishes in us or through us as natural outcomes of our relationship with Him. When our rejoicing is in our relationship with Him as opposed to the blessings that accrue from the relationship, we develop character that keeps us steady, regardless of our circumstances.*

Does this mean we should not expect blessings
from God? Absolutely Not! The problem is,

> *rejoicing in the blessing rather than the*
> *giver of the blessing exposes us to temp-*
> *tation.*

We have seen how in 1Timothy 6:17, God gives
us all good things to enjoy, meaning God delights
in blessing us with things we enjoy that please
Him. In John 16:24, Jesus states,

Until now you have asked nothing in My name. Ask, and you will receive, that your joy may be full.

In Romans 8:32 we have the following words,

He who did not spare His own Son, but delivered Him up for us all, how shall He not with Him also freely give us all things?

The good news is God delights in blessing us with all good things to enjoy. We only need ask for what we need either by asking deliberately during our communion with Him or by pleasing Him via our seeking of His kingdom and His righteousness with all our hearts (Matthew 6:33). For our protection, we focus on Him, the giver not the gift.

Remark 39 *Giving thanks "in all things" keeps our focus on Jesus, the author and finisher of our faith, regardless of our circumstances.*

Remark 40 *When we give thanks in all things, we give God the opportunity to strengthen us to continue in faith, hope, and love.*

Recommended Prayer 9 *I thank you Father of my Lord Jesus Christ that you love me and desire to give me all things freely to enjoy. I recognize Father that you do not shield me from challenges in this life because if you did, I would not grow and would not have the opportunity to bring glory to your Holy name. I rejoice in your promise that whenever you allow challenges to come my way, it always is for your glory, glory you then lovingly share with me. Thank you Father for grace that enables me continue in thanksgiving whenever you accomplish* *great things in me, through me, or for me, and grace to continue in thanksgiving during periods within which I face challenges. I appreciate you Lord Jesus for the joy that is set before me whenever I face challenges. I thank you Holy Spirit for the help, strength, and power I need for reigning in this life through Christ Jesus my Lord and Savior. Blessed be your holy name Father. In Jesus Name. Amen.*

CHAPTER 9

Hearts that do not condemn

> VCL Key 2: Hearts that do not condemn

If we are to experience Victorious Christian Living, we must be able to approach God's throne, the throne of grace with confidence. When trials come or we feel tested, we must have the reassurance that either of trials or tests do not derive from willful sin in the past.

Remark 41 *An important key to having hearts that do not condemn us is the avoidance of willful sin.*

But does the Bible not say in 1John 1:8 that

> 'If we say we have that we have no sin, we deceive ourselves and the truth is not in us'?

The statement above indeed is true. It derives, however, from this statement in Romans 3:23, which states,

> For all have sinned and fall short of the
> glory of God.

Combined, 1John 1:8 and Romans 3:23 speak to our fallen sinful state in relation to God's righteousness or character. This, however, is the essence of grace or unmerited favor, which is,

> For He (God) made Him (Jesus) who knew
> no sin to be sin for us, that we might **be-
> come** the righteousness of God in Him -
> 2Corinthians 5:21.[1]

We see here again the word "**become**" that we discussed in the preceding chapter. Clearly, regardless of the dimension within which we attempt to become, becoming requires a process.

If a person wants to become a finance professional by obtaining a PhD in Finance (my professional discipline) for instance, he or she needs at the minimum 6 years of elementary school; 6 years of high school or secondary school; 4 years of college; and 5 to 6 years in a PhD program for a total of a minimum of 21 years. If this person believes some practical experience is necessary in the course of the process, we add either of an MBA and at least 2 years of working experience or 4 years of working experience for a new minimum of 25 years of training. Given minimum school age is 5, it is highly improbable to meet someone less than 30 years old who has become a finance professional

---

[1]Words in brackets mine.

via the attainment of a PhD in Finance. This illustration demonstrates the importance of time and
process in so far as attempts at becoming anything
good are concerned.

I obtained a PhD in Finance (Business & Management) at the age of 33.
So why am I writing about spirituality? A PhD confers a "Doctor of Philosophy" degree; that is, certifies the
holder of the degree has acquired the
knowledge and tools required to philosophize (create, discuss, teach, and
apply knowledge) within a particular
discipline. I write about spirituality
because I believe in the name of Jesus Christ, and because the tools that
enable me philosophize within my discipline also enable philosophization
within the realm of spirituality. Given
a PhD in Finance does not confer
spiritual knowledge, I have acquired
knowledge of the Scriptures and of
God - the focus of the Scriptures, in
the course of my personal study of the
word of God. In the penning of this
treatise on grace and truth - as revealed in Jesus Christ, I am functioning in no different a capacity as Simon
Peter, a fisherman who with only the
Holy Spirit as teacher helped us all arrive at a better understanding of the
grace of God.

So we fall short of the glory of God, that is, independent of God's help are unable to be who God created us to be originally because of the multiplier effects of original sin committed by Adam and Eve (Exodus Chapter 3). If we accept the help offered us in Jesus Christ, we are able once again to share in the glory of God.

Armed with the knowledge that 'becoming' is a process that takes some time,

> *how are we to avoid having hearts that condemn us while we are in the process of doing our best to become sons of God?*

The answer to this question lies in the first two facets of what Jesus has done for those who believe in His name; that is, Jesus' sinless life on earth and death on the cross of Calvary.

When we receive Jesus into our hearts or lives, Jesus' sinless life is credited to our account, such that whenever the Father sees us or we come into fellowship with the Father, He sees the righteousness of His Son, our Lord and Savior, Jesus Christ. Regardless of our weaknesses and imperfections then, so long as we sincerely believe in the name of Jesus Christ and put forth effort to become sons of God, we **never** come under the law. The law cannot speak against us because since we have the righteousness of Christ, every mouth that can be raised up against us is stopped. This stopping of every mouth that can speak against us Jesus achieved for us via His sinless life and death on the cross.

Consider these words in 2Corinthians 5:19,

> *That is, that God was in Christ reconciling the world to Himself, not imputing their trespasses to them...*

Since God no longer imputes our fallen state to us in light of our faith in the name of Jesus,

> Having been justified by faith, we have peace with God through our Lord Jesus Christ, through whom also we have access by faith into this grace in which we stand, and rejoice in hope of the glory of God - Romans 5:1-2.

and

> There is therefore now no condemnation to those who are in Christ Jesus, who do not walk according to the flesh, but according to the Spirit - Romans 8:1.

Since God does not impute our fallen state to us, we have peace with Him and feel no condemnation; that is, our hearts do not condemn us.

What does God require of us then since we cannot "continue in sin for grace to abound"?

> Therefore, brothers, we have an obligation - but it is not to the sinful nature, to live according to it. For if you live according to the sinful nature, you will die, but if by the Spirit you put to death the misdeeds of the body, you will live, because those who are led by the Spirit of God are sons of God.[2]

Remark 42 *The preceding verses make clear only those who live according to the Spirit do not have their sins imputed to them by God. While the sins of every single person are already forgiven in Christ,*

---

[2] *NIV.*

only those who choose to be reconciled to God through Christ do not have their sins imputed to them. This is no different from saying "a cashier's check for US$100 million does not enable the beneficiary afford anything until the check is deposited into the beneficiary's account or cashed across the counter"

So what are the misdeeds of the body that are to be put to death by those who live according to the Spirit? Galatians 5:19-21 states,

> The acts of the sinful nature are obvious: sexual immorality, impurity and debauchery; idolatry and witchcraft; hatred, discord, jealousy, fits of rage, selfish ambition, dissensions, factions and envy; drunkenness, orgies, and the like. I warn you, as I did before, that those who live like this will not inherit the kingdom of God.

If we are to have hearts that do not condemn us, we must ask God for virtue that enables us detest and put to death acts of the sinful nature listed in Galatians 5:19-21. This need of virtue is echoed in 2Peter 1:5, which states,

> For this very reason (the reason of "*becoming*" that is espoused in 2Peter 1:1-4), make every effort to add to your faith virtue (goodness or in this specific case, **"love of God"**).[3]

When we request virtue from God, the same virtue made available to us through the Holy Spirit

---

[3]Words in brackets mine.

enables us detest acts of the sinful nature and enables us begin to love the character of God, which in 1Corinthians 13:4-8 is characterized as follows,

> Love is patient, love is kind. It does not envy, it does not boast, it is not proud. It is not rude, it is not self-seeking, it is not easily angered, it keeps no record of wrongs. Love does not delight in evil but rejoices with the truth. It always protects, always trusts, always hopes, always perseveres. Love never fails.[4]...

So what happens when we discover weaknesses and hidden sins in our lives? Consider these words from 1John 1:9,7,

> If we confess our sins, he is faithful and just and will forgive us our sins and purify us from all unrighteousness.[5]

> *But if walk in the light, as he is in the light, we have fellowship with one another, and the blood of Jesus, his Son, purifies us from all sin.*[6]

Combined, the immediately preceding two verses make clear an important key to avoiding hearts that condemn us is willingness to acknowledge or confess any hidden sins or weaknesses brought to our notice by the Holy Spirit. When we are willing to acknowledge or confess our sins, God takes on the responsibility of purifying us from our unrighteousness or sin.

What is our part in this?

---

[4] *NIV.*
[5] Ibid.
[6] Ibid.

Remark 43 *We must remain in the light so we main-tain fellowship with God. So long as we remain in the light, we shall be purified of our sins. When we maintain our faith, hope, and love in Jesus Christ, we are remaining in the light.*

Consider the following words in Hebrews 12:1-2,

> Therefore we also, since we are sur-rounded by so great a cloud of witnesses, let us lay aside every weight, and the sin which so easily ensnares us *(let us be-lieve God as to what is good and what is evil)* and let us run with endurance the race that is set before us, **looking unto Jesus, the author and finisher of our faith,** who for the joy that was set before Him endured the cross, despis-ing the shame, and has sat down at the right hand of the throne of God.[7]

It is important to note at this point that from the timing of the conviction of sin by the Holy Spirit to the timing of the manifestation of our cleans-ing from sin, we never come under condemnation because all that is happening with us is part of the process of becoming the righteousness of God in Jesus Christ. If we do not become aware of our weaknesses, we cannot request help from God that enables us overcome our weaknesses. So long as we are sincere in our fellowship with God, we are throughout this process covered by the righteous-ness of Jesus Christ.

---

[7]Words in brackets mine.

Remark 44 *If we wallow in guilt or condemnation whenever the Holy Spirit points out sins or weaknesses in our lives, we are refusing to believe God when He says that He does not impute our sins to us because we have chosen to accept the payment made for our sins by Jesus Christ on the cross of Calvary and as a result, have exchanged our righteousness for the righteousness of Jesus Christ. Since refusal to obey God limits our fellowship with the Holy Spirit, it becomes even more difficult for us to receive the grace we need from God that enables us overcome our sins or weaknesses.*

So what are some of the confessions of faith that are appropriate when we are in the process of becoming and have to overcome a sin or weakness?

When we discover sins or weaknesses in our lives, we are to declare in similar words or phraseology:

ॐ I agree with you Lord Jesus Christ that this character trait or action or motive I have discovered is contrary to your character - IJohn 1:9

ॐ I declare according to your word that I have died to sin through Jesus Christ, and as such am freed from sin; sin no longer has dominion over me - Romans 6:7

ॐ I declare that given I am resurrected with Christ, I have newness of life in Jesus Christ, newness sufficient to enable me overcome any weakness or sin - 2Corinthians 5:17

ॐ Thank you Father of my Lord Jesus Christ that while I wait for the cleansing work of the blood of Jesus Christ and the light of the Holy Spirit to be completed in regard of this sin or weakness, this sin or weakness is not imputed to me because I am covered by the righteousness of Jesus Christ.

S Given you Father have declared that I have acquired your righteousness in Jesus Christ via my confession of faith in Jesus as Lord and Savior, I know your grace cannot fail and I shall become your righteousness in Jesus Christ - 2Corinthians 5:21

S Thank you Father of my Lord Jesus Christ that I put to death the misdeeds of the body not by focusing on the misdeeds but by fellowshipping with you, the Holy Spirit and the Father. Thank you Father for fellowship via study of your word, via interactions with other believers in person or online, via written works, videos, audio, or any other media. Thank you for enhanced fellowship that is possible whenever you Father and my Lord Jesus Christ make your home with me because I have demonstrated my love for you in sincere desire and effort to obey your command to walk in love (John 14:21,23). Thank you Father that you are the true and living God with whom fellowship is possible even when I am engaged in the most mundane activities of life.

S Thank you Father because having had your love poured into my heart by the Holy Spirit, I am patient, I am kind. I do not envy, I do not boast, I am not proud. I am not rude, I am not self-seeking, I am not easily angered, I keep no record of wrongs. I do not delight in evil but rejoice with the truth. I always protect, I always trust, I always hope, I always persevere. I never fail.

Remark 45 *All of the confessions in the preceding bullets confess who God has declared us to be and as such are rooted in the word of God. When we make these confessions, we declare what God already has declared so we can become who God has declared us to be. In this regard, Paul declares in Philippians 3:12 - "**Not that I have already obtained all this, or have already been made perfect, but I press on to take hold of that for which Christ Jesus took hold of me.**" If we press on to attain what God already has declared to be, we cannot fail. Since God is Love, Love never fails.*

Remark 46 *The key to having hearts that do not condemn is avoidance of willful sin; faith in God that if we confess our sins, He is faithful to forgive us our sins and cleanse us from all unrighteousness; joy that comes from knowing the Father of our Lord Jesus Christ covers us with the righteousness of Christ throughout the period we are sincerely trusting in Him for the grace we need to overcome sins or weaknesses; and a focus on acquiring virtues God has made available to us via the Holy Spirit.*

Remark 47 *If we have acknowledged our sin and are in the process of becoming, there is no condemnation, so we approach God's throne of grace with confidence because while in the process of becoming, we still are the righteousness of God in Jesus Christ.*

CHAPTER 10

Reckon Yourselves

VCL Key 3: "Reckon Yourselves"

The phrase *"Reckon Yourselves"* can be found in Romans 6:11. The spiritual meaning of this phrase is discussed extensively, and with the utmost spirituality in the book, *"True Spirituality"* by Francis Schaeffer. In this treatise, I provide a concise and summary discussion of the phrase, *"Reckon Yourselves"* because some understanding of this phrase is essential for *Victorious Christian Living*. For a more extensive discussion of the phrase, I recommend Francis Schaeffer's book, a book that in my opinion is a masterpiece on what it means to be saved by grace through faith.

Romans 6:6-7,11 states,

> Knowing this, that our old man was crucified with Him, that the body of sin might be done away with, that we should no longer be slaves of sin. For he who has died has been freed from sin. Likewise you also, **reckon yourselves** to be dead indeed to sin, but alive to God in Christ Jesus our Lord.

The message here is very simple yet profound.

When we believe in the name of Jesus Christ, we must believe that our capacity to sin has been nailed to the cross in Jesus Christ. We also must believe that we have received the capacity to love and obey God. That is, we must believe we have become a new creation in Jesus Christ who is dead to sin, but alive to God in Christ Jesus. In summary then, we must reckon ourselves dead to sin, but alive to God.

But are these mere beliefs or "*positive Christian thinking*"? Absolutely Not! Our reckoning is rooted in the five facets of what Jesus has done or is doing for those who believe in His name. Since Jesus lived a sinless life, so can we. In Jesus' death and resurrection we have the assurance that we can die to sin and resurrect to newness of life in the power of the Holy Spirit. We reckon ourselves not on some whim, caprice, or philosophy. Rather, our reckoning is rooted in what Jesus has done or is doing for those who believe in His name.

The rooting of our faith in actual events or actions undertaken by the Father, Son, or Holy Spirit is an important foundation of Christian doctrine. While visions are part of Christian theology, they are accepted because they fit into what God has done or said within the course of actual historical events or actions. While Christian philosophers help us better understand Christian doctrines and their applications, these philosophies or expositions are accepted because they fit into what God has done or said within the course of actual historical events or actions. We believe because there are events or actions that occurred right here on earth that provide a reasonable foundation for a small or large leap of faith.

Remark 48 *If we desire to live victoriously, we must reckon ourselves dead to sin and alive to God in Christ Jesus our Lord.*

> VCL Key 4: Faith that works by love

In order to reckon ourselves, we need faith. But is this all we need?

1John 3:10 states,

> Whoever has been born of God does not sin, for His seed remains in him; and he cannot sin, because he has been born of God.

Since the resurrection of Jesus Christ from the dead is the assurance of newness of life, we must exercise faith that so long as we abide in Jesus Christ we cannot sin. Since we cannot abide in Christ without faith, faith is a defense against sin. Faith, however, must be rooted and grounded in love and must have love as its objective else it can only be utilized as a tool for personal aggrandizement.

Why is this the case?

If we have faith and our faith is not rooted in love, then the faith we have must be rooted in self. While we profess faith in the name of Jesus Christ then, in reality, we utilize our faith only for the things of this world. In this regard, we need to ask ourselves,

♡ Have I ever utilized my faith for overcoming a sin or weakness?

♡ Have I ever utilized my faith in spiritual warfare for the benefit of others?

♡ Have I ever utilized my faith to enhance my relationship with Father, Son, and Holy Spirit?

♡ Have I ever utilized my faith for resisting the temptation not to walk in love?

♡ Have I ever utilized my faith to empower ability to love actively as opposed to passively in situations within which the decision not to love actively would be spiritually legal because I have been wronged?

If we make no attempt to hurt our neighbor intentionally, we love passively. Whenever we undertake actions that are a blessing to our neighbor, we love actively.

If we are unable to answer yes to any of the preceding five questions, we are utilizing our faith in the name of Jesus primarily as a tool for personal aggrandizement. The command from our Father in Colossians 3:1-3 is:

Since then you have been raised with Christ, **set your hearts on things above**, where Christ is seated at the right hand of God. **Set your minds on things above, not on earthly things.** For you died, and your life is now hidden with Christ in God.

Consider these words in Ephesians 3:14-19,

> For this reason I kneel before the Fa-
> ther, from whom his whole family in heaven
> and earth derives its name. I pray that
> out of his glorious riches he may strengthen
> you with power through his Spirit in your
> inner being, so that Christ may dwell in
> your hearts through faith. And I pray
> that you, being rooted and established
> in love, may have power, together with
> all the saints, to grasp how wide and
> long and high and deep is the love of
> Christ, and to know this love that sur-
> passes knowledge - that you may be filled
> to the measure of all the fullness of God.[1]

This verse reiterates some of the most important truths we have discussed thus far. If we grasp
the meaning of this verse, we propel ourselves towards experiencing the presence of God in a new
and living way. So what are the truths enumerated
in this verse?

- We receive the Holy Spirit by faith.

- The Holy Spirit establishes us in love by pour-
  ing the love of God into hearts

- The goal of receiving the Holy Spirit is that
  Christ (God) may dwell in or be formed in our
  hearts

- We have power to know God only when we are
  rooted and established in love. This means
  God will not reveal Himself to people who are
  not rooted and established in His love

---

[1] *NIV*

Ƀ The goal of our fellowship with God is to know the love of Christ, love that surpasses knowledge and embodies the fullness of God

Remark 49 *If we desire to overcome self, sin, the world, and the wiles of the devil, we must desire faith that is established in love and desire to know the love of Christ, or equivalently, the love of God.*

Recommended Prayer 10 *I thank you Father of my Lord Jesus Christ that my faith does not rest on human philosophies or visions, but on actions undertaken by You within the course of the history of this world in which I live. I ask Father that Paul's prayer in Ephesians 3:14-19 be fulfilled in my life; that I am rooted and established in your love, that Christ is formed in my heart, that I have power along with all the saints to comprehend your love because only in comprehension am I able to be filled with Your love to the measure of the stature of my Lord Jesus Christ. This I pray in Jesus Name. Amen.*

CHAPTER 11

Understanding the purpose of tests

> VCL Key 5: Understanding the purpose of Tests

Suppose a job in a company consists of management of a series of projects with different levels of difficulty. Within this context, each project can be regarded as a test of the ability of an employee who at the time in question fills the role required for this job. Since the employee's failure likely implies the company will lose money, clearly the company would prefer the employee achieve phenomenal success in management of the projects.

Suppose an employee makes some mistakes in management of projects assigned, but gets most things right, such that while the projects are successful, some learning points are developed that

could be helpful for management of similar projects
in future periods.

> *Do the best companies terminate the em-*
> *ployment of such an employee?*

Typically, the best companies find ways to ensure learning points generated are consolidated such
that they become part of the knowledge base of the
organization for prevention of similar mistakes in
the conduct of company business. Since the employee generating the knowledge (learning points)
likely is the best candidate for sharing, dissemi-
nating, or documenting the knowledge, the best
companies retain and reward good employees who
succeed in their roles albeit imperfectly.

While the foregoing analogy is not perfect in
that God is our Father and Jesus is our eldest
brother, the analogy highlights an important principle which is,

Remark 50 *When the Father of our Lord Jesus Christ*
tests us, He is acting like a benevolent or loving CEO
supervising an employee. He delights in our suc-
cess because our success is His success. If we do
not achieve 100 percent success, He finds ways to
consolidate the knowledge we have gained of Him,
of ourselves, of our relationships, and of our so-
cieties, such that we end up better off though we
made some mistakes along the way. The only way
we fail a test from God is if we abandon our faith
in the name of Jesus via refusal to walk in faith,
love, and hope, with maintenance of faith evident
in a spirit of thanksgiving towards God and a spirit
that rejoices in our common salvation.

If we abstract away from God's dealings with
the nations of Israel and Judah in the Old Testament Scriptures, one of the few unambiguous

records of a test from God involves interactions between God and Abraham. In Genesis Chapter 22,
God instructed Abraham to make a sacrifice of his
son, his only son - Isaac - whom he had received
miraculously from God and who was supposed to
be a forefather of the descendants promised by
God. Imagine Abraham's bewilderment at the contradiction implied in this instruction from God. Regardless of the contradiction, Abraham chose to
trust God.

The question is:

> Was obedience some irrational, blind, fa-
> natical religious decision on the part of
> Abraham? The kind of blind religious
> devotion that leads to destructive extrem-
> ism?

Consider these words in Hebrews 11:17-19,

> By faith Abraham, when God tested
> him, offered Isaac as a sacrifice. He who
> had received the promises was about to
> sacrifice his one and only son, even though
> God had said to him, "It is through Isaac
> that your offspring will be reckoned." Abra-
> ham reasoned that God could raise the
> dead, and figuratively speaking, he did
> receive Isaac back from death.

Why did God direct Abraham to go sacrifice his
son to Him then provide a substitute for the same
sacrifice so that figuratively, Abraham did receive
Isaac back from death?

> In this test, God wanted Abraham to
> experience what it means to give up a

son via sacrifice. In the pain he experienced leading up to the substitution made possible by God, Abraham got a glimpse of the pain that the almighty God, Creator of heaven and earth experienced when His Son, Jesus Christ, our Lord and Savior became the lamb slain from the foundation of the world to secure our salvation (Revelation 13:8).

Remark 51 *In His understanding of God's pain, Abraham gets the opportunity to understand and know God better than he did prior to this test from God. Ultimately, the purpose of any test is deeper knowledge of and fellowship with God; fellowship that enables access to additional resources or blessings available to us in God.*

Consider the following words in Deuteronomy 8:2-3,

Remember how the LORD your God led you all the way in the desert these forty years, to humble you and to test you in order to know what was in your heart, whether or not you would keep his commands. He humbled you, causing you to hunger and then feeding you with manna, which neither you nor your fathers had known, to teach you that man does not live on bread alone but on every word that comes from the mouth of the LORD.

These words from the Book of Deuteronomy make very clear:

Remark 52 *God tests only so He can teach us things we do not yet know. God's purpose for tests is that we arrive at a better understanding of Himself and the principles of His kingdom.*

Another context within which God tests His people is located in Deuteronomy 13:1-4. The verses read as follows:

> If a prophet, or one who foretells by dreams, appears among you and announces to you a miraculous sign or wonder, and if the sign or wonder of which he has spoken takes place, and he says, "Let us follow other gods" (gods you have not known) "and let us worship them," you must not listen to the words of that prophet or dreamer, The LORD your God is testing you to find out whether you love him with all your heart and with all your soul. **It is the LORD your God you must follow, and him you must revere.** Keep his commands and obey him; serve him and hold fast to him.

Why is this constituted as a test from God?

Since God is all knowing and foresees the prophet or dreamer will attempt to lead people astray, He can ensure the event foretold does not come to pass. God allows the events to come to pass as foretold, however, so the people can reveal the state of their hearts towards God; that is, reveal whether they honor God's word and ways. In the same vein, since God sometimes repents of events He sets in motion, such as the destruction of Nineveh, non-occurrence of a prophecy does not, as is the case with the Prophet Jonah imply a false prophet.

A prophet or dreamer who foretells an event that comes to pass, then attempts to lead the people astray demonstrates his lack of allegiance to God. A prophet who prophesies an event that does not come to pass is not a false prophet if his life and actions pass litmus tests of allegiance to God's word and ways. These words make clear,

Remark 53 *A false prophet is not identified by failure of a predicted event. A false prophet is identified by attempts to lead people away from God or truths established by God.*

The words in Deuteronomy 13:1-4 make clear,

Remark 54 *We must never get so carried away with miracles, displays of word of knowledge, word of wisdom, or healings to the extent we begin to revere a prophet, apostle, worker of miracles, or healer and as a result lose sight of God. The command is clear. It is our Father and our Lord Jesus Christ alone we must follow and revere.*

So what was the Father's response to Abraham as recorded in Genesis 22:15-18?

> Then the Angel of the Lord called to Abraham a second time out of heaven, and said, "By myself I have sworn, says the Lord, because you have done this thing, and have not withheld your son, your only son - blessing I will bless you, and multiplying I will multiply your descendants as the stars of the heaven and as the sand which is on the seashore; and your descendants shall possess the gate of their enemies. In your seed all the nations of the earth shall be blessed, because you have obeyed my voice.

In relation to previous promises, God blesses Abraham with three new promises.

For a discussion of how God assesses us in the roles assigned to us within His Kingdom, see Chapters 2 and 4 of my book titled, "Truths that Create or Enhance Loving Relationships: The Christian Perspective" available on Amazon.com.

First, while God had previously promised in Genesis Chapter 15 that Abraham's descendants would be as numerous as the stars - which we know in modern times can be counted - now God adds an uncountable element to the numbers of his descendants - the sands on the seashore.

Second, for the first time, God tells Abraham that Jesus Christ - the seed - would be of his lineage.

Finally, God promises Abraham he would possess the gates of his enemies; that is, would be victorious over his enemies.

All of this because Abraham trusted in God and did what God demanded of him.

Remark 55 *Within the context of the existence of a controversy between God and Satan, or equivalently between good and evil, God tests us to demonstrate to loyal angels or principalities and powers in heavenly places (Ephesians 3:10) that we are deserving of whatever* **specific roles or promises** *that are entrusted to us by God. Ultimately, this demonstration is for our benefit.*

Recommended Prayer 11 *Father of my Lord Jesus Christ, I ask for understanding that enables me stand fast in faith in the things I know of you that are true and understanding that enables me yield and alter my views in the things I know of you that require some modification. I ask Father for grace*

to trust you in situations within which your direc-
tives to me seem not to make any sense because
in your infinite wisdom what appears not to make
any sense is a stepping stone to more blessings in
my Lord Jesus Christ. I thank you Father for the
grace I need to follow and revere you alone in Jesus
Name. Amen.

CHAPTER 12

Understanding the purpose of trials

Trials are not the same thing as tests.

Tests occur within the context of everyday life in the sense that whenever we do not uphold our beliefs in our actions or decisions, we fail the test of confidence in God or faith in the name of Jesus. If we ignore the presence of direct communication between God and Abraham in the test of Abraham discussed in the preceding chapter, the test of Abraham occurred within the context of everyday life. Why is this? Because other than Abraham, no one else knew Abraham was acting on a direct command from God; not even Isaac Abraham's son was aware of God's command to his father.

While it is better for us to pass God's tests, pass or fail, we become better off after a test from God. Does this not mean then that God is partial? Absolutely Not!

If we pass a test, we get to know God better and receive good and perfect rewards
from God for our faithfulness.[1]

If we fail a test, we get to know God better, we get to understand our weaknesses
better, receive grace from God for our
weaknesses, and are rewarded for maintaining our faith in God and not chasing
after other gods because we failed a test
of our faith in God or belief in the name
of Jesus Christ.

I believe David's maintenance of his faith in God
during periods within which he had failed God in
his character is one of the reasons God characterized David as a man "after God's own heart" in
1Samuel 13:14. In the accounts of David's failures
recorded in the Old Testament Scriptures, David
always accepted the consequences of his disobedience towards God without chasing after other
gods.[2] Solomon, David's son did not learn this
lesson, resulting in significant consequences not
only for his own family, but for the entire nation of
Israel.[3]

An important characteristic of tests from God
is,

Remark 56 *Tests from God never involve attempts
at taking from us wealth God already has given to
us. A test from God can, however, as demonstrated
in the preceding chapter require us to demonstrate
our relationship with God and love for what is right
transcends and is more important to us than opinions of spouses, children, parents, brothers, sisters,*

[1]James 1:17.
[2]1Chronicles 21:1-8; 2Samuel Chapters 11 & 12.
[3]1Kings Chapters 11 & 12.

or friends. This is why Jesus said in Matthew 12:50, "For whoever does the will of My Father in heaven is My brother and sister and mother."

Do we have any evidence that while failing a test can induce some negative consequences, such failings do not induce any direct penalties from God and are associated with blessings from God?

Abraham and Sarah I

In Genesis 20:1-18, Abraham colluded with his wife Sarah to lie about their relationship. Within the context of the collusion, Sarah would tell people in the new community within which they were settling that she was Abraham's sister, as opposed to Abraham's wife. The rationale for this collusion?

"Abraham's fear that he could be killed by local men who might become interested in his wife who is characterized as an extremely beautiful woman."

While Abraham was not attempting to hurt anyone via the collusion to lie, the decision to lie exemplified lack of faith that God could protect both himself and Sarah from any harm whatsoever. In the final analysis, we find the local men, including their king actually became interested in Sarah because they assumed she was not engaged to anyone within the context of marriage. God, however, protected Sarah from being compromised by the local men and revealed to the king the true state of affairs between Sarah and Abraham.

So did Abraham fail God? *Yes.*

Did God protect Abraham in spite of his failing, *Yes.*

Do we observe any direct penalty from God in this regard? *No.* Why is this the case?

Abraham lied not to hurt anyone but out of fear for his own life or welfare. Whenever people bear false witness against their neighbor, the intent is to hurt their neighbor.

Whenever people lie out of fear for their lives or welfare without any attempt at putting anyone else in trouble via false witness, they do not have faith that God can protect them or think the truth will get them in trouble. In these situations, while God does not approve of lies, he understands the weakness that produces the lies. For those who have faith in Jesus name, this demonstration of weakness is covered with the righteousness of Jesus Christ until the believer receives strength from the throne of grace to trust God and speak the truth in similar circumstances.

Illustration   Subsequent to God's rejection of Saul as king over Israel, God instructed Samuel to go and anoint David as king over Israel (Samuel did not know who at this point; obviously, however, God already knew the identity of the next king). On receipt of this instruction from God, Samuel responded in 1Samuel 16:2,

How can I go? If Saul hears it, he will kill me.

God responded as follows in 1Samuel 16:2-3,

Take a heifer with you, and say, 'I have come to sacrifice to the Lord.' Then invite Jesse to the sacrifice, and I will show you what you shall do; you shall anoint for Me the one I name to you.

1Samuel 16:4 states,

So Samuel did what the Lord said, and went to Bethlehem...

The aftermath?

Many years later, Samuel has grown in faith and in 1Samuel 19:18-24, Samuel risks his life to protect David and with miraculous interventions from God succeeds in protecting both his life and David's life from Saul.

Remark 57 *God applies His grace to our weaknesses not because He condones or winks at sin, but because it is His graciousness that produces faith, strength, and greatness in us. 2Samuel 22:36 states* **"You have also given me the shield of Your salvation; Your gentleness has made me great."** *The grace or gentleness from God works only if we agree with God on what is good and what is evil.*

Were there any consequences to the failing on Abraham's part in so far as inability to trust God is concerned?

God blessed Abraham through the king of this foreign land with wealth. Isaac, Abraham's son, Isaace would, however, display exactly the same weakness as his father in Genesis Chapter 26.

Abraham and Sarah II

In Genesis 16:1-16, Abraham and Sarah doubted God's promise that they would have a child that would be borne by Sarah. Abraham and Sarah eventually received this promise from God in spite of the failing of their faith. The outcome of their faith, however, was Ishmael, the forefather of the Arabs, who have become enemies to the promised descendants of Abraham - Israel. So Abraham and Sarah received the blessing, but incurred extremely significant, but negative consequences for posterity. The huge cost imposed on their descendants by Abraham and Sarah is a warning to every Christian to realize that just because God does not impose any direct penalties on us for our failings or imperfections does not mean the consequences of such failings always are trivial.

Moses

In Numbers 20:1-13, instead of speaking to a rock to spew out water for the people of Israel to drink, Moses struck the rock, but more importantly took credit for the miracle, as opposed to giving glory to God (verses 10&11). As a consequence of this failing that occurred within the context of everyday life, Moses died shortly after, and as such was not allowed by God to enter the promised land along with the people of Israel. Combined, Jude 1:9 and Matthew 17:3 demonstrate God resurrected Moses after he died and took him to heaven. After Moses' failings then, there were consequences - lack of entry into the promised land, and blessings - resurrection and translation to heaven to be with our Lord Jesus Christ. In light of the resurrection of

Moses from the dead, God prevented Moses from entering the promised land only so that the people would realize that only He, the almighty God, Creator of heaven and earth is deserving of worship. If Moses was mortal, clearly he was not God. In reality then, Moses' death was the means to his blessing.

> So why does God act like it is okay for us to fail tests that occur within the context of everyday life?

Remark 58 *If we are imperfect by nature because we have fallen short of the glory of God (Romans 3:23), a God that is merciful, and gracious, and just must needs take this state of affairs into consideration in His dealings with us. This means while wilfull disobedience or rebellion is punished, errors of judgment, errors induced while angry, and weaknesses of character that occur within the context of desire and effort to live a life that is pleasing to God are forgiven and clothed with the righteousness of Jesus Christ. When we are merely imperfect, as op posed to rebellious or disobedient, it is grace - power to become sons of God - that we need not punishment.*

VCL Key 6: Understanding trials

Trials, as opposed to tests are the outcome of direct opposition to us either by the devil or the world. Only people who are living righteously can experience trials. This means of course only people who are living righteously have the opportunity to overcome and receive blessings reserved for overcomers from the Father of our Lord Jesus Christ.

2Timothy 3:12 states:

> Yes, and all who desire to live godly in
> Christ Jesus will suffer persecution.

In 1Peter 4:12 we have the following words,

> Beloved, do not think it strange con-
> cerning the fiery trial which is to try you,
> as though some strange thing happend
> to you; but rejoice to the extent that you
> partake of Christ's sufferings, that when
> His glory is revealed, you may also be
> glad with exceeding joy.

The immediately preceding two verses make clear
that when we endure trials or persecutions by faith
without giving up on the love of God or the hope
of sharing the glory of God, we are participating
in the sufferings of Jesus Christ and accumulating joy for ourselves in our fellowship with Father,
Son, and Holy Spirit.

Hebrews 12:1-2 states,

> Therefore we also, since we are sur-
> rounded by so great a cloud of witnesses,
> let us lay aside every weight, and the
> sin which so easily ensnares us, and **let
> us run with endurance the race that
> is set before us**, **looking unto Jesus**
> the author and finisher (*perfecter*) of our
> faith, **who for the joy that was set be-
> fore Him endured the cross**, despis-
> ing the shame, and has sat down at the
> right hand of the throne of God.[4]

Consider these words in 2Corinthians 4:17,18,

---

[4]Word in bracket mine.

> For our light affliction, which is but for
> a moment, is working for us a far more
> exceeding and eternal weight of glory,
> while we do not look at the things which
> are seen, but at the things which are not
> seen. For the things which are seen are
> temporary, but the things which are not
> seen are eternal.

So how does God lead us into joy from out of our
sufferings, or equivalently, out of our endurance of
persecution or trials for the sake of the name of our
Lord Jesus Christ into joy?

1Corinthians 10:13 states,

> No temptation has overtaken you except
> such as is common to man; but God
> is faithful, who will not allow you to be
> tempted beyond what you are able, but
> with the temptation will also make the
> way of escape, that you may be able to
> bear it.

Remark 59 *The word of God makes clear God always has a way of escape from out of our trials
into inexpressible bottomless joy, full of glory (1Pe-
ter 1:8). Hallelujah!*

The question then is,

> *"Why does God allow trials to come upon
> those who believe in the name of Jesus
> Christ?"*

We find the answer to this question in 1Peter
1:6-7, which states,

In this (*all of the blessings of the gospel
enumerated in verses 3 through 5 of the
same chapter*) you greatly rejoice, though
now for a little while, if need be, you
have been grieved by various trials, that
the genuineness of your faith, being much
more precious thann gold that perishes,
though it is tested by fire, may be found
to praise, honor, and glory at the revelation of Jesus Christ.[5]

This text from 1Peter affirms our faith in God
is tested at times because the genuineness of our
faith has been called into question by principalities
or powers in heavenly places. In order to provide
proof of our faith in God, God allows these principalities or powers to bring trials or persecutions to
us, reposing confidence in our ability to pass the
tests of faith, and with the provision prior to the
commencement of the trial of a way of escape into
inexpressible joy full of glory.

The experience of the Patriarch Job

The patriarch Job experienced the loss of his children, wife, and possessions because God allowed
the devil to bring on him fiery trials of his faith.
In Job Chapter 1, the devil accuses Job of having
faith in God only because he was wealthy and had
never really had any difficulties in his life due to
the protection afforded him in return for his faith
in God. In order to demonstrate the genuineness
of Job's faith, God allowed the devil to tempt Job,
but with the strict command that the devil was not
to make any attempt on Job's life.

---

[5]Words in brackets mine.

The good news is that Job held on to his faith in God in the face of the loss of all things precious to him, including his health. At the end of his trials, God restores all that Job had lost, such that Job was no worse off from having passed through his trials. Even more important than the restoration of Job's possessions, and provision or restoration of wife and children was the improvement in Job's relationship with and understanding of God made possible by fellowship with God in the midst of his trials or sufferings.

In Job 42:2-6, Job responds to God's words to him as follows,

> I know that You can do everything,
> And that no purpose of Yours can be withheld from You.
> You asked,
> "Who is this who hides counsel without knowledge?"
> Therefore I have uttered what I did not understand,
> Things too wonderful for me, which I did not know.
> Listen, please, and let me speak;
> You said, "I will question you, and shall answer Me."
> **I have heard of You by the hearing of the ear,**
> **But now my eye sees You.**
> Therefore I abhor myself,
> And repent in dust and ashes.

At the end of his trials, Job confesses that prior to his trials, he had faith in God based on what he had heard either from whatever Scriptures were available back then or from the testimonies of those from prior generations who had walked with God like Enoch did, but now at the end of his trials, he sees God for himself; that is, has come to know God for himself. Out of this knowledge of God for himself, Job comes to a realization of his sinfulness and states, **"I abhor myself, and repent in dust and ashes"**.

Our journey to God as believers in the name of Jesus Christ commences exactly as did Job's, by faith in the word of God and the testimonies of those who have experienced God. As we fellowship with Father, Son, and Holy Spirit, we begin to acquaint ourselves with, understand, and know God until we believe not because of what we have heard or read or the testimonies of others but because of what we have come to know in the course of our relationship with God.

In John 6:68-69, Peter confesses as follows,

> Lord to whom shall we go? You have the words of eternal life. Also, we have come to believe and know that You are the Christ, the Son of the living God.

But can we arrive at knowledge from belief or faith if we do not abandon ourselves to God by faith as exemplified in these words from Job 13:15,

> *Though He (God) slays me, yet will I trust Him. Even so, I will defend my own ways before Him?*[6]

Absolutely Not!

Remark 60 *If we are to go on from faith to know Father, Son, and Holy Spirit, we must trust God regardless of our circumstances; that is, our hearts*

---

[6]Words in brackets mine.

*and our words must be filled with thanksgiving to
God in all things.*

So we see Job restored and full of joy after he
had endured a fiery trial of his faith. The question
then is,

> Did God restore Job's fortunes because
> he was perfect or because he demon-
> strated the genuineness of his faith in
> God, genuineness of faith evident in his
> words, decisions, and actions?

Consider these words spoken by God in Job
38:1-4 & 42:7,

> Then the Lord answered Job out of
> the whirlwind and said,
> *"Who is this who darkens counsel by
> words without knowledge?*
> *Now prepare yourself like a man; I will
> question you, and you shall answer Me.*
> *Where were you when I laid the foun-
> dations of the earth? Tell Me, if you have
> understanding?*
> *Have you commanded the morning since
> your days began,*
> *And caused the dawn to know its place?"*

And so it was, after the Lord had spoken
these words to Job, that the Lord said to
Eliphaz the Temanite (one out of three
of Jobs' friends), "My wrath is aroused
against you and your two friends, for you
have not spoken of Me what is right, as
My servant Job has."[7]

---

[7]Words in brackets mine.

Combined, God's words in Job Chapters 38 and 42 demonstrate that while Job's understanding of God was relatively good and better than that of his friends, he was still so far away in understanding of God, God has to tell him what he Job considers to be knowledge is counsel that darkens rather than enlighten.

Do we have any evidence of counsel from Job that darkens rather than enlighten?

In Job 1:21, Job states,

"...The LORD gave and the LORD has taken away, may the name of the LORD be praised."

In Romans 11:29, 2Timothy 2:11-13, and also in 2Corinthians 1:20, however, the Holy Spirit tells us,

"God's gifts and his call are irrevocable"

Here is a trustworthy saying: If we died with him, we will also live with him;

if we endure, we will also reign with him. If we disown him, he will also disown us;

*if we are faithless, he will remain faithful (**to His promises**), for he cannot disown himself.*

For all the promises of God in Him are Yes, and in Him Amen to the glory of God through us.[8]

These texts from the New Testament make clear God never gives then decide to take away. God has

---

[8]*NIV*. Words in brackets mine.

demonstrated this in the giving of His only begotten Son to identify with man, such that the "*Son of God*" also could be referred to while He was on earth as the "*Son of Man*". In Jesus Christ, God has given us "every spiritual blessing in the heavenly places".[9] If we deny Christ we lose access to the blessings, not because God takes the blessings away, but because we choose to take ourselves outside of Christ.

Jesus states the principle of God's faithfulness to His promises in this manner in John 15:5&4,

> I am the vine, you are the branches. He who abides in Me, and I in him, bears much fruit; for without Me you can do nothing. Abide in Me, and I in you. As the branch cannot bear fruit of itself, unless it abides in the vine, neither can you, unless you abide in Me.

We see then that regardless of Job's faithfulness to God, his knowledge of God was extremely imperfect at the commencement of his trials. The imperfection of Job's knowledge is evident in the fact that the account of Job's trials states clearly Job's trials emanated from the devil, not from God. In allowing Job to be tested, God demonstrated the genuineness of Job's faith, genuineness that hitherto had not been demonstrated because of God's protections over Job. While we know this, however, this knowledge of interactions between God and the devil in regard of Job's faith was not available to Job at the timing of his trials.

So was Job perfect throughout all of his trial? Absolutely Not! In his words, decisions, and actions, however, Job demonstrated the genuineness

---

[9]Ephesians 1:3.

of his faith, meaning he demonstrated his faith in God transcended the material things of this life. In addition, Job was real with God about his vexations and the state of his heart throughout his trials.

Remark 61 *If we are to get to know God in the midst of our trials, we must be real about ourselves before Him, at least to the extent to which we already know ourselves.*

> Personal Testimony

Starting sometime in mid-2010, my marriage, which had experienced significant turbulence in the past, began to fall apart more rapidly. Right about the same time, relationships I had at work, which I assumed were good and tried to save, also began to fall apart. No matter what I did, the slide continued all the way until the end of the year.

Sometime during the first quarter of 2011, I woke up one morning and the Holy Spirit had me singing the song with the following chorus,

> **Through it all, through it all, I learnt to trust in Jesus, I learnt to trust in God. Through it all, through it all, I learnt to depend upon His word**

over and over and over. I sang this song with tears streaming down my face, and with agony in my heart for perhaps three hours in my study. I sang standing up, bent over, sitting down until I felt a peace from God come all over me. At the end of this fellowship with God, I felt strengthened by God and knew I had been in God's very presence.

Naturally, this fellowship with God made me think God was about to work everything - family, work, and church relationships out for good.

I was wrong.

The peace was to steady me through even more troublous times of which I did not have any anticipation.

By the end of 2011, God made it clear work relationships were not going to be restored and provided the strength to resign from my job without first looking for another job.

By early 2012, I had the strength and the capital to start my own business.

By mid-2012, I had the strength to stop fighting to save my marriage and entrust the state of my marriage to the Father of my Lord Jesus Christ. The marriage was not restored and has been over since mid-2012.

By March of 2013, I had the strength to temporarily give up the form in which I was running my business, and relocate from the United States to my native country Nigeria as part of my search for income generating opportunities.

Without generating any new income between January 2011 and March 2013, I did not have to borrow a single dime from anyone. In spite of the fact that I have not seen my four children since my relocation to Nigeria in 2013, I am filled with the peace and joy of God.

What is it that strikes me the most about the love of the Father of my Lord Jesus Christ for me in the midst of these trials? As I look back my heart is filled with joy that the Father of my Lord Jesus Christ brought me into His presence to give me strength for the trials to come even before I came to the realization of how fiery the trial would yet become. At the time I was singing that song in my study in early 2011, I believed my work relationships would work out, and that my marriage would be saved. Neither of these two expectations worked out, yet I have been filled with indescribable, unfathomable, and inexpressible peace and joy because God brought me into His presence and strengthened me with might through His Holy Spirit ahead of time. I was so much at peace, people all around me wondered at the calmness with which I was dealing with all of the storms raging around me. Is such strength from God biblical? Absolutely! Jesus received strength from angels to endure His scourging and crucifixion while in His agony in the Garden of Gethsemane (Luke 22:43). In the midst of all the trials I endured and in light of evidence of my own imperfections, I not only believe but have come to know that the Father of my Lord Jesus Christ loves me. I have come to know what God means when He says, **"I am the apple of His eye"** (Psalms 17:8, Zechariah 2:8).

Trials that save us from ourselves

In Jeremiah 29:13, God speaks to us the following words,

> And you will seek me and find me when
> you search for me with all your heart.

But has God not already revealed Himself to us in the Scriptures and in the person of Jesus Christ?
Absolutely. Just as mathematical or financial principles already exist, but are not understood until they are studied, however, so also while God already has revealed Himself to us in Jesus Christ, we cannot and do not get to know Him if we do not exert effort to understand and know what He already has revealed about Himself.

Whenever we do not seek God with all our hearts, we have some other things in our lives we value as much as our relationship with God, meaning we have yet to abandon ourselves to God in the sense of Job's statement, "**though He slay me, yet will I trust Him**".

Why are we to trust God?

We trust God because He has declared to us in Jeremiah 29:11 and Romans 12:1-2 that every will of His for us is good, acceptable, and perfect, meaning there is no evil purpose in God for anyone who believes in the name of Jesus Christ. In the sacrifice of Jesus Christ not only for those who believed in God before Jesus was born but for all men, dead, living, or yet to be born, God declares there is no evil purpose in Him for any man, male or female. When we believe this of God we are able to give thanks in all of our situations because we know there always is a way of escape from trials into inexpressible joy.

So what happens when we profess faith in God but do not seek Him with all our hearts?

Remark 62 *Whenever we do not seek God with all of our hearts, God judges us so we do not lose our salvation.*

This state of affairs is set forth in 1Corinthians 11:31-32, which says,

> For if we would judge ourselves, we would not be judged. But when we are judged, we are chastened by the Lord, that we may not be condemned with the world.

When we are real with God, we are able to search our hearts or ask the Holy Spirit to search our hearts during trials to reveal to us hidden motives that are evil or evil actions of which we need to repent. If we are convinced via our fellowship with God that we do not have any such known deficiencies, we go boldly before God's throne of grace to ask for grace to see us through a trial of the genuineness of our faith. This confidence means "**our hearts do not condemn us**". It is important to note, however, that just because our hearts do not condemn us does not mean we do not have any room for improvements in our obedience to God.

In 1Corinthians 4:4, Paul states,

> For I know of nothing against myself, yet I am not justified by this; but He who judges me is the Lord. Therefore judge nothing (*that accords with spiritual decisions or actions only; morality or relationship issues are to be moderated or*

judged by the Church in holiness) before
the time, until the Lord comes, who will
bring to light the hidden things of darkness and reveal the counsels of the hearts.
Then each one's praise will come from
God.[10]

During his trials, Job asserted to his friends
the fact that he was not aware of any sin in his
life of which could be the source of his trials. It
was Job's friends refusal to believe his assertions
of purity via their insistence that a righteous man
could not experience bad situations that got them
in trouble with God. Lest we be too harsh on Job's
friends, many Christians today consciously or sub-
consciously continue to relate to other believers
with these same attitudes. Whenever a pastor tells
believers "**You do not have because you do not
have faith**" he or she is saying it is impossible for
someone in the process of a trial like Job's to be
in his congregation. While it is true that we need
faith to receive from God, God has demonstrated
strongly in the life of Job that lack of material possessions at some point in time is not evidence of a
person who lacks faith in God.

If we find our hearts do condemn us, trials bring
us to the throne of grace to confess our sins and
receive the grace that we need to lay the sin and
whatever weaknesses that facilitate the sin aside.
All the while, we keep our eyes on Jesus, and do
not allow our hearts to experience condemnation.
If God has judged us **so we are not condemned
with the world** (1Corinthians 11:31-32), then He
has judged us so we can rejoice in our salvation
and the resurrection power that enables us over-

---

[10]Words in brackets and italics mine.

come and live victoriously in relation to sin that manifests in our lives. This is one of the most important keys to victorious living, which is, the realization that God judges us so we can rejoice in His salvation and the glory we expect will engulf us as we transition from the identified sinful state to the glorious state made possible by the grace of God and faith in the name of Jesus Christ, our Lord and Savior.

Remark 63 *When our hearts condemn us, the key to overcoming is confession of our sin and rejoicing in the salvation that we have in Jesus Christ and the resurrection power that frees us from our sins and weaknesses. We focus not on our hearts or the sin we need to overcome. Rather, we focus on our fellowship with Jesus Christ, confessing who we are in Jesus Christ and receiving grace to become who He says we are: believers who have been freed from sin and made alive unto God.*

Recommended Prayer 12 *I thank you Father of my Lord Jesus Christ that you love me so much you will allow trials to come my way to prevent me from losing my salvation whenever I stray away from the paths of life. I thank you Father of my Lord Jesus Christ that whenever the genuineness of my faith is doubted, you will allow trials that provide proof of my faith for all time, for my edification, and for the glory of your Holy name. I thank you Father that you have said,* **I am the apple of Your eye**. *Thank you for your grace that enables me reign in life and have life abundantly to the praise of the glory of Your holy name. In Jesus Name. Amen.*

CHAPTER 13

Weapons of Righteousness

VCL Key 7: Weapons of Righteousness

Within the context of the existence of a great controversy between the Father of our Lord Jesus Christ and the devil, every single person on the face of the earth that is capable of choosing between right and wrong, good or evil, is involved in spiritual warfare. Since every single person makes choices in life, no one can abdicate and declare neutrality in this warfare. Either we choose righteousness and enlist on Jesus' side; vacillate from side to side, with choice of side only a function of what seems to benefit us the most; or choose evil and enlist on the devil's side.

Since Jesus already won the victory on the cross

of Calvary, the wise choice is enlistment on Jesus'
side.

The question then is,

> Given there are three sides to the great
> controversy, with two of the three sides
> essentially aligned with the devil, are we
> fighting on two different fronts against
> two different armies when we enlist on
> Jesus' side?

The answer is,

Remark 64 *A believer in the name of Jesus Christ
never fights people.*

> So what do we fight or for what do we
> fight?

The answers are found in 1Timothy 6:12 and
2Corinthians 10:3-5, which state, respectively,

> Fight the good fight of the faith. Take
> hold of the eternal life to which you were
> called when you made your good confes-
> sion in the presence of many witnesses.

> For though we live in the world, we
> do not wage war as the world does. The
> weapons we fight with are not weapons
> of the world. On the contrary, they have
> divine power to demolish strongholds. We
> demolish arguments and every preten-
> sion that sets itself up against the knowl-
> edge of God, and take captive every thought
> to make it obedient to Christ.

The first of the two immediately preceding verses makes clear we fight to maintain and advance our faith, such that we are able to take hold of the eternal life promised us in Jesus Christ. In John 17:3, Jesus states very clearly we take hold of eternal life by getting to know Him and His Father, our Father. When we fight the good fight of faith then we fight to ensure we stay on course with respect to continual growth in the grace and knowledge of our Lord Jesus Christ.

Remark 65 *Every believer in the name of Jesus Christ is a soldier fighting to maintain their faith in Jesus Christ, and fighting to stay on course with respect to continual growth in the grace and knowledge of our Lord Jesus Christ. When we win the fight to maintain our faith and grow in our faith, we are accruing to ourselves victories already won for us by Jesus Christ, the author and finisher of our faith.*

The text in 2Corinthians 10:3-5 complements the text taken from 1Timothy 6:12 in that we fight not only to maintain our faith and to achieve continual growth in the grace and knowledge of Jesus Christ, but also to enable these outcomes in the lives of fellow believers or in the lives of people yet to believe, but whom are interested in knowing truth that enables abundant living. In this fight, we utilize the weapons of our warfare, which are spiritual, to enable people see past philosophies, arguments, pretensions, strongholds, or occultic practices that prevent faith in Jesus Christ or prevent believers from achieving continual growth in the grace and knowledge of our Lord Jesus Christ.

Remark 66 *Every believer in the name of Jesus Christ fights not only for himself or herself, but also* *for other believers or people yet to believe in Jesus Christ that are within their sphere of influence. Just as soldiers fight not only for their freedom but for the freedom of their fellow citizens, so also believers in the name of Jesus Christ are supposed to receive victories for themselves and for others from the Father of our Lord Jesus Christ within the context of the "good fight of the faith".*

The question then is,

> *What are these weapons of our warfare, which have divine power, but are not weapons of the world?*

The standard imagery of the weapons of our warfare is found in Ephesians 6:10-18, which lists the following weapons, the workings of which I have either discussed to varying degrees in preceding chapters or plan to discuss in following chapters (within the context of this treatise). These weapons are:

> ### The Helmet of Salvation

✣ The Confession that we are saved by grace through faith

> ### The Shield of Faith

✣ The confession that we have died with Christ to sin and now are alive only unto God; The confession that sin no longer has dominion over us because we walk not in the flesh but in the Spirit

The Breastplate of Righteousness

☙ The confession that we are the righteousness of God in Jesus Christ

The Sword of the Spirit

☙ Confession of the word of God as appropriate in different situations

The preparation of the gospel of peace

☙ The Holy Spirit

The Belt of Truth

☙ Knowledge of the word of God in truth as opposed to error; the word of God makes clear believers in Jesus Christ who do not endeavor to know the truth will be deceived by supernatural works of the devil in the last days; 2Thessalonians 2:9 states, *"The coming of the lawless one is according to the working of Satan, with all power, signs, and lying wonders,*

*and with all unrighteous deception among those
who perish, because they did not receive the
love of the truth, that they might be saved."*
The word of God makes clear there can be
people who perish - people who do not love
the truth - participating in Church.

> **Prayer**

꽃 Communion with God that in essence acknowledges our dependence on God.

There exist many well written expositions of this
stylized rendition of the weapons of our warfare in
Ephesians 6:10-18. Note, however, that none of
the weapons listed relate directly to how we interact with people around us. While the components
of the armor God listed in Ephesians 6:10-18 relate to the spiritual state of readiness in which we
need to be in order to fight the good fight of the
faith successfully, they do not relate directly to
how we walk in love towards people in our sphere
of influence.

In this treatise, I want to focus on some attributes of a believer in the name of Jesus Christ
that along with the weapons of our warfare *"commend us to God"* as we fight the good fight of the
faith.

These attributes that commend us to God are
found in 2Corinthians 6:4,6-7, which reads,

> **Rather, as servants of God we com-
> mend ourselves in every way:....in pu-
> rity, understanding, patience and kind-**

**ness; in the Holy Spirit and in sin-
cere love; in truthful speech and in
the power of God;** with weapons of righteousness in the right hand and in the left.

If the attributes listed in 2Corinthians 6:6-7 commend us to God, they are of extreme importance in
addition to the weapons of our warfare. Why is this
the case?

Remark 67 *While the weapons of our warfare declare the state in which we must be in order to fight
the good fight of faith successfully, attributes listed
in 2Corinthians 6:6-7 declare who we must be or
what we must be doing in order to be successful
in the good fight of the faith. A perfect state of being means we are prepared for an attack from an
enemy. The attributes listed in 2Corinthians 6:6-7
declare what we must be doing or be in order to advance the kingdom of God and His righteousness.*

Is this dichotomy evident in Ephesians 6:10-
18? Consider verse 13, which states,

Therefore put on the full armor of God,
**so that when the day of evil comes,
you may be able to stand your ground**,
and after you have done everything, to
stand.

Remark 68 *The armor of God declares our state
in Jesus Christ, which we must be operating in by
faith in order to resist the wiles of the devil whenever the day of evil come. Only believers who already have the armor on before the day of evil ar-
rives have capacity to remain standing in the face
of trials or temptations.*

A few words on attributes that commend us to God in the good fight of the faith.

> **Purity** means our motives must be pure in our daily interactions. This of necessity implies our motive always must be love. Since love chastises and judges when necessary, but for restoration or righteousness, as opposed to condemnation, purity of motives is consistent with chastisement of fellow believers or people yet to share our beliefs.

> *In order to develop **Understanding**, we must be fellowshipping with God so we understand and know Him (Jeremiah 9:23). When we understand and know Him, we understand ourselves, others, and the state of the world around us, and as such are able to walk with wisdom in our decisions, actions, and relationships.*

Most people can be patient or kind sporadically. God, however, expects those who have faith in the name of Jesus to *continue* in **Patience and Kindness**. Since only those who can forgive have capacity to continue in patience and kindness, patience and kindness mean we must have forgiving hearts. Since capacity to forgive implies we understand the meaning of grace, only those who have truly experienced the grace of God have capacity to continue to forgive. The Father of our Lord Jesus Christ expects those who believe in the name of Jesus Christ to have capacity to continue in

patience and kindness. As already discussed, however, distancing ourselves from
people whose adherence to worldly philosophies justifies attempts at taking advantage of our patience and kindness is demonstration of a godly attribute. The Father of our Lord Jesus Christ demonstrated this attribute when He allowed
the nation of Israel to be relocated away
from the promised land because they refused to have relationship with Him and
grieved Him with worship of idols.

*In order to fight successfully, we must
walk in the Spirit; that is, fellowship with
the Spirit and allow the* **Holy Spirit** *to
guide us in all of our ways.*

In order to always have **Sincere Love**,
we need the love of God, which as already discussed, we receive from the Holy
Spirit. Sincere love is love that is not
displayed merely for the personal gain of
the person who is expressing love. Sincere love cares about its own well being, but will not wield love as a stick
over recipients of its love to demand unrighteous or evil actions as evidence of
reciprocal love. Sincere love lets go of
the loved whenever it is rejected by the
recipient of love. In letting go, sincere
love entrusts the relationship in question to God. Sincere love focuses not so
much on what it can get, but on what it
can give and what it can receive. *When
we focus on what we can get out of a relationship, our focus is on some predeter-*

mined benefit we already have in mind before we express love. When we focus on receiving, our focus is on whatever good thing the recipient of our love has capacity to give to us in return for our love. This is not to say anything we receive in return is acceptable. If we are rewarded with evil in exchange for our love, God expects us to distance ourselves from people with such responses, but continue to operate in sincere love in interactions we engage in subsequently. The command not to be weary in doing what is good (Galatians 6:9) applies to our actions, as opposed to a demand that we continue to do good to a certain group of people. In this regard, Jesus told His disciples in Matthew 10:14, "*If anyone will not welcome you or listen to your words, shake off the dust off your feet when you leave that home or town.*" In essence, Jesus is saying "sticking with people who refuse to respect our beliefs is not a response required from people who have faith in the name of Jesus."

When we engage in **Truthful Speech**, *we do not practice deception in our dealings with people. While imperfection means we may not always do what we say, it is important that we mean what we say at the time during which the words were uttered. Whenever we do not do what we say then, it is not because we lied, but because of the weakness of our flesh. If we are to overcome every sin, however, we must tolerate weakness of the flesh*

*only in so far as it applies to promises we
make to people that ultimately we are unable to fulfill. Whenever we make promises
to people but are unable to fulfill them,
let us rest in God concerning our failings,
and relate to the persons in question with
truthful speech, purity, and sincere love.
Against such treatment of people that we
fail there is no law.*

Jesus is the **Power of God** (1 Corinthians 1:24). If we are to fight the good
fight of the faith successfully, we must
have Jesus in our hearts and be rooted
and built up in Him. We must be looking
always to Jesus Christ, the author and
finisher of our faith (Hebrews 12:1-2).

The **Weapons of Righteousness** we hold
in our hands are the Sword of the Spirit
or the word of God (Ephesians 6:17). When
we know or understand the word of God,
speak the word of God, and apply the
word of God in our daily lives, we are ad-
vancing the Kingdom of our Lord Jesus
Christ.

Recommended Prayer 13 *Thank you Father of my
Lord Jesus Christ for grace that enables us commend ourselves to you in purity, in understanding,
in patience and kindness, in forgiving spirit or graciousness, in the Holy Spirit and sincere love, in
truthful speech, in the word of God, in prayers with
thanksgivings, by faith in the name of Jesus Christ,
the wisdom of God and power of God. In Jesus
Name. Amen.*

CHAPTER 14

Putting it all together: Applications

What are some of the interactions between the keys to *Victorious Christian Living?*

> *If we do not give thanks in all things, we cannot have hearts that do not condemn because absence of a heart filled with thanksgiving implies presence of a heart filled with murmuring or complaints. If we murmur or complain rather than give thanks, we are unable to know the will of God and cannot use events that are transpiring as stepping stones to greater glory.*

Whenever our weaknesses or sins are exposed by the Holy Spirit, we are not to be filled with guilt and shame. Rather, we are to recognize that this is part of the process of our reconciliation to God. What we have to do is confess, repent, ask for grace, thank our Father that He has heard and as such as supplied the grace, then go on confessing who God has declared us to be in Jesus Christ.

If we do not give thanks in all things, we do not have the right attitudes towards either of tests or trials.

By operating in faith, hope, and love that is evident in a spirit of thanksgiving towards God and a spirit that rejoices in our common salvation, we maintain our place in Jesus Christ, or equivalently, are able to abide in Him and bear much fruit during both favorable and unfavorable times.

By operating in faith, hope, and love that is evident in our reckoning of ourselves dead to sin and alive to God, we overcome sins and weaknesses.

When we are tested, it is so we can know Father, Son, and Holy Spirit better. When we face trials, it is so the genuineness of our faith can be demonstrated or so we can come to a realization of imperfections that require application of the cleansing power in the blood of Jesus Christ. When we give thanks in the midst of tests or trials we allow the objective of the test or trial to be realized in our lives.

When we operate in purity, in understanding, in patience, kindness, forgiving spirit, or graciousness, in the Holy Spirit and sincere love, in truthful speech, in prayer, and in faith in the name of Jesus Christ, we fight the good fight of the faith that advances the kingdom of God and His righteousness; we also are making progress in our knowledge of Father, Son, and Holy Spirit.

When we utilize the weapons of righteousness made available to us by God, we fight the good fight of the faith with hope and love, keeping our eyes fixed on our Lord and Savior Jesus Christ.

Application: Overcoming Addictions

In this life now filled with so much pressure, it has become ever so easy for everyone, including Christians to fall into addictions. While some addictions are evidently destructive such as pornography, alcohol, drugs, adultery etc. there are other addictions, such as television, food, masturbation etc. which while not necessarily destructive do not enhance how we see ourselves during times within which we are able to look ourselves in the eye and are honest with ourselves in so far as the life we live is concerned.

If an addiction is destructive, we do not need any guidelines to identify that activity as an addiction. In so far as the "*not necessarily destructive addictions*" are concerned, the following guideline serves as a guide in recognizing that activity as an addiction:

Remark 69 *Whenever an activity is such that we*

are no longer able to make **normal progress** *to-wards righteous life objectives, such as professional, lifestyle, spiritual, physiological, or educational objectives, that activity is becoming an addiction that needs to be addressed.*

So how do we overcome an addiction?

Up until about 2009, I battled an addiction on and off for about 8 years. I choose not to reveal the addiction because I want to focus on the fact that:

Remark 70 *For those who believe in the name of Jesus Christ, the process for overcoming addiction is exactly the same for each and every addiction.*

While I battled the said addiction for 8 years, on receipt of the revelationary knowledge of what I really needed to do in order to overcome, it took less than 6 months to overcome the said addiction.

The mistake I made for almost 8 years while trying to overcome my addiction?

I prayed for victory out of feelings of guilt and shame. I saw myself as failing my Lord Jesus Christ because I was not living up to the standard I knew He expected of me. I prayed because I did not know the solution to my problem. **The problem with all of these? Jesus lived, died, resurrected on the third day, ascended to the Father and intercedes for me in the heavenly sanctuary so I do not have to relate with Him in this manner.**

Remark 71 *When we pray about an addiction, we bring the addiction into even more focus in a spiritual sense, resulting in a heightening of the temptation to succumb to the addiction. Praying about an addiction is a definite no-no for those who seek to overcome addiction because we are confessing in our prayers that we are weak and do not know what to do. The good news of our salvation is: "**God has told us what to do but the enemy of our souls does not want us to know these truths**".*

So what did the Holy Spirit teach me? Whenever I succumbed to the addiction, I made a confession which went somewhat like this:

Keywords for locating these verses in an E-Bible or the E-Book version of this book in bold.

Recommended Prayer 14 *Thank you Father of my Lord Jesus Christ that I am a **new creation** in Christ Jesus. Thank you that old things are passed away and all things have **become new**. Father of my Lord Jesus Christ I agree with your word that my **members** (my body) are made for righteous actions and declare according to your word that since I am **born of God** I cannot continue in sin. Sin cannot reign over me because I have died to sin in the body of Christ and have resurrected to **newness** of life in Jesus Christ. I declare that the life I now live, I live by faith in Jesus Christ who gave His life for me that I might become the **righteousness of God** in Him. Father you have declared that wherever sin abounds, your grace **abounds** even more. I thank you Father that I have grace and **power** through the Holy Spirit to overcome every weakness or sin; grace that reconciles me to you in every facet of my life. Thank you Father that I am an overcomer and more than a **conqueror** through Christ Jesus my Lord and Savior. In Jesus Name. Amen.*

Every sentence in the preceding prayer is from a verse in the Bible. I prayed this sort of prayer laying hold on every promise available to me in the word of God with which I was familiar. Within 6 months, it was not the case that I was resisting the addiction; rather, it was the case that the addiction no longer was an addiction to me. Since my initial overcome in 2009, I only remember that I once had this addiction whenever I need to discuss addictions; I am totally free because I achieved or received a spiritual victory over sin, as opposed to some strategy I implemented with my own wisdom and in my own strength. I achieved victory not with a strategy, but by calling into play the infallible promises God says are mine by virtue of the faith I have declared in the cleansing blood of Jesus Christ and the power of God available to me in the Holy Spirit.

> But how will we ever be able to confess
> promises given us by God to enable us
> live victoriously if we never become aware
> of these promises?

Remark 72 *If we do not study the word of God for ourselves, we do not become aware of the promises that have been made to us by God and cannot declare or act upon these promises by faith in what God has accomplished in our behalf via the five facets of what Jesus has done or is doing for those who believe in His name.*

Do we have any spiritual support for this approach to overcoming addictions or sins in our lives? Consider these words in 2Peter 1:2-4, and Ephesians 1:3,

> Grace and peace be yours in abun-
> dance through the knowledge of God and

of Jesus our Lord. His divine power has given us everything we need for life (*cars, houses, talents, expertise, spouses, children, income generating resources etc.*) and godliness (*ability to walk in faith, hope, and love*) through our knowledge of him who called us by his own glory and goodness. Through these (His own glory and goodness) **he has given us his very great and precious promises, so that through them you may participate in the divine nature and escape the corruption in the world caused by evil desires.**[1]

Blessed be the God and Father of our Lord Jesus Christ, who has blessed us with every spiritual blessing in the heavenly places in Christ.

What are some of the truths made clear in these verses?

- Grace or power comes from knowledge of God and of Jesus our Lord

- Peace of mind - the peace of God that passes all understanding - requires knowledge of God

- Everything we need for life and godliness comes via our knowledge of God who has called us by his own glory and *goodness* meaning He desires to do us good

- It is through the promises given us by God that we escape the corruption in the world and become partakers of the divine nature. **This means God already has revealed to**

---

[1] *NIV*. Words in brackets mine.

us how to overcome. How then shall we pray as if we do not know what to do? It is not miracles in which we do not participate that we need in this aspect of our lives, it is victories won exactly how God has declared they should be won - via our active participation and receipt of grace from God. If we do not win the right way, it is difficult for the victory to be permanent

ॐ In Christ Jesus, we have been blessed with every spiritual blessing that is available in God, the Father of our Lord Jesus Christ

ॐ Some of these blessings have been made available to us via promises given to us by God through Jesus Christ or the Apostles. Some of these blessings we receive via our personal fellowship with Father, Son, and Holy Spirit

Remark 73 *If we are to overcome addictions, sins, or weaknesses, we must confess the promises given us by God, not our sins, addictions, or weaknesses. Confessing the promises made to us by God places our focus on God. Praying about our addictions, weaknesses, or sins implies the power to overcome lies outside of ourselves so we need a miracle. This is not true. The word of God states clearly the power to overcome lies in us - in our knowledge of God; in our confession of who God says we are; in our confessions of the promises given us by God; and in what God says our experience of Him should be. In so far as sin is concerned, we are not weak; rather we have been made strong in Jesus Christ.*

Lest I begin to come across as smug, remember I got it wrong before I got it right, and that only with the help of the Holy Spirit. In essence then, it is the Holy Spirit teaching us all. I merely am a participating bearer of good tidings or good news from the Holy Spirit to the Body of Christ.

Recommended Prayer 15 *Thank you Father of my Lord Jesus Christ for your exceedingly great and precious promises that enable me escape the corruption that is the world and become a partaker of your divine nature. Thank you Father of my Lord Jesus Christ for grace that keeps my eyes focused on the righteousness of my Lord Jesus Christ and keeps me rejoicing in the cleansing power of the blood of Jesus and the power of the Holy Spirit even as I continue in fellowship with you Father, my Lord Jesus Christ and the Holy Spirit. In Jesus name. Amen.*

CHAPTER 15

Resting in God

Having understood all that we need to know or do in order to overcome, we must learn to rest in God concerning what we now know.

If we experience setbacks, we rejoice in our salvation because we have confidence in our ultimate victory. How do we achieve this? By confessing who we are in Jesus Christ and declaring victories won for us by our Lord Jesus Christ, as opposed to whatever defeat or failing we seem to have experienced.

When we experience victories, we give thanks for all that our Father has done to secure every spiritual victory for us.

When it appears as if nothing new is happening in our spiritual lives, we trust our Father that in His own time, we shall receive new and refreshing mercies from His throne of grace.

In Isaiah 30:15 we find the following words:

> This is what the Sovereign LORD, the Holy One of Israel, says: "In repentance and rest is your salvation, in quietness and trust is your strength..."[1]

The peace of mind we need for rest, quietness, and trust is promised us in Philippians 4:6-7, which reads,

> Be anxious for nothing, but *in everything by prayer and supplication, with thanksgiving,* let your requests be made known to God, and the peace of God, which surpasses all understanding, will guard your hearts and minds through Christ Jesus.

If God shields everyone who confesses faith in Jesus Christ from challenges, every single person capable of decision making would confess faith in Jesus Christ. Within this scenario, however, some people will confess faith in Jesus Christ just for His protection without any interest in the development of a personal relationship with God. This was the reason for Job's trial and is the reason God allows challenges in the life of a person who confesses faith in the name of Jesus Christ. God brings good out of challenges, however, by lifting us up to a higher plane in every facet of our lives to the glory of His holy name.

"In everything by prayer and supplication, with thanksgiving" means, we ask God for help, guidance, strength, direction, solutions or whatever else

---

[1] *NIV.*

we need during challenging periods with thanksgiving in our hearts, not for the challenges but for
His promises to us, including the following three
promises:

> *"In all things God works for the good of
> those who love him, who have been called
> according to his purpose (Romans 8:28)"*

> "For I know the thoughts that I think
> toward you, says the Lord, thoughts of
> peace and not of evil, to give you a future
> and a hope (Jeremiah 29:11)."

and

> *"For if, by the trespass of the one man
> (Adam), death reigned through that one
> man, how much more will those who re-
> ceive God's abundant provision of grace
> and of the gift of righteousness reign in
> life through the one man, Jesus Christ
> (Romans 5:17)."[2]*

Remark 74 *If every challenge ultimately works out
for our good, we should be joyful in thanksgiving for
His love, grace, mercy, and strength. When we have
peace of mind in every situation and every situation
ultimately resolves for our good, we are reigning in
this life. If we will rest in God, we will experience
what it means to reign in this life.*

When it appears as if we are under seige from
the world or the devil, we are to hold on to this
promise in Psalms 62:1-2,

---

[2]Words in brackets mine.

> My soul finds rest in God alone; my sal-
> vation comes from him. He alone is my
> rock and my salvation; he is my fortress,
> I will never be shaken.[3]

In Luke 10:17-20, we have the following words,

> Then the seventy returned with joy,
> saying, "Lord, even the demons are sub-
> ject to us in Your name." And He (Jesus)
> said to them, "I saw Satan fall like light-
> ning from heaven. Behold, I give you
> the authority to trample on serpents and
> scorpions and over all the power of the
> enemy, and nothing shall by any means
> hurt you. Nevertheless do not rejoice in
> this, that the spirits are subject to you,
> but rather rejoice because your names
> are written in heaven."

In these words of Jesus are encoded the secret
to not falling flat on our face during times within
which God is accomplishing great things in our
lives. Jesus tells us not to rejoice in the great
things that He accomplishes in us. Rather, we are
to rejoice in our salvation, our fellowship with God,
the gift of eternal life that we have from God, that
becomes part of us via our knowledge of God (John
17:3).

In essence, Jesus tells us to rest in our Father
at all times.

Recommended Prayer 16 *Thank you Father of my
Lord Jesus Christ for peace that passes all understanding, and for the joy of my salvation. Thank
you Father for your grace that enables me rest in*

---

[3] *Ibid.*

*you and reign in life at all times. In Jesus name.
Amen.*

Part III

Some Specific
Relevant Truths

CHAPTER 16

What is Truth?

In the preceding chapters, we have discussed the importance of knowledge of Jesus Christ in so far as actualization of the purpose of grace in the life of a believer in Jesus Christ is concerned. We have also discussed principles that enable *Victorious Christian Living*. As discussed in the Preface, since a proper understanding of the grace of God and principles that enable *Victorious Christian Living* results in a proper understanding of truth for people who have faith in the name of Jesus Christ, all of the discussions in the preceding chapters enable a proper practical understanding of truth as it is in Jesus Christ.

In this chapter that sets the stage for all of the remainder chapters in this treatise, I want to re-state the meaning of the word truth to ensure the Christian notion of truth is unambiguously understood. In doing so, I address the age old question that has plagued man, which is,

Is truth objective or subjective?

If truth is objective, there is truth and everything else in life must be viewed within the context of known objective truth. If truth is subjective, there really is no truth and society functions on agreements between people as to what constitutes acceptable behavior, beliefs, attitudes, actions, and relationships.

So then,

"What is truth in so far as faith in the name of Jesus Christ is concerned?"

The answer to this question is very simple, yet profound, and is found in John 14:6, which states,

> Jesus said to him, "I am the way (*the path to God*), the truth (*the demonstration of the character of God*), and the life (*the source of eternal life*). No one comes to the Father except through me".[1]

In so far as Jesus being the way is concerned, Hebrews 10:19-20 says,

> Therefore, bretheren, having boldness **to enter the Holiest by the blood of Jesus, by a new and living way which He consecrated for us, through the veil, that is, His flesh,** and having a High Priest over the house of God, let us draw near with a true heart in full assurance of faith, having our hearts sprinkled from an evil conscience and our bodies washed with pure water.

---

[1] Italicized words in brackets mine.

With respect to eternal life, Jesus states in John 11:25,

> I am the ressurection and the life. He who believes in Me, though he may die, he shall live. And whoever lives and believes in Me shall never die. Do you believe this?

In so far as Jesus being the revelation of the Father, we have the following statement in John 1:18,

> No one has seen God at any time. The only begotten Son, who is in the bosom of the Father, He has declared Him.

Combined, John 1:18 and John 14:6 make very clear that

In so far as faith in the name of Jesus is concerned, "The character of God is Truth."

Remark 75 *In so far as faith in the name of Jesus Christ is concerned, and within context of the objectivity or subjectivity of truth, truth is objective and the character of God is truth.*

Remark 76 *Since God is love (1John 4:8), love is truth.*

Remark 77 *Since love is patient and kind, patience and kindness are demonsrations of truth. Since love does not insist on its own way, willingness to yield whenever yielding induces better outcomes is truth. Since love does not envy, does not boast, and is not proud, a life devoid of envy, boastfulness, or* *pride is a life that demonstrates truth. Since love is not rude, self-seeking, or easily angered, courteous talk, interest not only in one's own welfare, but the welfare of others, and slowness to anger are demonsrations of truth. Since love does not keep a record of wrongs, forgiveness is truth. Since love does not delight in evil but rejoices with the truth, a life that rejoices over what is good is a life of truth.*

Within the context of the objectivity of truth, if a person were to be moral in the sense of the six commandments that mediate relationships - *you shall honor your father and your mother*; you shall not commit murder; *you shall not commit adultery*; you shall not steal; *you shall not bear false witness against your neighbor*; you shall not covet your neighbor's wife; and *you shall not covet your neighbors' property*; while there is commendation or reward from God for honoring these principles that are reiterated in the New Testament (see my discussion in Chapter 3), it is impossible for any person to have relationship with God on the basis of these commendable behaviors.

Remark 78 *The only way to relationship with God the Father, our Father is through the body of Jesus Christ. Without confession of faith in the five facets of what Jesus has done or is doing for those who believe in His name, we cannot have relationship with God. There is no middle ground; no room for shades of gray. Either we have relationship with the Father, Son, and Holy Spirit via confession of faith in the name of Jesus Christ or we are moral beings that do not have relationship with the Father of our Lord Jesus Christ, God of Abraham, Isaac, and Jacob, Creator of heaven and earth.*

If you would like to know why you should believe the Bible is what it claims to be, that is the
"**word of God**", please flip to the next chapter. If
you would like to accept Jesus Christ as Lord and
Savior at this point in time, I encourage you to pray
this prayer right now on this day, a day of salvation,

Recommended Prayer 17 *Thank you Father of my
Lord Jesus Christ that while I was yet a sinner,
Christ died for me and resurrected so I can be reconciled to you. Thank you Father that because Jesus
ascended to you and lived a perfect life that now is
credited to me, I can receive your Holy Spirit. Thank
you Father that Jesus lives forever more to apply
His blood to my life so I can be cleansed of my sins
in the power of the Holy Spirit. I receive Jesus into
my life and acknowledge Him Lord and Savior to
the glory of your Holy name. Thank you that having
received Jesus, I now can receive the Holy Spirit to
the glory of your Holy name. I ask now Father, that
you fill me with your Holy Spirit so I can be filled
with your power, that is, your love; in Jesus Name.
Amen.*

CHAPTER 17

A reason for faith

So far, we have discussed truth and grace, taking the validity of the word of God or the Bible as a given or proven truth. Even among professed Christians, however, there exist differences in attitudes in so far as the validity of the Bible is concerned. While it is impossible to prove the validity of the Bible as a fact, we can ask a less tasking question to which we can provide an answer, which is:

Are there reasons why we should we trust the written word of God - the Bible - to be what it claims to be, God's revelation of Himself to man?

In the Bible, God has revealed Himself to us within the context of events, as opposed to revealing Himself merely as a philosophy. In this regard, many of the events documented in the Old Testament have been validated by historians and archaeologists, some of whom are not Christians. Until the present day, the Jews regard Saturday, the Sabbath day as a day of rest - evidence events in the Bible relate to real interactions between the God of Abraham, Isaac, and Jacob, Father of our Lord Jesus Christ and the nations of Judah and Israel. I have discussed some of these interactions in my book titled, *"Truths that Create or Enhance Loving Relationships: The Christian Perspective"*.[1]

In so far as the person of Jesus Christ is concerned, historians agree on the fact that Jesus was an actual person who lived, worked miracles, and died. The only point of departure relates to His resurrection. We know for a fact, however, that a dead body has never been produced, though Jesus died and was properly buried; that is, did not die via a fiery plane crash or drowning in the ocean.

We know the Apostles who preached His resurrection paid the ultimate price - death - rather than say Jesus did not resurrect. While it is not impossible for people to lie and die rather than tell the truth and live free, we know the character of the Apostles demonstrated virtue or goodness. These were people who went about demonstrating the love of God by healing people and perforrming miracles alongside the preaching of the gospel of Jesus Christ.

In the restraint of prisoners from embarking on an escape subsequent to an earthquake that shook all of their fetters loose, an earthquake that was the outcome of hearts that were outpouring praise to God in the midst of a difficult circumstance, Paul demonstrated love for a Philippian jailer who

---

[1] Available for sale at (hard copy):
https://www.createspace.com/5680163 or (e-book)
https://www.smashwords.com/books/view/546344.

likely would have been executed if some prisoners were to have escaped.[2] This was love in action - the love of God.

In the healing of a soothsaying girl who followed Paul around for some days while he was preaching and healing people, Paul showed he cared more for the condition of this girl who was being taken advantage of than he was angered by her actions. In the healing of this girl, Paul focused on her condition not on the annoyance that she had become to him in the conduct of his ministry. When we are filled with the love of God, our response to people derives not only from what improves our welfare, but also what we believe to be the loving action that improves the welfare of people that are relating with us. Paul improved his welfare and the welfare of this girl at the same time.[3]

The question then is:

"Why would people who spent their lives doing good to others lie and die, rather than tell the truth and live freely?"

If we think through the evidence carefully, the only conclusion we can arrive at is that the Apostles do not fit the mould of liars. So either they told the truth that Jesus ressurected or they suffered from a delusion, a delusion that resulted in miracles, healings, and the turning of the world upside down with good works, as opposed to military conquest.

Consider these words in 1John 1:1-4,

That which was from the beginning, which we have heard, which we have seen

---

[2]Acts 16:25-29.
[3]Acts 16:16-18.

with our eyes, which we have looked upon, and our hands have handled, concerning the Word of life - the life was manifested, and we have seen, and bear witness, and declare to you that eternal life which was with the Father and was manifested to us - that which we have seen and heard we declare to you, that you also may have fellowship with us; and truly our fellowship is with the Father and with His Son Jesus Christ. And these things we write to you that your joy may be full.

Either these words above are true or they are a delusion. There is no middle ground.

A Litmus Test

Jesus Himself said the nature of a thing is judged by the kinds of fruit it produces (Matthew 7:17-18). So what sort of fruit has true Christianity - the practice of the principles outlined in the Bible, as opposed to mere affiliation with a religious body or concept - produced?

I do not presume Christianity is solely responsible for the fruit enumerated. In all instances, however, Christianity has played a significant role in the development of the enumerated fruit.

✠ A formal education system that provides opportunities for people to achieve self actualization not possible to their parents or elderly immediate relatives. Outside of a formal educational system, it is virtually impossible for children to self actualize outside of the professions of their parents or immediate relatives. Many economists today lament the growing inequality between the middle and upper classes of society, inequalities that are supposed to be ameliorated by formal education.

✠ A formal healing industry that studies how to heal diseases.

✠ The printing press invented primarily to make the Bible available to every believer in the name of Jesus Christ. The printing press is an important component of the exponential growth in knowledge we have witnessed the world over.

✠ Scientists such as Sir Isaac Newton whose faith in God made them believe the world could be a better place for us all; that is, a place we understand more and more as time goes by, as opposed to a planet from which we all seek to relocate.

✠ A world in which the fruit of the delusion (resurrection) is regarded as good except in so far as the opinions of islamic extremists who oppose *formal education*, which they conveniently refer to as *western education*, are concerned. The question is, however, "*are the objectives of formal education good for society*?" The answer of course is *Yes!* In this regard, even if we recharacterize *formal education* as *western education*, clearly it is not the origin of the educational philosophy that is important; on the contrary, acceptance or rejection of formal education must be grounded in the objectives of the educational philosophy.

If the fruit of the supposed delusion (resurrection of Jesus Christ from

**the dead) is good, must we not con-
clude the supposed delusion is grounded
in reality?**

An important caveat

The validity of the Bible must be assessed on
the basis of:

ঙ The principles outlined

ঙ The validity of the events documented or discussed, and

ঙ The character and ministry of Jesus Christ.

While the failures of people who profess to be
Christians at displaying the character of Christ casts
doubts on the validity of their faith and can make it
difficult for searchers after truth to affiliate with a
church, it cannot be construed as evidence against
validity of the Bible.

Why is this?

The grace we have from God derives only from
the five facets of what Jesus has done or is doing
for those who believe in His name. If the events
discussed in the Bible are true, and there is indeed
a true and living God whose only begotten Son's
name is Jesus Christ, neither my shortcomings
nor any other Christians' shortcomings should prevent a seeker after truth from confessing faith in
the name of Jesus Christ.

Cursory Historical or Archaelogical Evidence on Biblical Events or History

All of the evidence I proffer in the following bulleted points are culled from the reference text titled,

> *History of the World: Earlist Times to the Present Day*, Hall, J.W., and J.G. Kirk, eds. World Publications Group, East Bridgewater, MA USA. In what follows, I refer to this reference text as *HWE*.

Consider the following archaeological or historical evidence in relation to the validity of Biblical events or history.

There supposedly is a discrepancy of about 4 years in the dating nomenclature in so far as the actual year of Jesus' birth is concerned.

✠ The timing of the birth of Jesus Christ has become the reference point in so far discussions of the history of the world are concerned. When we say *698 BC* we mean *698* years before the "birth" of Jesus Christ. When we say *50 AD* we mean *50* years after the advent of Christ. This is evidence historians the world over agree Jesus is a real person who lived on this earth.

✠ God called Abraham out of Ur of the Chaldees (Genesis Chapter 11), a city that was part of Mesopotomia. Mesopotomia is widely regarded among historians as the very first civilization (Coe, M.D., Civilization, *HWE*).

✠ The earliest evidences of writing come to us from about *3000 BC*, with words written on cuneiform; that is, tablets of stone (Coe, M.D., Civilization, *HWE*). This is about the time period of Biblical figures like Methuselah and Noah.

✠ The Israelite kingdom is regarded as one of the ancient civilizations (Coe, M.D., Civilization, *HWE*).

✠ Consistent with the possibility that an army could starve a city by massing around city walls (2Kings 6:24-25), Coe, M.D. states as follows: "*some civilizations were so thoroughly urbanized that, as in much of modern Sicily, the farmers lived within its walls by night, and ventured to distant fields in the dim light of dawn.*" - Coe, M.D., Civilization (pg. 23), *HWE*.

✠ While historians regard history recorded in the Bible as legends up until the time of Joshua, commencing at the time of Joshua, the history of the conglomerate tribes of Judah (Judah, Simeon, and Levi) and Israel (the remainder nine tribes) is regarded as historical fact. Saul, David, Solomon, Jehu all are regarded as powerful historical kings of Judah or Israel - Laffan, W.M., The Ancient Near East (pg. 48), HWE.

✠ Accounts in the Bible such as the destruction of Jerusalem are regarded as historical facts and have corresponding validation in historical sources external to the Bible - Laffan, W.M., The Ancient Near East (pg. 51), HWE.

But do not the same historians say the world we live in is millions of years old and that we evolved from ape like men to the form in which we find ourselves today?

Historians and archaelogists agree as follows:

> We now know that modern man, Homo
> sapiens, has existed in his present form
> for at least *40,000* to *50,000* years and
> that the present disparate populations
> of mankind form a single species - Pil-
> beam,, D., Emergence of Man (pg. 10),
> *HWE.*

If man has been in his currrent form for roughly
50,000 years, it is possible whatever lived on this
earth was destroyed, then God began the process
of creation. Were the living things that were destroyed creations of the God of the Bible or creations of some other deity? Is the God of the Bible
via His own creative agenda demonstrating to 'principalities and powers in heavenly places' (Ephesians
3:10-11) who had previously created on earth the
wisdom of creating "*in His own image after His own
likeness* (Genesis 1:26-27)?" as opposed to creating merely for His own pleasure? I do not have
any definite answers to these questions. What we
do know from the Bible is there exists a possibility
that whatever lived on earth could have been destroyed in similar manner as accounts recorded in
Genesis Chapters 6 through 9 prior to a creative
process that commenced on earth about *50,000*
years ago. Regardless of the aggregate time frame
of 50,000 years, historians and archaeologists provide a time frame of no more than 6,000 years for
intellectual activity on earth, with the most reli-
able evidence dating back no more than 4,000 BC
(Laffan, W.M., The Ancient Near East (pgs. 26-29),
HWE). This is exactlly the same time frame that is
implied in Biblical accounts of the history of man.

> *Is it possible all of the supposed prede-
> cessors of man were created by some other*

principality attempting to prove a point to God, with God commencing His own creative agenda about 6,000 years ago?

The length of time it took for man to evolve in basic knowledge from 50,000 BC to about 7,000 BC and evolution of knowledge man has achieved in merely 6,000 years raise questions as to whether man has a different creator from all of the supposed antecedents such as *Australopithecus (Pilbeam, D., Emergence of Man, HWE)* etc.. The possibility of a purposeful creative agenda is manifest in that if man in his current form consists of a single species differentiated not by genetics but by culture (Pilbeam, D., Emergence of Man, *HWE)*, this genetic homogeneity is more consistent with planned creation than unplanned genetic evolution. If we assume genetic evolution is part of some grand master plan, we arrive at evolutionary creation, as opposed to evolution by chance, such that the only difference between creationists and evolutionists is the nature of the creative process as opposed to the existence of a mastermind creator.

What can we conclude for a fact from the historical evidence in so far as the history of man is concerned?

Summary 1 *Something happened on this earth about 6,000 years ago that accelerated man's intellectual development. Within 3,000 years, this accelerationn of intellectual development had resulted in man's ability to write on cuneiform. The Bible says the event that occurred about 6,000 years ago was God's creation of man in His own image.*

Remark 79 *God never asks us to believe in a vacuum. He provides us with evidence to support any leap of faith He demands of us. My leap of faith may be large while yours is small. On the basis of the evidence, however, we all are required to make a leap of faith. This is no different a leap of faith, however, than occurs when an entrepreneurs on the basis of initial evidence decides to start a business. There is evidence the business can be successful and there is faith the business will be successful. How we live and make decisions is exactly how God expects us to relate with Him.*

Recommended Prayer 18 *Thank you Father of my Lord Jesus Christ that there exists sufficient evidence that the Bible contains your revelation of yourself to man. Thank you Father that while I cannot prove for a fact that the Bible is the revelation of the true and living God, there is enough evidence such that my leap of faith is a small step of faith supported by a large body of evidence. Thank you for all of the good fruit that your revelation of yourself in the person of our Lord Jesus Christ has sparked - education, healing, inventions etc. Thank you Father of my Lord Jesus Christ that all of your promises to me find their fulfillment in my Lord and Savior Jesus Christ. In Jesus Name. Amen.*

Recommended Prayer 19 *Thank you Father of my Lord Jesus Christ that while I was yet a sinner, Christ died for me and resurrected so I can be reconciled to you. Thank you Father that because Jesus ascended to you and lived a perfect life that now is credited to me, I can receive your Holy Spirit. Thank you Father that Jesus lives forever more to apply His blood to my life so I can be cleansed of my sins in the power of the Holy Spirit. I receive Jesus into* *my life and acknowledge Him Lord and Savior to the glory of your Holy name. Thank you that having received Jesus, I now can receive the Holy Spirit to the glory of your Holy name. I ask now Father, that you fill me with your Holy Spirit so I can be filled with your power, that is, your love in Jesus Name. Amen.*

CHAPTER 18

A Universal Reward System

Reward systems are integral components of daily
life. Parents offer their children rewards for good
behavior. Companies offer employees rewards for
helping the firm achieve or exceed stated goals or
objectives. Countries and states, cities, towns, or
villages within countries reward citizens or residents with honors, recognitions, or awards for outstanding achievements that benefit society to one
degree or another.

By their very nature, reward systems are like
coins in the sense that they have two sides. In so
far as reward systems are concerned, penalties are
the dual opposites of rewards. Parents penalize
their children for bad behavior. Companies sus-
pend or terminate employees that hurt the company's business via unethical conduct or severely
sub-optimal performance. Countries and recog-

nized civil entities within countries penalize citizens or residents for immoral or illegal conduct.

Much the same as man within the context of organized society, God, the Father of Jesus Christ has a well developed reward system consisting of rewards and penalties. If God the Father really is Creator of heaven and earth, it matters not whether people believe in Him; regardless of belief or unbelief, He, the Father has jurisdiction over affairs on earth in so far as rewards and penalties for behavior are concerned.

The question then is:

> *Is it possible for the Father's reward system to be just to everyone regardless of the presence or absence of faith in the name of Jesus Christ?*

Consider these words by Jesus in Matthew 16:27, and Revelation 20:12,

> For the Son of Man is going to come in his Father's glory with his angels, and then **he will reward each person according to what he has done**.

> And I saw the dead, great and small, standing before the throne, and books were opened. Another book was opened, which is the book of life. **The dead were judged according to what they had done** as recorded in the books.[1]

These words by Jesus show His reward system is quite similar to a well functioning reward system instituted within organized society in the

---

[1] *NIV.*

sense that regardless of whether we say we have faith in the name of Jesus Christ or not, the Father rewards us on the basis of our actions. So just like a good company rewards a top performer for top performance and an average performer for average performance, the Father rewards us on the basis of our actions.

What then is the point of faith in the name of Jesus Christ?

Remark 80 *Faith in the name of Jesus Christ brings to those who believe in Jesus as Lord and Savior the power of the Holy Spirit, such that we have the virtue or the power that renders the doing of what is right easier than it would be if we had to depend on our strength alone.*

Consider these words in John 3:16-19:

For God so loved the world that he gave his one and only Son, that whoever believes in him shall not perish but have eternal life. For God did not send his Son into the world to condemn the world, but to save the world through him. Whoever believes in him is not condemned, but whoever does not believe stands condemned already because he has not believed in the name of God's one and only Son. This is the verdict: *Light has come into the world, but men loved darkness instead of light because their deeds were evil. Everyone who does evil hates the light, and will not come into the light for fear that his deeds will be exposed.*

Remark 81 *In relation to the grace of God revealed in the person and ministry of Jesus Christ, condemnation does not come from God because we are imperfect or sinful; rather, it is the outcome of rejection of God's offer to help us become the righteousness He created us to be originally. Whenever God shines the light of His righteousness into our hearts and we retreat into darkness rather than embrace the light, we by our actions condemn ourselves. We of course leave God no choice but to respect our decision to remain in darkness and under condemnation.*

In the sending of Jesus Christ to reconcile us to Himself, the Father, our Father demonsrated sincere love for us because regardless of Jesus' ministry in our behalf, the Father's reward system is exactly the same: we are rewarded for our actions. The Father sent Jesus Christ to provide us with power that would make it easier for us to do what is right so it is easier for us to be on the right side of His justice system. In Jesus Christ the Father declares the reason He judges is not because He is capriciously looking for people who fail to live up to His standards of behavior; rather He judges because in the absence of justice the spiritual realm would devolve into chaos. If the Father does not enforce justice on earth, people who choose to continue to do evil via retreat into darkness and refusal to accept help from God go from bad to worse because their evil plans succeed. Similarly, people who choose to accept the help offered by the Father do not receive any reward for doing good. If we accept the power made available to us in Jesus Christ, we no longer have any fear of the Father's justice because we only receive good from the Father.

Consider the following words spoken by Jesus in Matthew 6:25-33,

> "Therefore I tell you, do not worry about your life, what you will eat or drink; or about your body, what you will wear. Is not life more than food, and the body more than clothes? Look at the birds of the air; they do not sow or reap or store away in barns, and yet your heavenly Father feeds them. Are you not much more valuable than they? Can any one of you by worrying add a single hour to your life?
>
> *"And why do you worry about clothes? See how the flowers of the field grow. They do not labor or spin. Yet I tell you that not even Solomon in all his splendor was dressed like one of these. If that is how God clothes the grass of the field, which is here today and tomorrow is thrown into the fire, will he not much more clothe you - you of little faith? So do not worry, saying, 'What shall we eat?' or 'What shall we drink?' or 'What shall we wear?' For the pagans run after all these things, and your heavenly Father knows that you need them. But seek first his kingdom and his righteousness, and all these things will be given to you as well.*

I discuss the concept of *prosperity* in greater detail and context in Chapter 25.

In light of comparisons to pagans and the Father's declaration that there will not be any pagans in the new heavens and new earth (John 3:18), clearly Jesus is talking about how those who have faith in His name are to comport themselves while here on earth. The reference to clothes, food, and

water or beverages provides support for these in-
ferences. In so far as the Father's reward system is
concerned then, Matthew 6:33 makes it very clear
the Father rewards us on earth for seeking first
his kingdom and his righteousness. This of course
implies God empowers us to prosper financially,
physiologically, intellectually, socially, spiritually,
and in resources in response to our willingness to
seek first the kingdom of God and His righteousness.

What then does it mean to seek first God's
kingdom and His righteousness?

Remark 82 *When we operate in faith that works
by love; that is, operate in faith, hope, and love with
our faith reposed in the five facets of what Jesus
has done or is doing for those who believe in His
name, we are seeking first God's kingdom and His
righteousness.*

Chapter 7 of this
treatise discusses
the importance
of resisting the
temptation not to
walk in love in so
far as maintaining
our relationship
with God is con-
cerned.

Jesus explains the objective of seeking God's
kingdom and His righteousness in The Lord's Prayer
as follows (Matthew 6:10):

> *your kingdom come,*
> *your will be done,*
> *on earth as it is in heaven.*

Since the kingdom of God arrived on the day of
Pentecost when the Holy Spirit was given to man
for the very first time, any efforts we expend such
that the will of God is done on earth as it is in
heaven helps establish the kingdom that has already arrived on earth. Since God is love, we are
seeking God's kingdom and righteousness on earth
whenever we resist the temptation not to walk in
love.

Eternal Life

Alright, so we get rewarded on earth for doing things that please the Father of our Lord Jesus Christ. We also are bestowed with eternal life at the timing of our acceptance of Jesus as Lord and Savior.

> So does eternal life begin while we are on earth or do we have to wait for the second coming of Jesus Christ to begin to experience eternal life?

Jesus answered the question of the timing of commencement of eternal life in the following words recorded in John 17:3,

> Jesus spoke these words, lifted up His eyes to heaven, and said, "Father, the hour has come. Glorify Your Son, that Your Son also may glorify You, as You have given Him authority over all flesh, that He should give eternal life to as many as You have given Him. *And this is eternal life, that they may know You, the only true God, and Jesus Christ whom You have sent.*

These words spoken by Jesus demonstrate quite clearly that eternal life begins on earth as we get to know our Father, the only true God and Jesus Christ. Clearly then, in addition to everything that we need for life on earth as a reward for seeking God and His righteousness, we also get to begin to enjoy eternal life while on earth.

Ephesians 1:13-14 and 2Corinthians 5:5 reinforce the notion that eternal life begins on earth in
this manner.

> And you also were included in Christ
> when you heard the word of truth, the
> gospel of your salvation. Having believed,
> you were marked in him with a seal, the
> promised Holy Spirit, who is a deposit
> guaranteeing our inheritance until the
> redemption of those who are God's pos-
> session - to the praise of his glory.
> *For while we are in this tent (earthly
> body), we groan and are burdened, be-
> cause we do not wish to be unclothed but
> to be clothed with our heavenly dwelling,
> so that what is mortal may be swallowed
> up by life. Now it is God who has made
> us for this very purpose and has given
> us the Spirit as a deposit, guaranteeing
> what is to come.*[2]

Since Jesus Christ lives forever and we are in-
cluded in Him, we have eternal life. The Holy Spirit
is a spiritual deposit of this eternal life which is
consummated at the second coming of Christ when
we receive glorious bodies that match up with the
spiritual reality of eternal life in Jesus Christ; that
is, the spiritual reality of fellowship with Father,
Son, and Holy Spirit.

Remark 83 *In light of the fact that the Holy Spirit
is our gurantee of eternal life, clearly it is no small
matter to ensure we have fellowship with the Holy
Spirit.*

---

[2]Words in brackets mine.

So what are believers in the name of Je-
sus Christ rewarded for at the second com-
ing of Jesus Christ?

> Jesus said to them, "Truly I tell you,
> at the renewal of all things, when the
> Son of Man sits on his glorious throne,
> you who have followed me will also sit on
> twelve thrones, judging the twelve tribes
> of Israel. And everyone who has left houses
> or brothers or sisters or father or mother
> or wife or children or fields for my sake
> will receive a hundred times as much
> and will inherit eternal life. But many
> who are first will be last, and many who
> are last will be first - Matthew 19:28-30.

In the immediately preceding verse, Jesus makes
clear those who believe in His name are rewarded
for sacrifices that relate to possessions or relationships in order to maintain faith in Him at His second coming. In addition to rewards for sacrifices
made, those who have faith in the name of Jesus
inherit eternal life; that is the eternal life that was
up to that point in time a spiritual reality via fellowship with and knowledge of Father, Son, and
Holy Spirit becomes a physical reality via the glorification of our bodies.

Let us get this straight then. God rewards us for
operating in faith, hope, and love here on this earth
but rewards us for sacrificing relationships and
possessions at the second coming of Jesus Christ.
Does this seem right? If we love our neighbors, we
get rewarded on earth. If a spouse chooses not to
believe in Jesus Christ and we experience divorce,
we have to wait until the second coming of Jesus
Christ to receive a reward for our sacrifice. What

is it God is trying to tell us within the context of this *seemingly lopsided reward system?*

Remark 84 *If divorce is predicated on spiritual differences, this will be evident in the actions of a Christian spouse post-divorce; that is, a divorcee who endures divorce in order to honor faith in Jesus Christ operates in faith, hope, and love in interactions with their estranged spouse. In reality then, whenever a believer in the name of Jesus Christ endures divorce from a spouse or separation from children for the sake of Jesus Christ, the sincerity or truthfulness of the spiritual rationale for divorce is evident in how they relate to their spouse or children subsequent to divorce. If a believer is truthful and sincere in so far as the divorce outcome is concerned, they treat their spouse with faith, hope, and love and receive a good reward for this on earth. The sacrifice made for the sake of the name of Jesus Christ is rewarded, however, at the second coming of Jesus Christ.*

Remark 85 *The seemingly lopsided reward system outlined by our Father ensures we do not break up our homes simply because we are looking for God to bless us here on earth. Simultaneously, it ensures people who have to endure such break ups for the sake of Jesus Christ are rewarded within the context of how they would have lived if they had stayed married; that is, within the context of their willingness to operate in faith, hope, and love in interactions with other people, including ex wives or ex husbands. This seemingly lopsided reward system ensures home break ups are last resorts in so far as our desire to honor the name of Jesus Christ in our lives is concerned.*

In the foregoing, we have established the Father's reward system, which regardless of faith in the name of Jesus Christ rewards people for right actions, but makes clear right actions are not sufficient to induce relationship with Father, Son, and Holy Spirit. Do we have any other evidence from the word of God for this universal system of justice? Consider these words recorded in Galatians 6:7-10,

> Do not be deceived. God is not mocked. A man reaps what he sows. The one who sows to please his sinful nature, from that nature will reap destruction; the one who sows to please the Spirit, from the Spirit will reap eternal life. Let us not become weary in doing good, for at the proper time we will reap a harvest if we do not give up. Therefore, as we have opportunity, let us do good to all people, especially to those who belong to the family of believers.

If a person who does not believe in the name of Jesus mistreats people around him **intentionally**, the Father says that person will reap what is sown. If a person who believes in the name of Jesus mistreats people around Him **intentionally**, the Father says that person will reap what is sown. As already discussed then,

Remark 86 *Faith in the name of Jesus Christ is not license for sin, because the goal of faith is becoming like Jesus Christ. Whenever a person professes faith in Jesus, but lives however he or she chooses, the Father regards such a person as not having faith in the name of Jesus.*

This is the message implied in the following words from James 2:17-18,

> **In the same way, faith by itself, if it is not accompanied by action, is dead**. But someone will say, "You have faith; I have deeds." **Show me your faith without deeds, and I will show you my faith by what I do.**

We conclude then that the Father of our Lord Jesus Christ imposes the same standard of judgment on everyone, regardless of faith in the name of Jesus Christ. The difference? Faith in the name of Jesus Christ makes it easier to earn a passing grade and be eligible for all of the rewards and blessings available in God. In so far as the God of Abraham, Isaac, and Jacob is concerned, we are commended or condemnend by our willingness to live right. Willingness not accompanied by effort is judged by Him, however, to be pretense. If we truly desire to live right, we will exercise effort towards achieving the objective. God recommends we start by receiving Jesus Christ into our hearts or lives.

Fruit of Imperfection

We all are by nature imperfect. This is the rationale for the following statement in Romans 3:23,

> For all have sinned and fall short of the glory (character) of God.

If we are by nature imperfect, since every seed that springs from imperfection cannot be expected in of itself to produce good fruit or outcomes, surely a God who "delights in lovingkindness, justice, and righteousness" cannot insist seeds that are the product of our imperfections must bear fruit. In order to ensure seeds of imperfection do not automatically bear bad fruit, God sent Jesus Christ to pay the price for our sins or imperfections and live a perfect life that can be credited to our account. In the sacrifice of Jesus Christ on the cross we have assurance from God that if we believe in the name of Jesus Christ, seeds of imperfection we sow will not automatically bear fruit that is detrimental to our welfare. So if a person who believes in Jesus Christ mistreats someone unintentionally as derived from character imperfections - e.g. shouting at a friend while angry or forgetting to appreciate a loved one during a period within which it is appropriate so to do - the grace of God covers this person's imperfections, and the Father ensures the seed sown by imperfections does not germinate. In this regard, Romans 8:28 states:

> And we know that in all things God works
> for the good of those who love him, who
> have been called according to his purpose.

Suppose, however, a person who does not believe in the name of Jesus mistreats someone unintentionally. In such a scenario, only that person's righteousness can speak for him. If he is so righteous relative to the character of God (the Father of Jesus Christ) as man can conceivably be without the grace of God, such that the seed dies, so be it. If his righteousness is not sufficient to kill the seed sown by his imperfections, however, the seed will germinate and bring forth fruit, albeit this person still may obtain mercy from God if perhaps he or she were to begin to know God in the process of the growth of the seed.

The importance of character in so far as application of the Father's universal system of justice is summed up in these words from Revelation 21:7-8, which reads,

> He who overcomes shall inherit all things, and I will be his God and he shall be My son. But the cowardly, unbelieving, abominable, murderers, sexually immoral, sorcerers, idolaters, and all liars shall have their part in the lake which burns with fire and brimstone, which is the second death.

Remark 87 *Jesus has overcome so it is easier for us to overcome predispositions to sin, inherent weaknesses, systems in the world that encourage evil or sin, and the devil. If we do not utilize the grace of God for the purpose of overcoming, we will not inherit all things.*

An important Caveat

In so far as relations between people are concerned, an important caveat suffices here in so far as the principle of sowing and reaping is concerned. The caveat here is,

> Whenever a person stands up in defense of himself or others, this is not desire to hurt others; rather, this is part

of seeking first God's kingdom and His righteousness.

In this day, we celebrate the rising up of *Allied Forces* to defeat Hitler during the Second World War. While the Japanese have requested they no longer have to apologise for dragging the entire world to war, their willingness to apologize in spite of horrendous losses of Japanese lives during the war reflects acceptance of the wrongness of their motives - oppression or subjugation of other peoples - for the war. In order for Hitler and Japanese forces to be defeated, Allied Forces had to kill German soldiers. Since the motive behind the killing of German soldiers was freedom for people that were being subjugated against their will, the killing of German soldiers was not an end in of itself and was backed by righteous motives.

In order to ensure people who love righteousness can stand up in defense of any group of people in need of help, Exodus 20:13 states,

"*You shall not murder*" as opposed to "*You shall not kill*".

Expressed as a principle applied outside of the legal system, which has its own code, but whose code ought to approximate the code of the one true God, Father of our Lord Jesus Christ, Exodus 20:13 implies,

Remark 88 *Whenever a person kills another person and the motive for such is not self defense against oppression or defense of other people being oppressed by the person killed, this is murder. This is the reason Cain was a murderer. Cain killed out of envy; that is, for self gratification. Whenever a person kills*

*another person merely for self gratification, this is
murder.*

Do we have any support for differentia-
tion of '*killing*' from '*murder*'?

In order to rescue Abraham's descendants from
Egypt, God killed all of the first born sons of the
Egyptians (see Exodus Chapter 11). The motive:
rescue of people being oppressed. But was this
killing of the first born sons of Egypt a wanton exercise of power on God's part? Definitely Not! God
commenced with persuasion and inflicted nine different plagues on the Egyptians to induce their co-
operation prior to resorting to the killing of all of
the first born sons of Egypt (see Exodus Chapters
6 through 11). Since God is righteous and cannot sin, killing people to stave off oppression or
to rescue people from oppression is not murder as
derived from God's own actions. In addition to this
illustration, there exist many more illustrations in
the Old Testament that self defense or defense of
other people against oppression is not murder.

An important principle that should give
us confidence in the godhead of the Father of our Lord Jesus Christ?

Remark 89 *Throughout the Bible, we see a God
who sets up principles for man to live by that are
derived from principles that simultaneously are His
own codes of behavior. We do not see a God who
sets up priniciples for man to live by, then tells man,
"Since I am God I can do whatever I want". Ought
we not to respond to a God who lives by the same
principles He has set up for His creation with love
and appreciation, as opposed to stubborn rejection,*

pride, or indifference? He already has demonstrated His love for us in the life (good deeds), death, and resurrection of Jesus Christ in our behalf. He loves us.

Remark 90 *The good news of salvation is that God has given us life - the grace we need to sow seeds that germinate to produce love, faith, hope, goodness, blessings, prosperity and all other good things in our lives - and this life is in His Son, Jesus Christ.*

Recommended Prayer 20 *I thank you Father of my Lord Jesus Christ that You do not desire to see seeds generated by my imperfections germinate for evil, but for good. I thank You Father for Your grace, the blood of Jesus Christ, and the power of the Holy Spirit, all of which work together to enable me overcome imperfections and weaknesses as they are brought to my notice by Your word. I do not nullify your grace by utilizing grace as excuse for imperfections; rather, I rejoice that in my Lord Jesus Christ I have access to all the power I need to reign in life over imperfections in the mighty name of my Lord and Savior Jesus Christ. In Jesus Name. Amen.*

CHAPTER 19

God really has chosen everyone, but...

The beautiful words spoken by Jesus that have become sort of an emblem of the gospel of God concerning Christ in John 3:16 make it very clear God has predestined every single person born into this world to be saved. John 3:16 states,

> For God so loved the world that He gave His only begotten Son that whosoever believes in Him should not perish but have everlasting life.

The word "**whosoever**" makes clear all are called to everlasting life; no one is excluded.

Regardless of the explicit nature of God's proclamation in John 3:16, some persons still have confusion as to the nature of Gods' predestination, with confusion induced within the context of some verses in the Bible. A verse that seems to induce confusion is Matthew 22:14, which states,

For many are called but few are chosen.

Some persons interpret this verse to mean that while Jesus draws all men to Himself as proclaimed in John 12:32, ultimately He chooses some and rejects others. This interpretation of Matthew 22:14 is biblically sound. The question, however, is:

What is the basis for rejection?

If Jesus' criterion for choosing from within the entire population of the "*called*" is the same for everyone, then everyone is predestined to be saved and chosen by God. This implies rejection is predicated on failure to meet up to a condition imposed by God in order for *the called* to transition from just being called to being chosen.

In Matthew Chapter 13, Jesus told the Parable of the Sower in which a sower sowed the seeds of the gospel of Jesus Christ and the seed fell by the wayside, on stony ground, on thorny ground, and on good soil. Jesus explains very clearly that the seed which falls by the wayside refers to those who hear the gospel, do not understand it, and have the words snatched out of their hearts by the devil. The *seed on stony soil* refers to those who receive the word with joy - are drawn to Jesus - but withdraw from Jesus in the face of persecution. The *seed among thorns* refers to those who love the things of this world more than the things of God, and as such choose to give up eternal wealth for the deceitfulness of riches. The *seed on good soil* refers to those who hear the word of God, understand it, and as a result bear good fruit.

Jesus' parable reveals seed on stony soil or thorny ground do not bear fruit because they either *choose* not to abide in Jesus Christ to avoid persecution or *choose* to give up faith in the name of Jesus for promise of monetary riches. In so far as either of these two groups are concerned, it is the people called who choose not to abide in Jesus Christ. Since they choose not to abide in Jesus Christ, Jesus has no choice but to reject them. We find then that the Father and the Son do not call then reject. In reality they have called and desire to choose everyone. Not everyone however, is willing to pay the price necessary in order to ensure they ultimately are chosen by God. In this regard Jesus states in John 15:9-12,17,

I have demonstrated in Chapter 3 that the command to *love as Jesus has loved us* is superior to the Old Testament command to *love our neighbor as ourselves*.

As the Father has loved me, so have I loved you. **Now remain in my love**. **If you obey my commands, you will remain in my love**, just as I have obeyed my Father's commands and remain in his love. I have told you this so that my joy may be in you and that your joy may be complete. **My command is this: Love each other as I have loved you**. This is my command: Love each other.

We have discussed the concept of "*faith that works by love*" in Chapter 10.

Notice Jesus' usage of the word *remain* within the phrase "*Now remain in my love*". In this phrase, Jesus states very clearly that after having being called we have a choice as to whether to remain or not to remain in Jesus Christ. If we desire to remain in Jesus Christ, we resist any temptation that attempts to induce us not to love one another as Jesus has loved us.

I reiterate here that love is not weakness. In Jesus' character as recorded in the Bible we see a perfect balance of strength, purposefulness, empathy, care for the welfare of others, and other attributes of good character. Regardless of the depths of His love for His disciples, Jesus never allowed His disciples hijack His ministry with their views of the objective of His ministry. Jesus rebuked His disciples when they did wrong or attempted to do wrong. While on earth with us Jesus was a strong leader who totally walked in love in the face of great opposition, yet achieved every objective of His ministry. When we understand how to operate in love like Jesus did, we will understand that operating in the love of God does not turn us into weaklings. In Part IV - the final 9 chapters - of this treatise I discuss (in Bible study form) some of the principles necessary to apply to ensure we do not misapply the love of God in course of interactions with people within our sphere of influence.

If we allow ourselves to be dissuaded from operating in *faith that works by love*, ultimately we are not able to remain in Jesus Christ, and as such are not chosen by Him. Do we find, however, any arbitrariness in Jesus' decision not to choose those who refuse to remain or abide in Him? Absolutely Not! Jesus' decision not to choose people who do not remain in Him ratifies their decision much the same as a teacher assigns a failing grade to a student who via negligence or refusal to do what is required has performed poorly on an exam.

The good news?

> *Jesus has time proven remedies for stony hearts and thorny grounds. If anyone has natural bent towards stony heart or thorny ground, but truly desires to be saved, all they need do is ask Jesus for time proven remedies that enable stony hearts become receptive hearts, and remedies that transform thorny ground into high yield fertile soil.*

Remedy for Stony Hearts

Concerning those with stony hearts, the Father declares as follows in Ezekiel 36:26,

> I will give you a new heart and put a new spirit within you; I will take the heart of stone out of your flesh and give you a heart of flesh. I will put my Spirit within you and cause you to walk in my statutes, and you will keep my commandments and do them.

Based on the promise in Ezekiel 36:26, no one can say:

> "I have a heart that is naturally stony, so while God has called me, He has not given me the capacity to respond to Him".

The word of God demonstrates God not only has called but also has provided the promise that enables a response. In the promise in Ezekiel 36:26 God declares He can infuse people that have naturally stony hearts with the capacity to love as Jesus loved via a change of heart and the gift of the Holy Spirit.

Remark 91 *God does not condemn us because our genetic make up predisposes us to hate, indifference, emotional detachment, or inability to love others. He condemns us because rather than allow Him supply the capacity to love, we choose to love the genetic make up.*

Remedy for Cares

In regard of those burdened with cares (thorns) of this life, the Holy Spirit declares as follows in 2Peter 1:2-4,

Grace and peace be yours in abundance through the knowledge of God and of Jesus our Lord. His divine power has given us everything we need for life (*cars, houses, talents, expertise, spouses, children, income generating resources etc.*) and godliness (*ability to walk in faith, hope, and love*) through our knowledge of him who called us by his own glory and goodness. Through these (His own glory and goodness) **he has given us his very great and precious promises, so that through**

them you may participate in the divine nature and escape the corruption in the world caused by evil desires.

Based on the promise in 2Peter 1:2-4, a person cannot say:

> "I fret too much over the things I need in this life, I am unable to rest in Jesus Christ concerning my needs." or

> "I have a heart that is bent towards the pleasures of this world, so while God has called me, He has not given me the capacity to respond to Him".

> The word of God promises *peace in abundance through the knowledge of God and of Jesus our Lord* and promises *every need or godly want is already provided for in Jesus Christ.*

Is there some other specific promise that applies? Matthew 6:25-33 states,

> "Therefore I tell you, do not worry about your life, what you will eat or drink; or about your body, what you will wear. Is not life more than food, and the body more than clothes? Look at the birds of the air; they do not sow or reap or store away in barns, and yet your heavenly Father feeds them. Are you not much more valuable than they? Can any one of you by worrying add a single hour to your life?
> *"And why do you worry about clothes? See how the flowers of the field grow.*

They do not labor or spin. Yet I tell you
that not even Solomon in all his splendor
was dressed like one of these. If that is
how God clothes the grass of the field,
which is here today and tomorrow is thrown
into the fire, will he not much more clothe
you - you of little faith? So do not worry,
saying, 'What shall we eat?' or 'What
shall we drink?' or 'What shall we wear?'
For the pagans run after all these things,
and your heavenly Father knows that you
need them. But seek first his kingdom
and his righteousness, and all these things
will be given to you as well.

Remedy for Spiritual Blindness

Concerning people who do not understand the
good news of the gospel, we have the following words
in 2Corinthians 4:3-4,

But even if our gospel is veiled, it is
veiled to those who are perishing, whose
minds the god of this age has blinded,
who do not believe, lest the light of the
gospel of the glory of Christ, who is the
image of God, should shine on them.

How do such people end up with their minds
blinded by the god of this age? The answers can
be found in John 3:19-21 and 1John 1:5-7 which
state,

And this is the condemnation, that
the light has come into the world, and

men loved darkness rather than light, because their deeds were evil. For everyone practicing evil hates the light and does not come to the light, lest his deeds should be exposed. But he who does the truth comes to the light, that his deeds may be clearly seen, that they have been done in God.

This is the message which we have heard from Him and declare to you, that God is light and in Him is no darkness at all. If we say that we have fellowship with Him, and walk in darkness we lie and do not practice the truth. But if we walk in the light as He is in the light, we have fellowship with one another and the blood of Jesus Christ His Son cleanses us from all sin.

Remark 92 *People who become insensitive to right and wrong are not born that way. Their insensitivity is the outcome of successive choices to back away from light that says "your actions are wrong or evil".*

The solution for people who find themselves insensitive to truth or *right versus wrong* is Jesus Christ. In John 8:12 and Luke 4:18-19, Jesus says,

"He who follows Me shall not walk in darkness but have the **light of life"**

and

The Spirit of the Lord is upon Me,
Because He has anointed Me
To preach the gospel to the poor;

He has sent Me to heal the broken-
hearted,
To proclaim liberty to the captives
And recovery of sight to the blind,
To set at liberty those who are op-
pressed;
To proclaim the acceptable year of the
Lord.

1 John 1:7 says,

**If we walk in the light as He is in
the light**, we have fellowship with one
another and **the blood of Jesus Christ
His Son cleanses us from all sin**.

Revelation 3:18&20 adds (Jesus speaking):

I counsel you to **buy from me** gold re-
fined in the fire, so you can become rich;
and white clothes to wear, so you can
cover your shameful nakedness; and **salve
to put on your eyes, so you can see**.
Here I am! I stand at the door and knock.
**If anyone hears my voice and opens
the door, I will come in**, and eat with
him, and he with me.[1]

Remark 93 *God has provided every remedy necessary for stony ground, blinded eyes or minds, and
thorny ground meaning God desires to choose everyone He has called. If we desire to be chosen, all we
need do is ask for the help He already has ensured
is available to us via the five facets of what Jesus
has done or is doing for those who believe in His
name. If we do our part, the probability of success
is 100 percent.*

---

[1] *NIV.*

Remark 94 *Regardless of their respective beliefs, everyone regards the Bible as a "good book" and Jesus as a "good man". Whoever finds themselves in darkness, but truly wants to find themselves in light should pick up a Bible, begin reading from the first chapter of the Book of John and ask for Jesus to reveal Himself so they can have the light of life.*

Remark 95 *The reason few are chosen is because many choose riches, evil, and ease of life (absence of persecution) over true wealth, love, and meaningful existence. Those who choose ease of life are not, however, immune from the effects of sin in this world. In choosing ease of life over faith in Jesus Christ in order to avoid persecution, people operate on the probability that by avoiding persecution they will avoid losses or bad experiences in life. It is a fact of life, however, that this play on probability fails more often than it succeeds. Based on the laws of probability then, it is much better to choose faith in Jesus Christ, meaningful existence, and victory over persecution than to choose ease of life.*

Recommended Prayer 21 *Thank you Father of my Lord Jesus Christ that there is no state of heart for which you do not have a solution. For those whose hearts are darkened, you have the light of life. For those whose hearts are stony, you have the heart of flesh. For those burdened with the cares of this world, you have made the promise that if they receive Jesus Christ into their hearts, they shall have peace that surpasses understanding and not lack any good thing. Thank you Father for your lovingkindness in making a way for everyone who desires to be saved to receive your salvation and become a new creation in Jesus Christ. In Jesus name. Amen.*

CHAPTER 20

Our Place in the Kingdom of God

In the preceding chapter, we have established how, regardless of our spiritual state prior to coming in contact with the Holy Spirit, God the Father really has chosen everyone to receive salvation or eternal life through Jesus Christ. Having being saved from our sins, God declares each and every believer has been saved for a predefined good purpose in Jesus Christ.

In this regard, we have the following words in Ephesians 2:8-10, which states,

> For by grace you have been saved through faith, and that not of yourselves; it is the gift of God, not of works, lest anyone should boast. For we are His workmanship, created in Christ Jesus for good works, which God prepared beforehand that we should walk in them.

In the book, *"Purpose Driven Life"*, Rick Warren does a great job of helping us understand the importance of purpose in the living of our everyday life. In this treatise, I focus on what it means when God declares He has predestined us to fill certain roles within His kingdom. An important insight in the passage from the Book of Ephesians is:

Remark 96 *God has created us in Jesus Christ for good works. This means there is no believer in the name of Jesus Christ who is created for bad or evil works.*

If God has prepared us for good works which He had in mind before we were born, He also must have provided resources we require for the performance of these good works. Consider these words in Ephesians 4:7-8, 11-13,

> But to each of us grace was given according to the measure of Christ's gift. Therefore He says:
> When He ascended on high,
> He led captivity captive,
> And gave gifts to men.
> And He Himself gave some to be apostles, some prophets, some evangelists and some pastors and teachers, for the equipping of the saints for the work of ministry, for the edifying of the body of Christ, till we all come to the unity of the faith and of the knowledge of the Son of God, to a perfect man, to the measure of the stature of the fullness of Christ.

In order for believers in Jesus Christ to be able to perform their functions as apostles, prophets, evangelists, pastors, or teachers, God has given His church some gifts through the Holy Spirit. These gifts are enumerated in 1Corinthians 12:4-11.

> There are diversities of gifts, but the same Spirit. There are differences of ministries but the same Lord. And there are diversities of activities, but it is the same God who works all in all. But the manisfestation of the Spirit is given to each one for the profit of all: for to one is given the *word of wisdom* through the Spirit, to another the *word of knowledge* through the same Spirit, to another *faith* by the same Spirit, to another the *working of miracles*, to another *prophecy*, to another *discerning of spirits*, to another d*ifferent kinds of tongues*, to another the *interpretation of tongues*. But one and the same Spirit works all these things, distributing to each one individually as He wills.

All of the preceding verses make clear that the Father gives us ministries (abilities that have to do with the edification of the church), gifts (manifestations of the Spirit that enhance the effectiveness of our spiritual abilities), and activities (professional, recreational, religious etc.) according to His will. In so far as our spiritual abilities and gifts are concerned, our Father, who knows us better than we know ourselves decides what we receive.

Remark 97 *God already has provided the resources we require to achieve the good works for which we are created in Jesus Christ.*

The passage in 1 Corinthians discusses the ministries, gifts, and activities that accrue as gifts to the Church. In relation to people who have yet to confess faith in the name of Jesus Christ, however, Revelation 1:4-6 declares concerning those who are created in Jesus Christ for good works as follows:

> John, to the seven churches which are in Asia:
> Grace to you and peace from Him who is and who was and who is to come, and from the seven Spirits who are before His throne, and from Jesus Christ the faithful witness, the firstborn from the dead, and the ruler over the kings of the earth, **To Him who loved us and washed us from our sins in His own blood, and has made us kings and priests to His God and Father**, to Him be glory and dominion forever and ever. Amen.

Priests intercede for people before a deity. If priests are faithful in their roles, they never seek to oppress people for whom they intercede; rather they seek improvements in their welfare. In the combination of the roles of kings and priests, the Father reiterates the fact that believers in the name of Jesus Christ are to seek to influence affairs on earth via our roles as Kings and Priests, with the objective of improvements in the welfare of everyone living right and discipline, deterrence, or punishments for those who indulge in evil against their neighbors, including those who have yet to confess faith in the name of Jesus Christ.

Since Kings influence affairs via edicts, God expects believers to declare righteous edicts in the

course of daily living.
When we confess,

> Thy will be done,
>
> On earth as it is in heaven

we are declaring righteous edicts in the course of daily living. When consistent with the Father's revelation of Himself in Jeremiah 9:23 we declare:

> The earth is filled with lovingkindness towards those who love Jesus Christ

> On this earth, love for what is right is rewarded with good; love for evil is rewarded with discipline, deterrence, or punishment

or declare:

> I am rewarded with everything I desire that is good for me and everything that is good for me of which I have yet to be aware because I seek first the kingdom of God and His righteousness

and declare

> "The earth is filled with righteousness and peace"

we are declaring righteous edicts in the course of daily living that are consistent with our roles as kings and priests.
Do our declarations matter? Answers can be found in Ezekiel 22:29-31 & 1Peter 3:10-12

The people of the land practice extor-
tion and commit robbery, they oppress
the poor and needy and mistreat the alien,
denying them justice. **I looked for a
man among them who would build up
the wall and stand before me in the
gap on behalf of the lad so I would not
have to destroy it, but I found none**.
So I will pour out my wrath on them
and consume them with my fiery anger,
bringing down on their own heads all
they have done, declares the Sovereign
Lord.

He who would love life

and see good days,

Let him refrain his tongue from evil,

And his lips from speaking deceit.

Let him turn away from evil and do good;

Let him seek peace and pursue it.

For the eyes of the Lord are on the righteous,

And his ears are open to their prayers;

But the face of the Lord is against those
who do evil.

Remark 98 *Kings do not beg. Rather they proclaim,
declare, and enforce edicts. If we do not declare,
proclaim, or enforce righteous edicts given us by
God in His word, we are not living as kings. We
recognize, however, that people in our sphere of influence have choices for which they alone are solely
responsible. So when people live contrary to our
righteous edicts this is not a failure of our edicts
but a choice on the part of people to live contrary to*

*the will of the Father. If the choice by Adam and
Eve to sin in the Garden of Eden was not a failure
on God's part, but rather demonstration of power of
choice, whenever people choose to love sin this is
not a failure of our righteous edicts. This is why we
proclaim justice or truth on this earth as opposed to
a declaration that everyone is saved.*

Kings Have Income Streams

Kings have sources of income generation that
enable wealth creation and accumulation. In order to function in our capacity as kings we need
sources of income that enable wealth creation not
only for our benefit but also so we can be a blessing to others. In addition to our roles in church
then, those of us who are not professional clergy or
support staff within the context of church administrative structures have need of means for income
generation and wealth creation, meaning we have
our own professional activities. The question is:

> *How do we figure out the will of God or
> the "good works we are created for in Je-
> sus Christ" in so far as our professional
> activities are concerned?*

Consider the following words in Colossians 1:9-
10 and Ephesians 5:17,

> For this reason we also, since the day
> we heard it, do not cease to pray for you,
> and to ask that you may **be filled with
> the knowledge of His will in all wis-
> dom and spiritual understanding**; that

you may walk worthy of the Lord, fully pleasing Him, being fruitful in every good work and increasing in the knowledge of God.

Therefore do not be unwise, but **understand what the will of the Lord is**.

The verse from Colossians encourages us to be filled with the knowledge of God's will so we can be fruitful in every good work - the good works God prepared us beforehand to perform, as indicated in Ephesians 2:8-10. The verse from Ephesians encourages us to be wise, with wisdom defined as understanding of the will of God for our lives. These two verses make very clear

Remark 99 *In so far as our activities our concerned - professional, recreational etc., every believer in Jesus Christ works out the path of their life in conjunction with the Holy Spirit.*

Remark 100 *In so far as choices of professions are concerned, no one in the Church of God can take upon themselves the right to determine what other believers in the name of Jesus Christ can be in the conduct of their secular lives. While the Church of God can to its detriment reject a ministry or gift that God has conferred on a believer, no one in Church has the right to attempt to determine other believers' professions. God of course does not expect us to engage in evil professional activities.*

The More Excellent Way

1Corinthians Chapter 12 concludes in the following manner in verses 29 through 31,

> Are all apostles? Are all prophets?
> Are all teachers? Are all workers of mir-
> acles? Do all have gifts of healings? Do
> all speak with tongues? Do all interpret?
> But earnestly desire the best gifts. And
> yet I show you a more excellent way.

What is this more excellent way (1Corinthians
13:2,8-10,13)?

> And though I have the gift of prophecy,
> and understand all mysteries and all knowl-
> edge, and though I have all faith, so that
> I could remove mountains, but have not
> love, I am nothing. Love never fails. But
> whether there are prophecies, they will
> fail; whether there are tongues, they will
> cease; whether there is knowledge, it will
> vanish away. For we know in part and
> we prophesy in part. But when that which
> is perfect has come, then that which is
> in part will be done away. And now abide
> faith, hope, love, these three; but the
> greatest of these is love.

Remark 101 *If we desire spiritual gifts or offices
more than we desire to walk in love, we are nothing
in so far as the Father's estimate of our spiritual
worth is concerned.* **When we desire and exert
effort to walk in love in the power of the Holy
Spirit, we are desiring to walk in the will of
God.**

The Holy Spirit emphasizes the importance of
love and our knowledge of God's will for our lives
in the following passage from Philippians 1:9-11,
which states,

And this I pray, that your love may abound still more and more in knowledge (*of God and His will*) and all discernment (*of spirits or spiritual things, including the will of God*), that you may approve the things that are excellent (*which we would not be able to approve were we not able to recognize them*), that you may be sincere and without offense till the day of Christ, being filled with the fruits of righteousness which are by Jesus Christ, to the glory and praise of God.[1]

Remark 102 *If we desire and exert effort towards walking in love, not in our own power, but in the power of the Holy Spirit, we will find, fill, and thrive in our place within the Kingdom of the Father of our Lord Jesus Christ. Since the Father promises us that we will not lack any good thing if we set our hearts on the well being of His kindgom and His righteousness (love), we thrive in this world while we await the glorification of our bodies at the second coming of our Lord Jesus Christ*

Love Never Fails

I grew up in a home in which my Dad was a minister of the gospel. Our home was located in a mission compound established to provide comforts of living to which missionaries from overseas were used to as they sought to build the kingdom of God in the Southwestern part of the Federal Republic of Nigeria (*FRN*). My elementary school, which used

---

[1]Words in brackets and italics mine.

to be owned by the church and was located within the mission compound, had been taken over by the *FRN* during one of those rash moments within which governments seek to destroy what is good in their own countries.

The rationale for taking over the schools was to liberalize admission so every child has access to the best schools in the country. In the take over of the schools then, the *FRN* was admitting schools run by missionaries or churches were better than government schools. The question is: *Does taking over church schools improve the quality of existing secular schools?* Moreover, if the government has hitherto been unable to run its schools as well as the church schools, why exactly would the quality of the church schools be maintained post take over? So what happened? **The church schools degenerated and eventually many years later, were no different from the secular schools post take over.** This is an apt illustration of the destructive effects of envy within society.

As could be imagined, and what with the emphasis on horticulture and landscaping, the mission compound in which I spent my boyhood was a much better living environment than the environment outside of the walls of the mission compound. In this nigh perfect living environment, the only thing that excited me as a young boy was becoming a minister of the gospel just like my Dad.

Years went by and my Dad was transferred to what then was the capital of Nigeria, Lagos and other parts of the country. I went on to attend one of the elite secondary schools in Nigeria run by the *FRN*, as well as the first and foremost university in Nigeria, The *University of Ibadan*. In all of this time, including the time I spent majoring in *Pure Mathematics* at the University of Ibadan, I never once desired to be anything but a minister of the gospel. Regardless of the existence of a seminary run by the church my Dad worked for, a seminary from which my older brother and younger sister would earn degrees, I attended a secular university and majored in the pure sciences. There was no point in time whatsoever during which I had any desire to attend seminary or major in theology.

Why do I emphasize the lack of desire to be anything but a minister of the gospel?

> *On the face of it, it makes no sense for a person desiring to become a minister of the gospel to attend a secular university and major in Pure Mathematics.*

During the final year of my program at The University of Ibadan, a program from which I graduated with top honors - a First Class Honors degree, I **consciously** asked God for the baptism of the Holy Spirit for the very first time. Does this mean I had never before asked for the Holy Spirit? This of course was not the case. As a Christian I had asked God for the Holy Spirit in preceding years. It was during my final year at the University of Ibadan, however, that I really began to realize the importance of the Holy Spirit. In my final year, I asked for the infilling of the Holy Spirit with knowledge, as opposed to asking because that was what God expected from me as a believer in the name of Jesus Christ. Somehow, but aided by my reading of the book *True Spirituality* by Francis Schaeffer, I had arrived at an understanding that I was supposed to be in fellowship with the Holy Spirit. I asked for the Holy Spirit with some but not full understanding. As promised by Jesus Christ, I received the baptism of the Holy Spirit.

Consequent on my infilling with the Holy Spirit, the Holy Spirit led me into a career in Consulting and Banking, subsequent to which I obtained a PhD in Business & Management, with specialization in Finance from the University of Maryland, College Park USA. Eleven years post doctorate degree, however, I am writing this treatise, which as is the case with any good work inspired by the Holy Spirit, is a blessing the Holy Spirit is conferring on the church. Without my training within the context of a rigorous and analytic PhD program, I would have the spiritual ability to write this book, yet lack the skills necessary to pull it off. By trusting the leading of the Holy Spirit, I have become a minister of the gospel but without any desire to become professional laity. I enjoy the work that I do in my profession - a profession in which by the grace of God I have achieved and continue to achieve tremendous success. In addition to my professional objectives, however, I am allowing the Holy Spirit to produce works such as this through me that bring spiritual blessings into the church of God.

In my experience of God, I have discovered that if we will obey Jesus Christ by doing our best in the power of the Holy Spirit to "**Love one another as Jesus has loved us**" and **exert effort towards**

increasing our knowledge of Jesus Christ and the Father, while we may make mistakes along the way, we will never fail to realize God's good purpose for our lives. *God really does mean the words,* **Love Never Fails.**

Recommended Prayer 22 *Thank you Father of my Lord Jesus Christ for your grace that makes it possible for me to be filled with the love of God alongside faith in the name of Jesus Christ and hope of sharing the glory of God. Thank you Father of my Lord Jesus Christ for revelation of your good will for my life as I fellowship with you, Jesus, and the Holy Spirit. Thank you Father that You are guiding me to my sources of income generation and wealth creation so I have resources required to function as a king and priest within the context of my good purpose in You. I thank You Father that Love Never Fails. In Jesus Name. Amen.*

CHAPTER 21

Does God really expect us to be perfect?

If our goal is to become like Jesus Christ, then perfection or holiness is an important goal of Christian living. Jesus states this goal in Matthew 5:48, which reads as follows,

> *Therefore you shall be perfect, just as your Father in heaven is perfect.*

While Jesus' words reinforce the notion of perfection as a goal of Christian living, we walk away from the words in Matthew 5:48 without an understanding of what it means to be perfect as our Father in heaven is perfect. Thankfully, as evidenced in the commencement of Jesus' statement with the word '*Therefore*', Jesus provides us with a definition of perfection in the verses that lead up to Matthew 5:48.

In Matthew 5:43-45&48, Jesus defines perfection as follows:

> You have heard that it was said, 'You shall love your neighbor and hate your enemy.' But I say to you, love your enemies, bless those who curse you, do good to those who hate you, and pray for those who spitefully use you and persecute you, that you may be sons of your Father in heaven; for He makes His sun rise on the evil and on the good, and sends rain on the just and on the unjust. Therefore you shall be perfect, just as your Father in heaven is perfect.

Remark 103 *It is clear from Jesus' words that perfection is not a state to which we attain. Rather, it is a character we seek to develop. In essence, whenever we resist the temptation to depart from love as the foundation of our actions or choices, we are seeking to be perfect as our Father in heaven is perfect. In order to be perfect then, we simply need to walk in faith in the name of Jesus Christ; walk in the love of God towards everyone - both those who love us and those who do not love us; and believe that as we operate in faith and love we shall be glorified, rewarded with good gifts from God, and become like God.*

> We need wisdom in order to love those who do not love us. For Bible Studies that expound on the wisdom we need in order to love those who do not love us, see Part IV of this treatise.

Holiness

A word that is commonly associated with perfection is 'Holiness'. The word holiness is commonly interpreted as the outcome of spiritual growth that makes us become like God in character. Is this, however, the correct interpretation of the word **'holiness'**?

Consider the following words in Ephesians 4:22-24, 1Thessalonians 3:11-13;

> *That you put off, concerning your former conduct, the old man which grows corrupt according to the deceitful lusts and be renewed in the spirit of your mind, and that you put on the new man which was created according to God, in true righteousness and holiness.*
>
> Now may our God and Father Himself, and our Lord Jesus Christ, direct our way to you. And may the Lord make you increase and abound in love to one another and to all, just as we do to you, so that He may establish your hearts blameless in holiness before our God and Father at the coming of our Lord Jesus Christ with all His saints.

Since "*our hearts are established blameless in holiness via increase and abundance of love in our lives*", true righteousness and holiness involves walking in love towards people around us.

This rendition of holiness is explicit in 1Thessalonians 3:11-13, which states it is the spirit of our minds - willingness to submit to God's definition of perfection - that enables us become a new man created in true righteousness and holiness. In so far as holiness is concerned then, holiness is perfection, and perfection is desire to and capacity to walk in love towards people around us. Any standard of righteousness or holiness that does not derive from desire to and capacity to walk in love is according to the Holy Spirit, false righteousness and holiness.

Ephesians 1:3-4 and Colossians 3:12-14 cast holiness in the following manner.

> Blessed be the God and Father of our Lord Jesus Christ, who has blessed us with every spiritual blessing in the heavenly places in Christ, just as He chose us in Him before the foundation of the world, that **we should be holy and without blame before Him in love**.
>
> Therefore, **as God's chosen people, holy and dearly loved** (*as people already placed in a state of holiness or provided with the capacity, right, or power to be holy*), clothe yourselves with compassion, kindness, humility, gentleness, and patience. Bear with each other and forgive whatever grievances you may have against one another. Forgive as the Lord forgave you. *And **over all these virtues put on love**, which binds them all together in* **perfect unity**.[1]

We have been talking about the love of God since Chapter 3 of this treatise. At this point and within the context of Colossians 3:12-14, we see the '*love*

---

[1]Words in brackets mine.

of God' is not merely the capacity to love but a gift from God. That is, while we can set our hearts to be compassionate, kind, humble, gentle, and patient - characteristics of love - we need the *'love of God'* or equivalently, the *'wisdom of God'* in order to know how to combine kindness with humility, humility with gentleness, gentleness with patience etc. That is, we need the mind of God or the Holy Spirit to perfect application of the attributes of love in our daily lives. In this regard, we have in 1Corinthians 1:24 that Jesus Christ is the wisdom of God. Since *God is love, Jesus is love.* We find then that Jesus Christ is the source of the love of God and source of the wisdom of God, all of which we receive via our fellowship with the Holy Spirit.

> *How do we know we have the wisdom of God?* James 3:17 defines the wisdom of God as follows:

> But the wisdom that is from above (from the Father of our Lord Jesus Christ) is first *pure*, then *peaceable, gentle,* willing to yield, full of mercy and good fruits, without partiality and without hypocrisy.[2]

Suppose we find we need wisdom what then are we to do? James 1:6 reiterates the fact that just as the love of God is a gift from our Father, so also is the wisdom of God. The passage reads,

> If any of you lacks wisdom, let him ask of God, who gives to all liberally and without reproach, and it will be given to him.

Remark 104 *Holiness is not a state we attain to; rather, it is a state in which we already find ourselves. We grow in holiness as the state of holiness*

---

[2]Words in brackets mine.

becomes part of our character. At every point in time
during our growth, however, we are holy. Holiness
then is not the outcome of our Christian life; it is
what we are at every point in time in our journey
towards God and what we become by virtue of our
faith in Jesus Christ. If we characterize holiness as
an outcome of the Christian life, it appears it is possible to have faith in the name of Jesus Christ and
yet not be holy. The Scriptures make very clear a
person who genuinely has faith in the name of Jesus Christ cannot be characterized as unholy even
when they are still deficient in their spiritual understanding. How is this? Because Jesus lived
a perfect life on earth so our imperfections are not
counted against us while we genuinely are in the
process of getting to know God so we can become
like God.

Remark 105 *God has demonstrated His wisdom
in that the principles by which we live in Christ
are exactly the principles of holiness and perfection.
Perfection or Holiness is a state (**a spiritual blessing in Christ***) in which we already find ourselves,
the reality of which we seek to actualize in our lives
via improvements in our capacity to walk in love towards people in our sphere of influence. We remember, however, that the 'love of God' is poured into our
hearts through the Holy Spirit whom He has given
to us. That is, the love of God is a spiritual gift we
receive from God that renders loving responses to
people around us natural. In addition to the love of
God, we need to be desirous of receiving the wisdom
of God.*

Remark 106 *In so far as spirituality is concerned
we become whatever God already has declared us
to be. Only people already declared to be holy by*

virtue of faith in the name of Jesus Christ have the right, power, or capacity to actualize holiness in their lives. While it is possible to strive for holiness without faith in the name of Jesus Christ, it is impossible to become holy via such striving. Why is this? Because we cannot by striving acquire the love of God. The love of God is a gift that grows as we appreciate and cultivate it in our lives, not a reward to the strongest, fairest, or richest.

Recommended Prayer 23 *Thank you Father of our Lord Jesus Christ that the principles by which we live in you are exactly the principles that declare us holy, righteous, or perfect in you. Thank you Father that You have declared us already complete in Jesus Christ (Colossians 2:10) so we never fall under condemnation while in the course of perfecting holiness; that is, while in the course of perfecting our capacity and ability to walk in love. I thank you Father that I do not need to switch from one set of principles for living from Monday through Friday, then put on some other principles for living on Saturday or Sunday. Thank you for the wisdom evident in the good news of your salvation, wisdom that simplifies so I can focus on knowing you and my Lord Jesus Christ within the course of my daily activities. Thank You Father for the love of God in my heart and the wisdom I need to love as Jesus would have me love. Blessed be your holy name Father. In Jesus Name, Amen.*

CHAPTER 22

What exactly is Christian Suffering?

We already know from preceding chapters that one of the attributes of love is patience. Patience is most useful whenever we do not fully understand some phenomenon or circumstance but choose to wait to find out more before arriving at some conclusion, action, or decision. If patience does not devolve into conclusions, actions, decisions, or outcomes, it is not consistent with the Christian notion of patience. Patience is active not passive. Patience is not passive subservience to some notion of fate. Patience works, that is engages in certain actions while choosing to wait in order to obtain conclusions, determine actions, arrive at informed decisions, and enable right interpretations of outcomes in respect of the object of patience.

Do we have any support for this in the Scriptures? Hebrews 6:11-12 states,

> We want each of you to show this same
> **diligence** to the very end in order to make
> your hope sure. We do not want you to
> become **lazy**, but to imitate those who
> through **faith and patience** inherit what
> has been promised.

Diligence implies some activity in which we are
involved; is an antonym to laziness, an attitude
we are implored to avoid; and is interpreted in
Hebrews 6:11-12 as commitment to faith and patience that is rewarded with inheritance of whatever is promised us by God. In so far as the importance of patience for overcoming the world, self, or
the devil is concerned, James 1:2-5 states,

> Consider it pure joy, my brothers (sis-
> ters), whenever you face trials of many
> kinds, because you know that the test-
> ing of your faith develops perseverance
> (*an attribute that requires and is a syn-*
> *onym of patience*).   Perseverance must
> finish its work so that you may be ma-
> ture and complete, not lacking anything.
> If any of you lacks wisdom (*as to how to*
> *persevere with joy in the midst of trials*),
> he (she) should ask God, who gives gen-
> erously to all without finding fault, and
> it will be given to him (her).[1]

If we are to ask God for wisdom in the event we
do not know what to do, clearly perseverance or
patience involves doing something while we wait.
This is evident from the fact that in the presence
of definitions of what is right or 'right things to do' -

---

[1]Words in brackets mine.

in this case, the goal of continuation in love regardless of circumstances - wisdom is knowing what to do and the right timing for the right thing to do.

Remark 107 *Patience is not passive waiting for fate. Patience is revealed in ability to continue working at what is right or continuance in right things while waiting for some event or outcome that is the objective of faith to transpire.*

I have commenced this chapter with a discussion of patience for two reasons. First, patience is essential to ability to translate *Christian Suffering* into *Christian Victory*. Second, in the event my assertions in regard of the concept of '*Christian Suffering*' seem shocking a priori, the reader has need of patience in order to stick with me until the end of this chapter and arrive at an informed decision or conclusion.

Referring to Jesus, Isaiah 53:4-6 states,

*Surely He has borne our griefs
And carried our sorrows;
Yet we esteemed Him stricken,
Smitten by God and afflicted.
But He was wounded for our transgressions,
He was bruised for our iniquities
The chastisement of our peace was upon Him,
And by His stripes we are healed.
All we like sheep have gone astray;
We have turned every one, to his own way;
And the Lord has laid on Him the iniquity of us all.*

In this regard, Matthew 16:21 states,

> From that time Jesus began to show
> to His disciples that He must go to Jerusalem,
> and suffer many things from the elders
> and chief priests and scribes, and be killed,
> and be raised the third day.

Remark 108 *Since Jesus has suffered for every-one who has faith in His name, we are not to de-sire to suffer in this world. If we **desire to suffer** in this world, we are heaping scorn and disdain on the suffering Jesus endured in our behalf.*

Do we have any evidence in favor of this assertion?

It is easily verifiable via a search within a digital Bible, that Jesus never used the word suffer or suffering in relation to those who believe in His name though He used the word in reference to Himself. Since Jesus never attributed suffering to those who believe in His name, faith in the name of Jesus precludes any delight in suffering.

In regard to suffering, Luke 22:15 says,

> Then He (Jesus) said to them, "With
> fervent desire I have desired to eat this
> Passover with you **before I suffer**; for I
> say to you, I will no longer eat of it until
> it is fulfilled in the kingdom of God."

Regardless of the absence of attribution of suffering to those who believe in His name by Jesus, we find Jesus' Apostles, Apostle Paul in particular speaking about sufferings in their writings to believers.

Consider the following texts taken from Philippians 1:29; Romans 8:15-17; and Philippians 3:10-11.

> For to you it has been granted on behalf of Christ, **not only to believe in Him, but also to suffer for His sake**.

> *For you did not receive the spirit of bondage again to fear, but you received the Spirit of adoption by whom we cry out, "Abba Father." The Spirit Himself bears witness with our spirit that we are children of God, and if children, then heirs - heirs of God and joint heirs with Christ, if indeed we suffer with Him, that we may also be glorified together.*

> That I may know Him and the power of His resurrection, and the fellowship of His sufferings, being conformed to His death, if by any means, I may attain to the resurrection from the dead.

Now if Christ has suffered for us and has not attributed any suffering to us, why are we suffering for Him or with Him? Can this attribution of suffering to faith in the name of Jesus be biblical?

> *"how exactly are we to interpret statements made by Jesus' Apostles that seemingly suggest suffering is part of the Christian's creed?"*

The key to reconciling Christ's sufferings on our behalf and the attribution of suffering to those who believe in His name can be found in 1Peter 5:8-9, and 2Timothy 3:12, which read,

Be sober be vigilant; because your adversary the devil walks about like a roar-
ing lion, seeking whom he may devour.
**Resist him, steadfast in the faith, know-
ing that the same sufferings** are experienced by your brotherhood in the world.

Yes, and **all who desire to live godly**
in Christ Jesus will **suffer persecution**
- 2Timothy 3:12

Remark 109 *Christian suffering embodies all of the
temptations or trials the devil targets at those who
have faith in the name of Jesus.*

Remark 110 *We are to resist the devil so as to be
able to maintain faith in the name of Jesus, continue
in our love walk, and continue in the sharing of the
glory of God.*

Remark 111 *If the devil or worldly systems in which
we live were to cease to attack us in order to get
us to give up our faith in the name of Jesus, there
would not be any Christian suffering.*

Remark 112 *Unless by choice or calling from the
Father of our Lord Jesus Christ, faith in the name
of Jesus Christ is not a calling to self abnegation or
rejection of self actualization.*

While Jesus never attributed suffering to His
disciples, He did speak about persecution.

*But I (Jesus) tell you: Love your enemies
and pray for those who persecute you -
Matthew 5:44*[2]

---
[2]Words in brackets mine.

> But before all this, they will lay hands on
> you and persecute you. They will deliver
> you to synagogues and prisons, and you
> will be brought before kings and gover-
> nors, and all on account of my name.
> This will result in your being witnesses
> to them - Luke 21:12-13.

Suppose the absence of persecution, with persecution predicated on faith in the name of Jesus.
Then the experience of those who have faith in the
name of Jesus is captured in the following words
penned in 3John 1:2,

> Dear friend, I pray that you may enjoy
> good health and that all may go well with
> you, even as your soul is getting along
> well.

Remark 113 *Gods' desire for us is prosperity in
our knowledge of Him and His grace, prosperity in
our professions, prosperity in the building of wealth,
prosperity in our marriages or families, prosperity in
our physiology, prosperity in our intelligence, knowledge, or wisdom, and prosperity in everything good
for us, including things good for us that God already
knows, but which we are yet to realize. The only an-
tithesis to this plan from God is persecution from the
devil. We have Jesus' promise that because He has
overcome the devil, if we maintain faith in Him like
Job did, we shall overcome and continue in prosperity in Jesus name.*

What are some of the specific promises provided us by our Father in regard of the reward for
steadfastness in our resistance to the devil's persecutions or persecutions of unreasonable and evil

men that reject faith in the name of Jesus Christ
(2Thessalonians 3:2)?

> You will be betrayed even by parents,
> brothers, relatives, and friends, and they
> will put some of you to death. All men
> will hate you because of me. But not a
> hair of your head will perish. By stand-
> ing firm you will gain life - Luke 21:16-
> 18.

> *But may the God of all grace who called
> us to His eternal glory by Christ Jesus,
> after you have suffered a while, perfect,
> establish, strengthen, and settle you. To
> Him be the glory and the dominion for-
> ever and ever. Amen - 1Peter 5:10-11.*

This verse from the Book of 1Peter states very
clearly that like Job we are to expect joy that is derived from our restoration whenever we pass through
any trials or resist temptations for the sake of the
name of our Lord Jesus Christ.   Job lost almost
everything during his trials, but become wealth-
ier subsequent to his trials.   This is the Father's
promise to us that if we are faithful, any attack
from the devil or evil men in this world ultimately
turns out for our blessing.

In addition to restoration here on earth, we receive spiritual accolades from God for our faithfulness. 2Timothy 4:7-8 states,

> I have fought the good fight, I have fin-
> ished the race, I have kept the faith. Fi-
> nally, there is laid up for me the crown of
> righteousness, which the Lord, the righteous
> Judge, will give to me on that Day, and
> not to me only but also to all who have
> loved His appearing.

Recommended Prayer 24 *I thank you Father of my Lord Jesus Christ that you have called me to prosperity in every facet of my life. Having the understanding that persecution by the devil or evil men in this world is inevitable, I rejoice always in your salvation and give thanks in all of my circumstances knowing you have promised to restore, strengthen, and settle me in your love and in prosperity after I have endured any persecution. I thank you Father that though persecutors can kill my body, not an iota of the essence of my being will be harmed even as I attain to eternal life in you by your grace in Jesus name. I thank you Father that whenever persecution is of unreasonable and evil men, you will deliver me and glorify your name and I shall participate in the glory that is revealed in Jesus Name. Amen.*

CHAPTER 23

The truth about Homosexuality

1Corinthians 6:9-11 states a profound and real truth concerning people who believed in the name of Jesus within the Greek metropolis of Corinth as follows:

> Do you not know that the unrighteous will not inherit the kingdom of God? Do not be deceived. Neither fornicators, nor idolaters, nor adulterers, nor homosexuals, nor sodomites, nor thieves, nor covetous, nor drunkards, nor revilers, nor extortioners will inherit the kingdom of God. **And such were some of you. But you were washed**, but you were sanctified, but you were justified (declared righteous) in the name of the Lord Jesus

and by the Spirit of our God.[1]

In Chapter 5, we discussed how it is impossible for believers in the name of Jesus Christ to enter into the Most Holy place where Jesus and the Father are without a conscious decision to allow our consciences to be washed with the word of God for the renewal of our minds, such that we begin to walk in the love of God. The verse quoted above makes clear many Greek believers were involved in all sorts of unrighteous behaviors prior to declaring faith in Jesus Christ. Upon confession of faith, however, they allowed themselves to be washed with the word of God and became new creations in Jesus Christ whom no longer practiced the unrighteous behaviors outlined in 1Corinthians 6:9-11.

> *As we have discussed in Chapter 6, God declares us righteous then gives us the power to become the righteousness He has declared us to be. If we do not activate this power in us via our desire to be washed with the word of God we never become what God has declared us to be and are unable to enter into intimate fellowship with Father, Son, and Holy Spirit.*

Remark 114 *In order for the believers in Corinth to have given up the unrighteous behaviors outlined, they had to believe the word of God that these behaviors were ungodly in nature and desire to receive the love of God so they could have grace that enables a change not only in behavior but in nature. The goal of the grace of God is not just that we are able to resist temptation, but that we receive the*

---

[1]Words in brackets mine.

life of God such that unrighteous behaviors cease to hold any sway over us. Jesus said (I paraphrase) of the devil in John 14:30 "He (the devil) has no hold on me".[2] The goal of the Christian life is to be filled with the light of God and have no darkness in our lives (1John 1:5-7).

"If any man be in Christ, He is a new creation" the word of God says in 2Corinthians 5:17.

We are saved from a tendency to homosexuality exactly as we are saved from a tendency to steal or commit adultery; that is, by rejecting a spirit of condemnation while confessing who we are in Jesus Christ - heterosexual male and female men. A Christian with homosexual tendencies cannot, however, be living with someone with whom they have a homosexual relationship, yet be confessing who he or she is in Jesus Christ because the actions do not correspond to the confession. As discussed in the immediately preceding chapter, patience or perseverance involves right actions as we await whatever promise is activated by faith in the name of Jesus. If a homosexual person becomes a Christian and continues to live with a homosexual partner, the decision to continue to live with contradicts the desire to become heterosexual. Since perfection requires perseverance in actions that are consistent with heterosexuality, the grace to overcome is difficult or nigh impossible to receive whenever we demonstrate patience as merely waiting as opposed to patience at doing what is right.

Homosexuals who become Christians must believe God that homosexuality degrades the nature, character, or glory of God in man, and ask of God

---

[2] *NIV*

the grace they need to become the new creation God has declared them to be in Jesus Christ. This is essential for maintenance of and growth in fellowship with God. In the presence of acceptance of God's declaration that homosexuality degrades His nature in us, Christians with homosexual tendencies can begin to confess who they are, receive strength to meet their needs, and have resources provided within the Church to help regain heterosexuality that is part of Gods' original plan for man.

There is no middle ground here in so far as God is concerned. If we do not believe God, we cannot go on to know Him as we ought to and as such cannot receive the fullness of His grace or love. Where does that lead then? What will it profit homosexual Christians if they participate in service to God and fellow men on earth, yet remain ineligible for eternal life? The Holy Spirit says in 1Corinthians 15:19,

> *If only for this life we have hope in Christ,*
> *we are to be pitied more than all men.*

What does this mean?

> Are we not pitiable if we receive Jesus as Lord and Savior then renounce all sin except the sin of homosexuality; a sin that keeps us out of fellowship with the Savior with whom we seek fellowship?

Remark 115 *Whenever we reject the work of the Holy Spirit in respect of any facet of our life that is contrary to the will of God, we are saying our interest in Jesus is only for this life.*

If we believe in the name of Jesus Christ, yet refuse to give up our sins so we can participate in the eternal life that accrues to faith in the name of Jesus, we are giving up the most important objective of the five facets of what Jesus has done or is doing for those who believe in His name, which is eternal life. Homosexual tendencies are the outcome of sin on this earth, including deliberate mixings of male and female chromosomes by the devil or his agents with a view to the degradation of God's original design. If homosexual tendencies are part of man's fallen nature, as opposed to God's original creation as represented in Adam, the source of these tendencies is not the Holy Spirit; rather, it must be the case these tendencies have come to be part of man's fallen nature via interactions with fallen angels, principalities, and powers that seek to corrupt God's image in man or the outcome of fantasies that arose in men's minds, fantasies that can be traced back as far as Sodom and Gomorrah; that is, as far back as about *2000 BC.* God does not condemn men or women who have homosexual tendencies because they have these tendencies; rather He condemns because when they come in contact with Jesus Christ and perceive there is power to make them whole they choose to retreat into darkness and remain homosexual.

If a homosexual male or female man desires to have fellowship with Jesus Christ, it is an exercise in futility to receive Jesus Christ, yet refuse to believe the same Jesus Christ when He makes clear to this man that he or she must begin to confess and rejoice in the heterosexuality that is part of God's original plan for man. *All that God expects from a homosexual man is that he believes God and acts on God's word. The rest of it is up to God and we know God's love never fails.*

Remark 116 *We are called not just to overcome ho-*

mosexuality, but to overcome tendency to or love for homosexuality.

A summary of keys to overcoming homosexual tendencies

✠ Acknowledging Jesus Christ as Lord and Savior

✠ Confessing that "since Jesus says homosexuality is sin, we are willing to lay down this sin so we can go on to know our Lord Jesus Christ"[3]

✠ Conforming our actions to our faith in Jesus Christ by distancing ourselves from interactions that feed on homosexual tendencies

✠ Confessing who we are in Jesus Christ - heterosexual male and female men

✠ Whenever we fall short of our confession via the giving in to homosexual tendencies, declaring that "having acknowledged I have fallen short of the glory of God, the grace of God keeps me complete, perfect, and righteous in Jesus Christ while I await receipt of the strength I need to overcome". This involves

  ☙ Approaching God's throne of grace to ask for more grace,

---

[3]I use the word '*we*' because the word of God makes clear none of us are exempt from temptations in any area of life. Also because these steps also are the very same steps required for overcoming any sin or weakness in our lives. If we believe "Jesus was tempted in every point as we are but was without sin" - Hebrews 4:15, it is the case Jesus overcame the tendency to homosexuality so we also can overcome.

✸ Believing immediately that we have received the needed grace,

✸ Resumption of the confession that we are heterosexual male and female men.

✠ Confession that the change in nature we desire cannot fail because God's promises to us cannot fail.

In regard of the impossibility of failure if we do our part, 2Peter 1:2-4 states,

> Grace and peace be yours in abundance through the knowledge of God and of Jesus our Lord. His divine power has given us everything we need for life (*cars, houses, talents, expertise, spouses, children, income generating resources etc.*) and godliness (*ability to overcome any weakness or sin*) through our knowledge of him who called us by his own glory and goodness. Through these (His own glory and goodness) **he has given us his very great and precious promises, so that through them you may participate in the divine nature and escape the corruption in the world caused by evil desires.**[4]

Remark 117 *The key to overcoming sin is believing God that He has freed us not only from sin but from the tendency to sin and provided us with power to live right. If we believe God, we will perfect holiness. If we do not believe God, we shall never be able to remain in the Most Holy Place after we have already gained admission.*

---

[4] *NIV*. Words in brackets mine.

Do we find any evidence in the Scriptures for the notion that we can lose our admission into the *Most Holy Place* if we do not live by faith in the promises of God that have to do with living righteously? 1Corinthians 10:1-6 and Hebrews 4:1-2 state as follows:

> For I do not want you to be ignorant of the fact, brothers (sisters), that our forefathers were all under the cloud and that they all passed through the sea. They were all baptized into Moses in the cloud and in the sea. They all ate the same spiritual food and drank the same spiritual drink; for they drank from the spiritual rock that accompanied them, and that rock was Christ. **Nevertheless, God was not pleased with most of them; their bodies were scattered over the desert. Now these things occurred as examples to keep us from setting our hearts on evil things as they did.**

> Therefore, since the promise of entering his rest still stands, let us be careful that none of you be found to have fallen short of it. For we also have had the gospel preached to us, just as they did; **but the message they heard was of no value to them, because those who heard did not combine it with faith**.

Remark 118 *We cannot say we have faith in Jesus Christ as Lord and Savior yet reject His definition of righteousness, or equivalently, reject His definitions of right and wrong. It is well documented historically that the demise of many world empires is preceded by sexual decadence or immorality.*

Remark 119 *The key to abundant life in Jesus Christ is believing God's declarations about the things He already has accomplished in our behalf through the five facets of what Jesus has done or is doing for those who believe in His Name.*

Recommended Prayer 25 *I thank you Father of my Lord Jesus Christ for calling me out of darkness into your marvelous light. I thank you Father that I am a new creation in Jesus Christ, old things have passed away, and all things have become new. I thank you Father that there is nothing contradictory to your nature that was in me prior to my transference into your marvelous light that can survive the cleansing power in the blood of Jesus and the overcoming power I receive via fellowship with the Holy Spirit. Thank you Father for loving me so much and for desiring friendship and fellowship with me in Jesus Name. Amen.*

CHAPTER 24

The Truth about Sex

We know from the word of God that God designed sex not only for child bearing, but for companionship. This is evident in the following words from Genesis 4:1, which reads,

> "Now Adam knew his wife, and she conceived and bore Cain..."

The verse above does not say,

> "Now Adam desired to have a child through Eve, and she conceived and bore Cain..."

Clearly,

Remark 120 *It was Adam's desire to know (understand, appreciate, and love) his wife that made it possible for Eve to conceive and bear Cain.*

251

The importance of sex in the consummation of a marital relationship is evident in the fact that marriages can be annulled if a man never attempts to get to know his wife within the sense of Genesis 4:1. If a man never gets to know his wife, the couple never are able to become one spiritually, an objective that is the will of the Father of our Lord Jesus Christ. The reason why God created a ranking within marriage after the fall of man in the Garden of Eden was to ensure the spiritual objective of oneness remained achievable. If the man and the woman are both in charge of affairs on earth without any understanding as to who should defer to the other whenever disagreements arise, this leaves room for spiritual chaos, the kind of chaos we are dealing with in the world today.

Remark 121 *In the Fathers' command to the woman to submit to her husband, God desired to ensure the man and the woman could become one spiritually. Within the context of the Father's command, even if a woman were to be 100 percent certain of the rightness of her opinions and as such sure she is right and her husband wrong, so long as a decision or direction on the part of her husband is not an unrighteous or immoral course of action, God expects the woman to abide by her husband's course of action. Why is this? Whenever a woman refuses to submit to her husband's course of righteous action, this brings division between man and wife and gives room for the devil to sow seeds of discord within a marriage. Since discord is the opposite of oneness, a woman's refusal to submit to her husband **in the Lord** enables a defeat of God's objective of spiritual oneness within marriage.*

While it is true men have in the past abused this directive from the Father, clearly this was not the objective of the command from God, else:

- ✣ God would not talk to Mary the mother of Jesus before talking to her fiance, Joseph - Luke 1:26-38,

- ✣ God would not talk to the mother of Samson the Nazirite prior to talking to his father, Manoah - Judges 13:1-5,

- ✣ or appoint a married female prophetess by name Deborah as a Judge over His people, Israel - Judges 4:4.

Many Christians in this age wonder at these commands from Paul recorded in 1Corinthians 14:33-35; and 1Timothy 2:11-14, which state:

> For God is not a God of disorder but of peace. As in all the congregations of the saints, women should remain silent in the churches. They are not allowed to speak, but must be in submission, as the Law says. If they want to inquire about something, they should ask their own husbands at home; for it is disgraceful for a woman to speak in the church.

> *A woman should learn in quietness and full submission. I do not permit a woman to teach or to have authority over a man; she must be silent.*

I pose here a very simple question, which is,

Outside of the church, could women in Paul's age interact freely with men who were not their own husbands?

The answer to this question of course is a re-sounding No!!! The intent of the instructions in 1Corinthians 14:33-35; and 1Timothy 2:11-14 is not the subjugation of women, but an attempt at ensuring the church is not seen to be subverting cultural standards that were common to the then known world, particularly within the Greek States. How do we know this? Paul encourages women to have spiritual discussions with their own husbands at home. Since women were not allowed to interact freely with men not their husbands, in order for a woman to ask questions in church, she would have to interact directly with men that were not her husband, a violation of a cultural norm within the then known world. If Paul allows women to violate the culture in church, this could lead to avoidable persecution because the church would be seen to be attempting to change the culture. Since the purpose the woman seeks by speaking in church can be achieved via the combination of discourse with her husband within her home, and discourse between her husband and other men in church, the objective of influencing the church remained attainable without any deviation from cultural norms or practices.

Remark 122 *In cultural matters that are not inimical to the principles of the Kingdom of our Lord Jesus Christ, God does not expect the church to be disruptive. The only area in which the church never compromises is with respect to the love of God. In this regard the Holy Spirit says in Romans 13:8,* **"Let no debt remain outstanding, except the**

continuing debt to love one another, for he who loves his fellowman has fulfilled the law."

It is a misunderstanding of messages in passages such as 1Corinthians 14:33-35 and 1Timothy 2:11-14 that induces some women to regard Christianiaty as a chauvinistic religion. Much contrary to the case, I have established how laws put in place by the Father of our Lord Jesus Christ provided significant protections for women, including protections of their sexuality in my book titled, *"Truths that Create or Enhance Loving Relationships: The Christian Perspective"*. In this discussion of what constitutes Christian sexuality, it is important to realize God's command that the woman submit to her husband was for administrative and spiritual order that enables spiritual oneness between husbands and wives. Since oneness within families translates into oneness in church and society, there is peace and unity in church or society whenever families are united spiritually.

In this age within which we live, with the exception of Islamic communities and some fringe religions, women interact with men freely. Since the culture has changed outside of the church, the culture within the church must change, but within parameters or boundaries established by God to ensure the possibility of spiritual oneness within families and the church. In this regard, the actions of the Prophetess Deborah are insightful. During periods within which God provided spiritual leadership through her, she led entirely by herself. During periods within which administrative leadership was needed in addition to spiritual leadership, she found a good man by name Barak to stand with her in leadership of the people. God has demonstrated in His word that a woman can provide spiritual leadership for His people. In so far as administration within church is concerned, however, God would have women whom He has called to be spiritual leaders have by their sides men who partner with them to provide administrative leadership. Any woman who desires to be a leader of God's people can learn from the life of the Prophetess Deborah.

Now Back To Sex

The most important issue with biblically legitimate sex in today's world is

"What makes a woman feel like having sex with, or equivalently, feel like knowing (getting intimate with) her husband?" and "What makes a man feel like having sex with his wife?"

Within the context of faith in the name of Jesus Christ,

♡ When a man is patient with and kind to his wife, this ought to make her feel like getting to know her husband better.

♡ *When a man does not insist on his own way because he acknowledges the merits of his wife's opinion, this ought to make her feel like getting to know her husband better.*

♡ When a man is gentle, not proud, and goes out of his way to bless his wife with good things, this ought to make her feel like getting to know her husband better.

I could go on and on, but the point is:

Remark 123 *If men and women would be excited by godliness or love, sex between husbands and wives will provide the spiritual oneness it is designed to provide within the context of marriage. Part of the problem with sex in today's world is that women are sexually excited by charm, physique, money, and power, but not by godliness.*

So what about the other side of the coin? Within the context of faith in the name of Jesus Christ,

♡ When a woman respects her husband even when he is not sure of himself or the paths on which he finds himself, this ought to make him feel like getting to know his wife better.

♡ *When a woman is a good mother to her children and makes the home a haven of peace for her family, this ought to make a man feel like getting to know his wife better.*

♡ When a woman knows when to press her husband for an answer and when to leave him to his thoughts during discussions or challenging times, this ought to make him feel like getting to know his wife better.

Remark 124 *If men would be excited by godliness or love, they will approach sex not with a desire to find release, but with a desire to share love with their wives. When correspondingly, a woman is excited by godliness, her focus is not achieving an orgasm, but on "getting to know her husband better".*

Remark 125 *Sex between husbands and wives creates spiritual oneness when the husband focuses on getting to know his wife during the act of sex and the wife focuses on getting to know her husband. In*

the focus on each other, more love is created along with spiritual oneness.

Remark 126 *In my personal experience, a focus on sharing love during sex makes it easier for a man to satisfy his wife sexually. My ex wife and I were married for 13 years and were romantically involved for 20 years. In all of that time, because sex had no meaning to me outside of getting to know my ex wife, I never once cheated or considered cheating sexually. Now that we are 'divorced', sex continues to have meaning for me only within the context of a loving relationship with another woman.*

Remark 127 *I note here that one of the problems men have in today's world is that most men marry before they fully self actualize within the context of their professions. Since men find it difficult to focus on their wives as they ought before they begin to see themselves as self actualized, sometimes well meaning men who desire to love their wives during the act of sex are unable to accomplish this objective to their heart's desire. Unless a man is able to put aside feelings that relate to pursuit of self actualization while at home, the only remedy for this is self actualization. If a man has need of this ability, all he need do is ask Jesus for help and help will be provided.*[1]

---

[1]PhD programs offered in top universities located in the United States are extremely demanding, perhaps because the professors are determined to give more work than is possible to get done perfectly within a particular space of time. During the course of my PhD program, I was reminded of how imperfect I was every week because every assignment had to be turned in 'imperfect' due to time constraints. I have few recollections of the times my ex wife and I spent having sex while I was a PhD student. Most recollections of sex between my ex wife and myself I retain are from periods during which because I had ac-

Sex in an Imperfect World

In an imperfect world, it is possible for a man to need his wife's help sexually in the sense that he comes into the sex act without any desire to please but to find some succour in copulation with his wife. When sex does not always occur within this context, a woman must understand that her husband can need her in this sense at times. When a man is going through challenging times professionally for instance, he may need his wife to give up her rights to his attention during sex so he can find the spiritual release that enables him master the effects of the challenges on his emotions or mental state. This of course applies to women as well. In an imperfect world, there may be times during which a woman needs to be selfish during the act of sex so she can find release for pent up energies that are destructive.

The word of God anticipates emotional objectives for sex in the following words recorded in 1Corinthians 7:3-4,

> The husband should fulfill his marital duty to his wife, and likewise the wife to her husband. The wife's body does not belong to her alone but also to her husband. In the same way, the husband's body does not belong to him

---

complished some objectives, and was beginning to regard myself as an expert in my field, I felt self actualized. Unless men wait until much later to marry, women will have to help their husbands make the most of sex during periods within which their men do not yet regard themselves as self actualized within their professions.

alone but also to his wife.

Remark 128 *In an imperfect world, no husband or wife can be required to be perfect in so far as sex is concerned. Sometimes a husband needs a free pass to focus on his needs in order to achieve some emotional release during sex. Sometimes it is a man's wife who needs a free pass to achieve emotional release during the act of sex. If this becomes the norm within a marriage, however, either of husband or wife or both parties in the marriage are not focusing on loving or getting to know each other.*

Sex Prior to a Wedding

In light of principles outlined, how are we to regard sex between two people who have yet to have a wedding? While the word fornication is commonly applied to the act of sex between two people yet to have a wedding, a search of the Scriptures reveals the word fornication is only ever applied to illegal sexual acts by married people.

In Jesus' words,

> And I say to you, whoever divorces his wife, except for sexual immorality (*NIV*: "marital unfaithfulness"; *YLT*: "whoredom"; *KJV*: "fornication"), and marries another, commits adultery; and whoever marries her who is divorced commits adultery - Matthew 19:9.[2]

---

[2]Words in brackets mine. *YLT* is acronym for *Young's Literal Translation*; *KJV* is acronym for *Kings James Version* of the Bible.

If two people who have yet to be married offi-
cially in church or by civil authorities are having
sex within the context of the principles enunciated
in this chapter,

 ☻ *They do not have multiple partners with whom*
  they are having sex

 ☻ At least one of the two people is financially
  responsible and as such is prepared, or can
  prepare for formalization of the marriage

 ☻ *Neither one of the two people is married (liv-*
  ing with, having sex with, and providing bene-
  fits only associated with marriage) to someone
  else

 ☻ Sex is not coerced or obtained via deceptive
  confessions that are not supported by thoughts
  in the heart. When a man tells a woman he
  loves her only so she can have sex with him,
  he cannot at the same time claim he is having sex so he can get to know the woman he
  is deceiving.

 ☻ *The couple desire to let people in their social*
  circles, including their families know they have
  decided to be together within the context of a
  loving relationship

 ☻ The couple desire to formalize their marriage
  either in church or within the context of civil
  authority at the earliest possible time

Consider these words in 1Corinthians 7:36,

  If anyone thinks he is acting improp-
 erly toward the virgin (if we are to be
 pragmatic as opposed to idealistic, the

word *woman* is more appropriate than *virgin* in these modern times) he is engaged to, and if she is getting along in years and he feels he ought to marry, he should do as he wants. He is not sinning. They should get married.[3]

According to the Holy Spirit, when a man begins to feel like having sex with a woman he is dating, meaning he desires to get to know her better, if he has decided she is the one, then they should go ahead and get married; that is, they should go ahead and begin to have sex within the context of a marital relationship, else the reiteration, "*He is not sinning*" is meaningless. If they are having sex within the context of a marital relationship, unless they work in different locations, meaning they come together at regular intervals in either location, they must be living together. The date of announcement of the marriage - the wedding date - well, that is another matter entirely, but an event that should occur as closely to the date of marriage as possible. **Note this is not a case of a try out marriage where people live together, test things out, then choose to opt out or get married. This is marriage till death do us part by faith in the name of Jesus Christ, with hope of success rooted in faith that all (good) things are possible in Jesus Christ, and with the love necessary received via fellowship with the Holy Spirit.**

As an illustration of these truths, consider the fact that Isaac had sex with and married Rebecca as his wife before he presented her to his father. The evidence? Genesis 24:66-67,

---

[3]Words in brackets mine.

> Then the servant told Isaac all he had done. **Isaac brought her into the tent of his mother Sarah, and he married Rebekah.** So she became his wife, and he loved her; and Isaac was comforted after his mother's death.

Consistent with Isaac's actions, marriage is not consummated until the act of sex transpires between husband and wife in Deuteronomy 22:13-29. An examination of the laws provided God's people in the Books of Genesis through Deuteronomy reveals no mention of weddings. Up until the time of Joshua then, we find no mention of weddings in the Bible. *Young's Literal Translation* of the Bible reveals the word wedding appears only once in the Bible in Luke 12:36 within the context of a parable told by Jesus. In discussing any feasting associated with marriage between the Church and Jesus Christ, Revelation 19:9 terms the feast a *marriage supper* not a wedding feast. It is clear from the Bible that predication of marriage on a wedding is a non-Christian tradition. In the Bible, marriage is predicated on sex between an unmarried man and an unmarried woman or in polygamous contexts, sex between a married man and a yet unmarried woman. Since God has instituted male man as head of his home, the Bible makes clear polyandry - marriage involving one woman and multiple men - is a non-Christian concept.

Remark 129 *If Isaac married Rebekah by having sex with her in his mother's tent without a wedding ceremony, marriage precedes a wedding ceremony. The concept of wedding night sex is not a Christian but a non-Christian concept. In a perfect world, the act of sex is the initiation of a marriage that is an-*

nounced to society via a wedding. Weddings an-
nounce marriages so no man or woman within a society can claim ignorance of the marital situations of
their neighbors. In a world within which society no
longer is as close knit as in Biblical times, weddings
no longer serve as effective deterrrents to adultery.
In today's world the only deterrent to adultery is a
couple's commitment to their marriage vows.

Recommended Prayer 26 *Thank you Father of our
Lord Jesus Christ for spiritual oneness that is the
objective of sex and marriage. As I focus on getting
to know my spouse during the act of sex, I ask that
the objective of spiritual oneness be achieved in my
marriage in Jesus Name. Amen.*

CHAPTER 25

Prosperity

God desires the prosperity of those whom He calls, whom we have seen He also automatically chooses unless those whom He calls refuse to go on to love God and their fellow man. How do we know this? Deuteronomy 8:18[1] states,

> But remember the LORD your God,
> for it is he who gives you the ability to
> produce wealth, and so confirms his covenant,
> which he swore to your forefathers, as it
> is today.

If God gives us ability to produce wealth as part of confirmation of His covenant, clearly He desires our prosperity in every facet of life.

Revelation 5:12 says of Jesus Christ,

---

[1]All texts in this chapter are from the *NIV* of the Bible.

In a loud voice they sang, "Worthy
is the Lamb, who was slain, to receive
power and wealth and wisdom and strength
and honor and glory and praise".

Since we are in Jesus Christ, we have access to
wealth, power, wisdom and strength, and as such
should desire to be wealthy. These words in Romans 8:32 reassure us of our access to everything
in Jesus Christ in the following manner:

He who did not spare his own Son,
but gave him up for us all - how will he
not also, along with him, graciously give
us all things?

Since all things are reposed in Jesus Christ, we
have access to wealth and only need ask that we
may receive.

But does God give us wealth or ability?

Deuteronomy 8:18 states clearly that God gives
us ability to produce wealth, meaning God typically does not magically produce wealth. On the
contrary, since wealth is produced by ability, there
is a process via which we attain to wealth such
that ex post we are able to describe our path to
attainment of wealth, with wealth attained via the
application of ability received from God.

*Does this imply then a spiritual difference
between wealth and riches?*

Remark 130 *Wealth connotes more than money or
assets that can be monetized. It connotes ability,
well being, accummulated resources, and 'on demand' access to resources that are yet to be associated with the wealthy person. If we need health*

that money cannot buy, we have access to this wealth in Jesus Christ. If we need peace that surpasses all understanding, peace we know money cannot buy, this wealth is available in Jesus Christ. If we seek to be blessed with all good things money can buy, Jesus advises us in Matthew 6:33 to stock up wealth in heaven so He can bless us with every good and perfect gift that brings us joy. When we seek to be wealthy, we seek to build up abundance of resources in God from which we can draw whenever we have any need.

Remark 131 *If we focus on becoming rich, our focus is on plans that enable us accumulate the things of this world, as opposed to plans that fit us into a grander purpose or plan that benefits us and people within our sphere of influence. We focus on how rich we can be as opposed to how much ability we can develop within the grand purpose of our lives, ability that in Christ enables us accummulate wealth. When we focus on being wealthy as opposed to being rich, we do not judge ourselves by how much money we are making or can make, we judge ourselves by how well we are progressing in the grand purpose of our lives as revealed to us by Father, Son, and Holy Spirit.*

Let me illustrate

I graduated from the University of Ibadan in 1995 with a First Class Honors degree in Mathematics; that is, with the highest possible honors. Alongside this achievement, I am a native of the Delta region of Nigeria - the region from which Nigeria extracts crude oil for exports, with crude oil the major source of revenue within the country. At the timing of my graduation, I heard the Holy Spirit tell me very clearly within my spirit that the Father wanted me to pursue a career in consulting. If I were to apply to oil exploration companies, such as Shell Oil, Chevron etc. I would have a double advantage in the recruitment process - highest honors possible in one of the most challenging sciences, and the fact that by hiring a native, the oil exploration companies could illustrate their commitment to sharing the oil wealth with people from the Delta area of Nigeria.

At the timing of my job search in 1996, oil exploration companies were paying somewhere in the neighborhood of US$9,000.00 per year in salaries. Consulting companies? Well, the best of these companies were paying about US$2,500.00 per year in salaries; that is, less than 30% of salaries that accrued within the oil exploration sector. If I wanted to be rich, I would apply to the oil exploration companies for a job. If I wanted to be wealthy, I would apply to the consulting companies. I chose wealth over riches, not only in accepting a job from a consulting company - what now is PricewaterhouseCoopers LLC - but in refusal to apply to any oil exploration company for a job. If the Father wanted me in consulting, I had no business applying to oil exploration companies for a job.

The Father's surprise? Within six months of commencement of my career at what then was Price Waterhouse LLC, my salary increased from about US$2,500.00 to about US$5,500.00. Within two years and four months of my working career, I was earning about US$9,000.00. In 1999, I emigrated to the United States to pursue PhD studies in Finance. Upon graduation from my PhD program in 2005, I started at well over US$100,000.00 per year. I chose wealth over money. The Father of my Lord Jesus Christ threw in everything else that was good and perfect for me, including the money I initially gave up to do His will. Choosing wealth over riches really does pay off if we trust the love of our Lord Jesus Christ.

Does the word of God advise us against a *"focus on becoming rich"*?

Consider the following words in 1Timothy 6:9 and Matthew 6:24?

People who want to get rich fall into temptation and a trap and into many foolish and harmful desires that plunge men into ruin and destruction. For the love of money is a root of all kinds of evil. Some people, eager for money, have wandered from the faith, and pierced themselves with many griefs.

No one can serve two masters. Either he will hate the one and love the other, or he will be devoted to the one and despise the other. You cannot serve both God and money.

If we choose wealth over becoming rich, money is not the most important determinant of our choices in this life. Our Father's needs in so far as the building of His kingdom and proclamation of His righteousness and goodness factor into our decision making. It is our willingness to honor our Father's needs that ensures we are storing up wealth in heaven in our everyday life on this earth. When we attend church services, it is to fellowship with

God and fellow believers. If we are not directly employed by church organizations, it is in our daily actions outside of church services that God expects us to choose Him (wealth) over money.

> *So what then is the place of money in the life of a believer who desires to be wealthy?*

Remark 132 *If we have faith in the name of Jesus, we are to view money as the outcome of good productive activities to which we are directed either consciously or unconsciously by the Holy Spirit. When we desire money without any supporting activities this translates into desire for money that is not accompanied by application of ability. Within such a context, our desire for money is not rooted in desire for wealth. When the money we desire out of productive activities leads us to cheat customers, suppliers, or employees, we are developing love of money that ultimately chokes the Holy Spirit out of our lives.*

Remark 133 *In support of our desire to be wealthy, we are to ask our Father, the Father of our Lord Jesus Christ to give us the ideas, direction, wisdom, power, strength, ability etc. we need to engage in good productive activities that generate income for us and through which we build the wealth that is of this world.*

Remark 134 *If we desire to be wealthy in the things of God, the recipe in Colossians 3:1-3 is: "Since then you have been raised with Christ, set your hearts on things above, where Christ is seated at the right hand of God. Set your minds on things above, not on earthly things. For you died, and your life is now hidden with Christ in God".*

Remark 135 *Since "all things are added to us if we seek first God's kingdom and His righteousness" and "since we grow in spiritual wealth if set our hearts on things above as opposed to earthly things" the recipe for success in accumulating grace, peace of mind, joy, health etc. is exactly the same recipe for receiving houses, cars, professions, money etc. from our Father. Clearly, our Father is not bipolar. His recipe for pleasing Him is exactly the same whether we are at work, at home, at play or in a church service. His recipe for receiving spiritual gifts is exactly the same as His recipe for receiving the things of this life. Jesus is the answer to bipolarity in today's world.*

Remark 136 *Since we accumulate faith, love, and hope in exactly the same manner we acccumulate earthly wealth or resources, if we succeed in accumulating the things of this world - cars, houses etc. - yet are poor in love, we have focused on becoming rich not on becoming wealthy. In the story of Job, the Father has demonsrated, however, that a believer can be wealthy in love yet due to trials designed for the glory of God be deficient in the things of this world at some particular point in time. We know, however, that in the long run just as was the case with Job, a believer who is wealthy in love will have all good things to enjoy in so far as the things of this life are concerned.*

Recommended Prayer 27 *Thank you Father of my Lord Jesus Christ that you desire my prosperity in every facet of life and have set up your kingdom such that exactly what I need to do to prosper as a citizen of heaven is exactly what I need to do to prosper in the things of this world that I need for daily existence and prosperity. Thank you Father*

that you are the answer to bipolarity in this world.
In Jesus Name. Amen.

Postscript

I left the United States for my native country Nigeria in 2013 consequent on the failure of my first
marriage. Like most righteous men in the Bible
who failed God in one area or the other (think Moses,
Abraham, Samson, Elijah etc.), this is one area of
my life in which I have failed at actualizing my visions of the future. I have failed in part because at
the timing of my first marriage, I did not know God
well enough to handle the marriage decision as a
mature Christian man. Like some other honest
men who have failed in their marriages, I naively
imagined that since I loved my ex wife and she
loved me and since we both professed faith in Jesus Christ, that would be enough to get us through
marital life. I note here that I am not necessarily
saying "*I made a mistake in the marriage decision*
though that may well be the case". The Father has
taught me that the most important question when
things do not work out right is not "**did I make**
a mistake?" Rather, the most important question
is: "**how do I use what I know now to create a**
better future?"
     One thing I do know?

> "*If I knew the things I know today and*
> *had the spiritual maturity I have today*
> *at the timing of my marriage decision in*
> *1999, I either would have had a better*
> *marriage with the same woman from whom*
> *I now am divorced or the two of us never*
> *would have married each other*".

What do I mean by this? God wooed Judah (the same nation) for thousands of years before the time was right for a lasting marriage through Jesus Christ our Lord and Savior. What was it God was wooing out of Judah? Her imperfections - imperfections such as idolatry that eventually would scuttle the marriage if they were to remain. While the Church still is not a perfect bride for Jesus Christ, we know this is a marriage that will be perfected and survive for all eternity. If I knew the things I knew today, I would have wooed better with the patience and wisdom God gives, and with the same woman *potentially* could have had a better marriage that would have been perfected in Jesus Christ. The good news is I have the opportunity to apply these principles within the context of courtship and marriage in the present and future.

Today whenever I have the opportunity to counsel young people, I tell them (in essence)

> *"If you do not ensure your choice of spouse fits within your understanding of God or His purpose for your life, and do not ensure you and your spouse are in agreement as to the guideposts you will adopt in arriving at decisions within your marriage, even if your marriage survives you will have many troubles to navigate".*

Why is this important? Many a times people do not necessarily mean the same thing when they say "*I believe in Jesus Christ as Lord and Savior*". Believers in the name of Jesus can have cultural, educational, or environmental philosophies that color applications of principles of the kingdom of God in their lives. If two people with different cultural colorings of their faith and differences in understanding of what it means to be a Christian get married, unless they experience some convergence in beliefs and applications of faith, their marriage is bound to experience many troubles that would be avoided if they resolved these colorings and understandings within the process of arriving at the marriage decision.   The mistake I made and which some other honest Christians have made is the assumption that confession of faith in the name of Jesus implies we have the same understanding of God, the place of God in our lives, or the same principles for decision making in critical situations.

I have written this treatise with a view to helping believers like myself and searchers for truth not yet Christians arrive at a common understanding of what it means to have faith in the name of Jesus.

This goal of a common understanding of the faith we share is not mine; rather it is the will of our Father who says in Ephesians 4:11-13,

And He Himself gave some to be apostles, some prophets, some evangelists and some pastors and teachers, for the equipping of the saints for the work of ministry, for the edifying of the body of Christ, **till we all come to the unity of the faith and of the knowledge of the Son of God, to a perfect man, to the measure of the stature of the fullness of Christ.**

It is my hope that you are arriving at a better and common understanding of what it means to have faith in the name of Jesus. In Jesus Name. Amen.

Recommended Prayer 28 *Thank you Father of my Lord Jesus Christ for knowledge, discernment, and wisdom that enables me turn every stumbling block into a stepping stone to greater glory in Jesus Name. Amen.*

CHAPTER 26

Sabbath Rest

In Mark 2:27, Jesus proclaims,

> "The Sabbath was made for man, not
> man for the Sabbath. So the Son of Man
> is Lord even of the Sabbath."

In these words, Jesus declares He the Lord of the Sabbath created the Sabbath to be a blessing to man. Since God does not embark on creative activities just to demonstrate His power but for a purpose, Jesus in these words declares there is purpose to the Sabbath. Consistent with these declarations, Genesis 2:1-2 states,

> Thus the heavens and the earth were
> completed in all their vast array. By the
> seventh day God had finished the work
> he had been doing; so on the seventh

day he rested from all his work. And
God blessed the seventh day and made
it holy, because on it he rested from all
the work of creating that he had done.

Every day created by God was declared good in
Genesis Chapters 1 and 2. Since "*there is none
good but God*" (Matthew 19:17), God has infused
every day created by Him with His righteous presence. In addition to the seventh day being good,
however, God declared the seventh day holy; that
is, set apart the seventh day for a righteous purpose because He had rested on the seventh day
from all the work He had done. Since God dwells
in eternity and as such is not bound by time, the
Sabbath could only have been instituted for man,
with God demonstrating to us the essence of the
Sabbath by Himself resting on the seventh day.
We may ask then,

"What is the purpose for which the seventh day was declared holy by God?"

"Is the purpose for the seventh day
implied in the fact that God rested from
all of His work on the seventh day?"

An Aside: Eternity and Time

*Ever wondered how God can dwell in
eternity yet be ever present in each time?*

If God already knows how everything
will shake out - who will embrace His

love and who will reject His love - why
does He bother to love everyone?

> *Why not just be partisan and love only*
> *those who He knows will love Him back?*
> *In fact, why not just kill off everyone whom*
> *He knows will not respond to Him and*
> *leave only those who love Him?*

God loves everyone because everyone must have a chance to make the choices foreseen by God before they can be judged by Him. This is the essence of the power of choice bestowed on man by God. God has demonstrated also that killing off all evil people at a particular point in time does not solve the problem of evil in the world, because children of righteous people like Noah do not all turn out righteous. Within a few years of the destruction of all evil people during the flood, there were enough evil descendants of a righteous Noah that God had to interfere in affairs on earth by confounding man's language, resulting in separation into different languages or ethnicities (Genesis 10:32 & Chapter 11).

Historians believe this confounding of languages is a fable, but agree man is of one essence or origin. Fable or not, the combination of one origin and multiple languages implies some confounding of languages at some point in time in the course of history.

The most wonderful implication I think of God's dwelling in eternity and presence in time is:

Remark 137 *He walks with us, talks with us, and enjoys the journey with us within the context of time and space. While He guarantees we will have victory over every challenge that comes our way (John 16:33; Romans 5:17; 1John 5:5), in the choice not to reveal every detail of the future He already knows, He ensures our walk with Him remains interesting and hopeful, with room for unanticipated newness, discovery, growth, knowledge, wisdom, relationships, or achievements. Only a God who loves deeply cares so much about meaningfulness of life*

He refuses to reveal every detail of our glorious future ahead of time.

Remark 138 *In the absence of any uncertainty in this life, life would be meaningless. The only certainty that we need in this life is the assurance that if we love God, meaning we desire and make effort to live a life of love, victory over every challenge that comes our way is guaranteed. Jesus ensured in time and space our assurance of this guarantee from God.*

Remark 139 *In so far as it relates to man or life on this earth, God uses His knowledge of eternity to ensure His purposes and judgments are established in the earth.*

> ### Back to Sabbath Rest

Consider the following words in Ephesians 5:1-2, and 1John 4:17

> **Be imitators of God**, therefore, as dearly beloved children and live a life of love, just as Christ loved us and gave himself up for us as a fragrant offering and sacrifice to God.

> Love has been perfected among us in this; that we may have boldness in the day of judgment; **because as He (God) is, so are we in this world.**[1]

Remark 140 *If we are to be imitators of God, we should desire to rest every seventh day from our*

---

[1] Words in brackets mine.

economic activities, devoting said time to fellowship with God, family, and friends. In the devotion of one day a week to fellowship with God, family, and friends, we remind ourselves of the importance of love and relationships.

Remark 141 *When we rest one day a week, we devote time to celebration of the spiritual rest we already have in Jesus Christ. The Sabbath does not give rest. Rest comes from our relationship with Jesus Christ. In the celebration of the rest we already have, however, we proclaim or declare Jesus as Lord and Savior.*

What then are we not to do on the Sabbath?

Remark 142 *So long as we focus on spending some of the Sabbath time with God, and some with family or friends no one can judge our Sabbath keeping. Attendance at church services on Sabbath enables us spend time with God, family, and friends at the same time. This is supposed to be the benefit of church services that hold on Saturday or Sunday morning, the days most Christians set apart for Sabbath rest.*

In regard of judgment concerning sabbath observance, Colossians 2:16 states,

> Therefore do not let anyone judge you by what you eat or drink, or with regard to a religious festival, a New Moon celebration or a Sabbath day.

This verse from Colossians does not say we are not to keep a Sabbath day. Rather it states we alone are the judge of how we keep a Sabbath day.

This principle is evident in the life of Jesus because He kept the Sabbath as He saw fit, not as defined by the religious authorities of His day.

In John Chapter 5, Jesus healed a paralytic who was lying by the Pool of Bethsaida on the Sabbath. As is wont with God, the paralytic had to demonstrate faith in Jesus' words in order to be healed since Jesus instructed him in verse 8 while still paralysed to take up the couch on which he lay and begin to walk. The man of course got healed the moment he began the process of attempting to rise up from his couch and as instructed took up his couch and began his journey home. When the healed man ran into Pharisees, they enquired as to why he was carrying a couch around on the Sabbath to which he replied it was Jesus who had made him whole. Consider then Jesus 'response to the Pharisees in John 5:16-17,

> **So, because Jesus was doing these thing on the Sabbath, the Jews persecuted him**. Jesus said to them, "My Father is always at his work to this very day, and I, too, am working."

While Jesus' words in John 5:16-17 demonstrate He kept the Sabbath as He saw fit or as guided by His Father, they simultaneously raise a seeming conundrum in the sense that

> If God always is at His work how could He have rested on the seventh day?

In reality, there is no conundrum because God dwells in time and space only in relation to man. Since God dwells in eternity except within the context of interactions with man or life on this earth,

God is not bound by time, as such the notion of continuous observance of the Sabbath is meaningless in relation to God. God rested on the first Sabbath during creation week merely to demonstrate by His own example to us the essence or purpose of Sabbath.

Rest and Newness

When the Bible says God rested from all the work He had done it means exactly what it says literally yet with a spiritual interpretation. Since God had seen and declared all He had created to be good, **God rested from all He had already done** via refusal to continue to tinker with what He had declared to be good. It was not that God was not working at all on the seventh day; rather it was the case that whatever He was doing on the seventh day was something entirely new.

Do we have any support for God moving on to new things from the Scriptures? Isaiah 43:18-19 states,

Some of the following verses are promises from God. I pray you receive them by faith in Jesus Name.

> Forget the former things; do not dwell on the past. **See, I (God) am doing a new thing!** Now it springs up; do you not perceive it? I am making a way in the desert and streams in the wasteland.[2]

In regard of people in rebellion against God, Numbers 16:30 states,

> **But if the LORD brings about something totally new**, and the earth opens its mouth and swallows them, with everything that belongs to them and they go

---

[2]Words in brackets mine.

down alive to the grave, then you will
know that these men have treated the
LORD with contempt.

Psalm 40:1-3 states,

> I waited patiently for the LORD; he turned
> to me and heard my cry. He lifted me
> out of the slimy pit, out of the mud and
> mire, he set my feet on a rock and gave
> me a firm place to stand. **He put a new
> song in my mouth, a hymn of praise
> to our God**. Many will see and fear and
> put their trust in the LORD.

Concerning the new covenant in which we stand
at the present time, God declares as follows (in
Jeremiah 31:31) prior to the consummation of the
covenant in the life, death, resurrection, ascension, and intercessory ministry of our Lord Jesus
Christ:

> The time is coming, declares the LORD
> when **I will make a new covenant** with
> the house of Israel and with the house
> of Judah.

In these words from Lamentations 3:22-23, we
are assured of the newness of Gods' love:

> Because of the LORD's great love we are
> not consumed, **for his compassions never
> fail. They are new every morning**; great
> is your faithfulness.

God declares His focus on new creative activities in Isaiah 65:17 as follows:

Behold, **I will create new heavens and
a new earth**. The former things will not
be remembered, nor will they come to
mind.

Concerning those who have desire for righteousness God declares in Ezekiel 36:26,

**I will give you a new heart and put a
new spirit in you**; I will remove from
you your heart of stone and give you a
heart of flesh.

Remark 143 *Our God Father of our Lord Jesus Christ
is a God of new things. Sabbath signifies rest that
is the beginning of new things. When we rest as
God rested we are telling God we are interested in
new things in a new week.*

At this juncture, it is clear from the Scriptures that the seventh day was created
for rest. But

Must we rest from our work on Saturday, the seventh day of the week?

Since God rested on Saturday, the seventh day and
set it apart for that purpose, to the extent possible we should desire to rest on Saturday, the seventh day of the week. In the current dispensation
within which civil and spiritual authority no longer
are conjoined as was the case in Biblical Israel or
Judah, however, the Father has in His magnanimity and graciousness freed us from condemnation
in the event we are unable to rest on the seventh
day. In the event then of jobs or responsibilities
that require us to work on Saturday we can rest

on any other day of the week as guided by the Holy Spirit.

Jesus declares as follows in John 4:21-24,

> Believe me, woman, a time is coming when you will worship the Father neither on this mountain nor in Jerusalem. You Samaritans worship what you do not know; we worship what we do know, for salvation is from the Jews. Yet a time is coming and now has come when the **true worshipers will worship the Father in spirit and truth**, for they are the kind of worshipers the Father seeks. **God is spirit, and his worshipers must worship in spirit and in truth**.

In these words, Jesus demonstrates His Father, our Father desires we get to know Him; hence, His interest in revealing Himself to us within the course of ordinary daily living.

If we are to worship in spirit and in truth, the day of worship, the location of worship, the posture of worship all become irrelevant in the determination of the acceptability of our worship. This more so given the commandment in 1Corinthians 10:31, which states,

> So whether you eat or drink or whatever you do, do it all for the glory of God.

Remark 144 *If we are living for the glory of God in each and every action on each and every day, we cannot at the same time consider any day a day of worship. A day designated for rest from economic activity so we can renew our strength and renew our relationships remains valid, however, because the rest is eminently spiritual, physical, and social.*

Will the seventh day Sabbath ever become binding on Christians again?

Combined, Colossians 2:16-17 and Isaiah 66:22-23 imply we will keep the seventh day Sabbath in the new earth subsequent to the Second Coming of Jesus Christ. The texts read:

> So let no one judge you in food or in drink, or regarding a festival or a new moon or sabbaths, **which are a shadow of things to come**, but the substance is of Christ.

> As the new heavens and the new earth that I make will endure before me, declares the LORD, so will your name and descendants endure. From one New Moon to another and from one Sabbath to another, **all mankind** will come and bow down before me, says the LORD.

We bow not as an act of servitude, but an act of appreciation for what Jesus has done for us.

Since civil and spiritual authority are conjoined in the rulership of Jesus Christ in the new earth, there no longer is any need for magnanimity or graciousness on God's part in so far as the keeping of the seventh day Sabbath is concerned.

Why Sabbath keeping is Important

If we spend all of our time on economic activities, in our actions we declare *"just being"* or *love* is not important. Simultaneously, we confess relationships are important only within the context of work. But if we work to support our dreams and our families, work in of itself is supposed to enhance our family relationships, meaning time spent *just being* with our families is important. Since we focus most of our energies on economic activities six days a week, a seventh day within which our relationship with God and relationships with family and friends are at the center of our plans and activities ensures we remain focused on what is most important, which is *being* or *becoming* and *love*.

We have discussed the importance of *"becoming"* in Chapter 6.

In addition to a beneficial effect on *being, becoming*, and *growing in love*, resting one day a week helps keep our minds, bodies, and spirits fresh so we can remain innovative and bring newness to life within the context of pursuit of economic activities. Ultimately then Sabbath keeping is designed for our benefit. If employers believe taking time every year to refresh our minds, bodies, or spirits is important, much more so weekly renewal that keeps us relevant and as such helps preserves our jobs until the next annual leave. **If we do not cherish Sabbath keeping we do not come under condemnation from God. We, however, also do not enjoy the physiological, intellectual, social, civil (within-family), and spiritual benefits of setting apart time for God and family.** If, however, we stubbornly reject personal reminders or promptings from the Holy Spirit that we need Sabbath rest, we disobey God within the context of our personal relationship with Him and can lose our relationship with Him.

Our Father has designed Sabbath rest for our benefit. We are wise to make the most of this blessing from God.

Recommended Prayer 29 *I thank you Father for creating Sabbath for my benefit. Thank you Father for newness as I rest in your grace and love once every week to the glory of your holy name. Thank* *you Father that by your grace I reap all of the bene-fits of Sabbath rest as I set apart one day a week to celebrate and enjoy your love and the love of fam-ily, friends, or loved ones. Thank you Father for for unanticipated newness, discovery, growth, knowl-edge, wisdom, relationships, or achievements made possible because I live by faith in the name of my Lord Jesus Christ. In Jesus Name. Amen.*

CHAPTER 27

Enoch

Abraham believed God and demonstrated his faith in righteous actions.

Noah found favor with God and saved his entire family.

Moses loved the people of God and was the humblest man that ever lived.

Enoch walked with God and was not for God took him.

Since the Holy Spirit had yet to be given while Jesus was on earth, He could not have been available to Enoch thousands of years prior.

At a time when Jesus Himself confides the Holy Spirit was not yet available to man (John 7:37-39), Enoch found a way to walk with God; that is, achieved a state promised by God that was not supposed to be possible or feasible until Jesus had lived a sinless life on earth, died, resurrected on the third day, and ascended to His Father in heaven.

If Enoch could walk with God during a time during which walking with God was supposed to be impossible, those of us who live in this age in which the Holy Spirit already has been bestowed upon us have no excuse for falling short of fellowship with Father, Son, and Holy Spirit.

Let us go on to know the Lord. In Jesus Name. Amen.

Part IV

Epilogue:
Understanding the
Love of God

In this section, I include a series of 8 Bible Studies that provide insights into how those of us who believe in the name of Jesus Christ are supposed to love people around us as Jesus has loved us.

Introduction to Study Series

The word of God says "God is Love" - 1John 4:8. In 1Corinthians 13, the Holy Spirit defines love in this manner:

> If I speak in the tongues of men or of angels, but do not have love, I am only a resounding gong or a clanging cymbal. If I have the gift of prophecy and can fathom all mysteries and all knowledge, and if I have a faith that can move mountains, but do not have love, I am nothing. If I give all I possess to the poor and give over my body to hardship that I may boast, but do not have love, I gain nothing.
>
> *Love is patient, love is kind. It does not envy, it does not boast, it is not proud. It does not dishonor others, it is not self-seeking, it is not easily angered, it keeps no record of wrongs. Love does not delight in evil but rejoices with the truth. It always protects, always trusts, always hopes, always perseveres.*
>
> Love never fails. But where there are prophecies, they will cease; where there are tongues, they will be stilled; where there is knowledge, it will pass away. For we know in part and we prophesy in part, but when completeness comes,

what is in part disappears. When I was a child, I talked like a child, I thought like a child, I reasoned like a child. When I became a man, I put the ways of childhood behind me. For now we see only a reflection as in a mirror; then we shall see face to face. Now I know in part; then I shall know fully, even as I am fully known.

And now these three remain: faith, hope and love. But the greatest of these is love.

An important fallout of these two passages is:

1. Love is the essence of God, but love cannot necessarily be deduced from actions because actions that appear to be "good" can have motives other than love. This is the rationale for the following words in 1Samuel 16:7 "...the LORD looks at the heart". Heart implies of course motives or sincerity of actions - 1Timothy 1:5; 1Peter 1:22.

2. While 1Corinthians 13 enables an understanding of what love is, it does nothing to teach us which attributes of love are most appropriate in any given situation.

Statement number 1 above is self explanatory. Let me illustrate Statement Number 2 with the following questions or scenarios:

✠ 1Corinthians 13 states "love rejoices in the truth" but also states, "love is patient, love is kind". The question is: Since rejoicing in the truth can run counter at times to patience and kindness, when is it better to be patient and kind vis-a-vis emphasizing the truth?

✠ Is it ever okay for love not to protect, trust, hope, or persevere? If a parent turns in a son or daughter who has never been involved in evil but whom they think or believe is planning evil to civil authorities, are they not walking in love because they are not protecting, trusting, hoping, or persevering in beliefs about the good character of their son or daughter?

✠ When a spouse gives up on a marriage, are they violating the requirement of perseverance and hence not walking in love?

We know the Word of God is neither deficient nor self contradictory. Whenever seemingly conflicting attributes of love apply in a particular situation, however, it can become unclear which attribute predominates or is more appropriate than the other.

In this series of Bible studies, I develop principles for managing the conflicting attributes of love using Jesus' response to different events that occurred in His life. While there are specific principles to be applied, the overarching principle that is revealed in the life of our Lord Jesus Christ and the Apostles is the importance of allowing our decisions and actions to be guided by the Holy Spirit. This is implied clearly in Romans 8:14, which says:

> For as many as are led by the Holy Spirit,
> these are sons of God.

The word of God states clearly, however, that the Holy Spirit leverages on our knowledge in guiding us. John 14:25-26 states,

> All these I have spoken while still with
> you. But the Counselor, the Holy Spirit,

whom the Father will send in my name,
he will teach you all things and will remind you of everything I have said to
you.

Remark 145 *Since the Holy Spirit teaches us, our knowledge of God is important for direction in decision making. Since the Holy Spirit helps us remember what we already know or have learnt, our ability to discern the Holy Spirit's direction is not independent of our knowledge of who God is and how He expects us to respond to different circumstances.*

John 14:25-26 makes clear that while the guidance of the Holy Spirit is the overarching principle for decision making, what we know of God, His ways, His approach to resolving conflicts between grace and justice or other conflicting principles renders discernment of the guidance of the Holy Spirit easier in specific situations.

The Father of our Lord Jesus Christ emphasizes the importance of our knowledge of Him in this declaration recorded in Jeremiah 9: 23-24:

Let not the wise man boast of his wisdom

or the strong man boast of his strength

or the rich man boast of his riches,

but let him who boasts boast about this:

that he understands and knows me

that I am the LORD,

who exercises lovingkindness, judgment

and righteousness in the earth,

for in these I delight, says the LORD.

Since God balances three different attributes, which are lovingkindness, judgment (equivalently, truth or justice), and righteousness, believers who know God must understand how to balance these attributes of God.

The specific contexts of applications of love we will explore in this Bible Study series are:

✠ **Lesson 1**: Knowing when to hand over your coat

✠ **Lesson 2**: Knowing when to walk two miles

✠ **Lesson 3**: Knowing when to endure affliction

✠ **Lesson 4**: It is okay not to want to bless if...

✠ **Lesson 5**: Knowing whether it is okay to quit

✠ **Lesson 6**: Knowing how to be angry, yet not sin

✠ **Lesson 7**: Knowing when to insist on your way

✠ **Lesson 8**: The essence of the Christian faith

The word of God says in James 3:17,

> *But the wisdom that is from above is first pure, then peaceable, gentle, willing to yield, full of mercy and good fruits, without partiality and without hypocrisy.*

I pray you will find wisdom in God as you make your way through these Bible studies in Jesus Name. Amen.

300

CHAPTER 28

Knowing when to hand over your coat

Context: "And if anyone wants to sue you and take your shirt, hand over your coat as well" - Matthew 5:40.

The statement above from Matthew 5:40 was spoken by Jesus. Who best then to illusrate this principle than Jesus Himself. Let us explore how Jesus exemplified this principle in His own life in so far as people wanting to hurt him is concerned.

Study Outline

1. What was Jesus' response at a point in time when people wanted to hurt him? John 8:59

2. What was Jesus' response to similar attempts to hurt him in John 10:31-39

3. What happened on one occasion where they sought to arrest Jesus? John 7:44-46

4. But did Jesus expect to be killed at some point in His ministry? Matthew 16:21

5. When did Jesus set His face to go to Jerusalem? Luke 9:51; Luke 18:31; John 11:5-16

6. When did Jesus come down to earth to save us? Galatians 4:4

7. Why is it not contradictory for Jesus to resist mistreatment at some point, then eventually submit to it? Hebrews 12:1-2

8. What did Jesus instruct his disciples to do if rejected in any town? Mark 6:11

Discussion

Unless directed by the Holy Spirit, God expects us to resist evil that is directed at us. Whenever God instructs us to not resist evil, however, there is *JOY* set before us (Hebrews 12:1-2). In the same manner Jesus, the author and finisher of our faith waited until submission to the Romans and the Jews would lead to *JOY* before allowing Himself to be crucified. In Jesus' statement that we should be willing to submit to an evil person who wants to take advantage of us or mistreat us, He puts us on notice that it is possible for the Holy Spirit to instruct us not to resist an evil person. Whenever the Holy Spirit instructs us to not resist such people, we are not feel stupid or suspect it is some false spirit attempting to mislead us. Rather, we are to rejoice at the *JOY* set before us.

The sequence of Jesus' actions is revealing. First, He taught like no one ever did, so the authorities got angry. Since even soldiers were getting carried away with Jesus' teachings, the authorities decided to try to get Him to say things that would justify stoning Him to death on the spot, as opposed to trying to arrest Him. Once the authorities began trying to stone Him, first Jesus hid Himself. Next, He escaped from them; then finally submitted to them. But when did He submit? When submission was the only route to glory and joy. Luke 9:51 states

> "*when the time had come* for Him (Jesus) to be received up, that He steadfastly set His face to go to Jerusalem".[1]

What was the outcome of Jesus 'submission to mistreatment?

> And you, being dead in your trespasses and the uncircumcision of your flesh, He has made alive together with Him, having forgiven you all trespasses, having wiped out the handwriting of requirements that was against us, which was contrary to us. And He has taken it out of the way, having nailed it to the cross. Having disarmed principalities and powers, He made a public spectacle of them, triumphing over them in it - Colossians 2:11-15.

Jesus defeated His enemies who sought to harm him by submitting to the mistreatment. Not only

---

[1]Word in bracket mine.

did He win, He won victory for you and me by rescuing us from under the law and placing us within His grace.

Life Lesson 1 *Like Jesus, we are to submit to evil persons or mistreatment only when the Holy Spirit indicates submission is the path to achieving victory or the path that brings joy to us and glory to God.*

The essence of Jesus' words in Matthew 5:40 is that we should never be surprised or resistant whenever the Holy Spirit instructs us to respond to evil persons in the manner directed, a response others, including fellow believers may consider foolish or stupid.

In Acts Chapter 21, Paul proceeded on a journey in spite of prior revelation from God to Himself and other believers as to the course of actions that would transpire if he were to proceed on his journey to Jerusalem; that is revelations of his arrest initiated by evil men who were in opposition to the gospel. Why did Paul proceed on this course of action regardless of remonstrations from fellow believers? Because the Holy Spirit instructed Him so to do.

> The lesson: Do not hand over your coat unless the Holy Spirit tells you so and assures you of *JOY* afterward as was the case for Job, Paul, and Jesus.

> But is not the case Paul was beheaded eventually after he had written all of the Books in the New Testament, the purpose for which God allowed him to be incarcerated?

Yes, it is true Paul died via a beheading. It is true also, however, that the person who beheaded him, the Ceasar who sentenced him, and the soldiers who guarded him all died and are dead. Death is not failure of the victory promised us by Jesus Christ. We know, however, that those of us who believe in Jesus Christ will have the last laugh over death at the Second Coming of Jesus Christ.

The word of God declares in 1Corinthians 15:52, 54-57 as follows,

> In a flash, in the twinkling of an eye, at the last trumpet. For the trumpet will sound,, the dead will be raised imperishable, and we will be changed. For the perishable must clothe itself with the imperishable, and the mortal with immortality. When the perishable has been clothed with the imperishable, and the mortal with immortality, then the saying that is written will come true: **"Death has been swallowed up in victory**." "Where O death, is your victory? Where, O death, is your sting?" The sting of death is sin, and the power of sin is the law. **But thanks be to God! He gives us the victory through our Lord Jesus Christ.**

It is fitting to end with the words in Hebrews 12: 1-2:

> Therefore we also, since we are surrounded by so great a cloud of witnesses, let us lay aside every weight, and the sin which so easily ensnares us, and let us run with endurance the race that is set before us, **looking unto Jesus, the author and finisher of our faith, who for the joy that was set before Him endured the cross, despising the shame,**

and has sat down at the right hand of the throne of God.

Recommended Prayer 30 *Thank you Father of my Lord Jesus Christ that whenever you ask me not to resist evil people it is because you have set before me inexpressible, bottomless joy. Thank you Father for your kingdom that is righteousness, peace, and joy in the Holy Spirit.*

CHAPTER 29

Knowing when to walk two miles

Context: "And whoever compels you to go one mile, go with him two" - Matthew 5:41.

How is the commandment above from Jesus different from the commandment in Matthew 5:40, the preceding verse?

In Matthew 5:40, an evil person wants to take advantage of you then leave. If they stayed with you, meaning in your situation they would not be taking advantage of you. This is the essence of the popular song by "Asa" in which she says (I paraphrase):

> "both the jailer and the jailed are exactly in the same situation because the jailed are incarcerated only when there

is a jailer living in the jail house and taking care of them."

I note here that *Asa* is singing a satire
in the sense that it is implied in her
song the jailed are actually righteous
or innocent people fighting for what is
right who have been incarcerated by
evil people. Asa emphasizes the irony
of these sorts of situations. Evidence
in the news of innocent people being
released from jail after 10 or 20 years
of incarceration is evidence innocent
people have been jailed in the past on
the basis of fraudulent evidence (if evidence can be shown to be fraudulent
after 10 or 20 years, clearly the evidence was fraudulent at the timing
of incarceration). *Nelson Mandela* of
South Africa and *Aung San Suu Kyi*
of Myanmar are two famous persons
that were jailed within the context of
a fight for what is right then subsequently released partly due to pressure from people, organizations, or
countries that believe in the concept
of freedom. *Let us join our faith together to proclaim* "**the innocent are
not jailed for the sins of evil persons and are not prey for evil persons in Jesus Name**". Amen.

In Matthew 5:41, an evil person compels a person who loves righteousness to share in his or her
experiences or burdens. What does Jesus' life teach

us about how to interpret this verse? In light of the fact that the beauty or glory of Jesus' character while here on earth prevented evil people from feeling comfortable around Him, we will derive the principles we seek from Jesus' responses to everyday people that sought His attention.

Study Outline: Jairus and his daughter - Mark 5: 21-42

1. What was Jairus' faith? Mark 5: 21-24

2. What happened as Jesus went along to Jairus' house? Mark 5:24-29

3. Did this event hasten Jesus' arrival at Jairus' house? Mark 5:30-34

4. What happened to Jairus' daughter while Jesus was delaying and what was Jesus' response? Mark 5:35-36

5. Did Jairus' daughter get healed? Mark 5:37-43

6. Could Jairus' daughter have been healed without Jesus going to Jairus' house, in which case she would have been healed before she died? Matthew 8:5-13

Discussion

In the events recorded in Matthew 8:5-13, we see Jesus could have healed Jairus' daughter simply by speaking the word of healing wherever he was located. The problem, however, was that Jairus did not have faith for such a solution - so Jesus agreed to heal his daughter based on the faith he already had, which was dependent on Jesus "laying hands on his daughter".

Life Lesson 2 *When it comes to matters in which we have a certain amount of faith in respect of the process for arriving at a godly outcome, God is willing to adopt that process and walk with us even when our process is not the most effective or efficient process. God honors our faith because in the honoring of our faith He enables us increase our faith such that next time around we perhaps have enough faith for His most effective and efficient process. In the honoring of the faith we already have, God demonstrates the following Love principle in 1Corinthians 13, which is: "Love does not insist on its own way." God, Our Father, the Father of our Lord Jesus Christ does not ask of us anything He Himself is unwilling to practice. He has called us to fellowship, relationship, citizenship, frienship, and sonship not subservience.*

Did God gain anything out of walking with Jairus when He could have sent Jairus home by himself to his healed daughter? The answer is a resounding *YES!*

✠ First, Jairus experienced what it is to walk with God

✠ Second, Jairus' faith got strengthened because a woman who had been ill got healed on the way to his house

✠ Third, in the healing of the woman with the issue of blood, God demonstrated that He honors faith that is put into action whenever the objective of the faith is godly and righteous

✠ Fourth, Jairus came to realize that Jesus not only can heal, He can raise the dead. Jairus got more miracle than he bargained for. *Hallelujah!*

✠ Fifth, Jairus got a new and improved daughter filled with the life of God

✠ Sixth, Peter, James, and John got to see God at work and have their faith in Jesus strengthened

So did Jesus walking with Jairus result in more glory for God in comparison with Jesus speaking the word of healing far away from Jairus' house and Jairus' daughter getting healed? The answer of course is a resounding YES.

Life Lesson 3 *Whenever God's name can be glorified, (i) we should be willing to walk with rather than send on their way; and (ii) we should be willing to walk two miles instead of one.*

So why did Jesus not want Jairus and his family, or his disciples to broadcast abroad what He had done?

Because His time had not yet come to be glorified by suffering, death, and resurrection. The moment Jesus raised Lazarus from the dead, the Word of God says in John 11:51

"So from that day on they plotted to take his life".

If Jesus had allowed Jairus and his family or his disciples to begin broadcasting what he had done, plots to take his life would have commenced at the wrong time. This links to the previous lesson in which we see Jesus refusing to allow himself to be stoned because his time had not yet come. In Jesus' life, we see the importance of a recognition of the time or season in which we are in at any particular point in time. It was not humility that Jesus was displaying when he dictated that the miracle not be announced. How do we know this? Because there was no attempt at keeping a similar miracle secret when He raised Lazarus from the dead. In fact, in John 12:12-17, Jesus accepted the adoration or celebration of His person that was the outcome of Lazarus being raised from the dead, events that further instigated the plot to put him to death.

Life Lesson 4 *Even when we know what God's purposes concerning us are, we need to understand there is a time for the fulfillment of that purpose. In Galatians 4:4, the Word of God says: "But when the fullness of the time had come, God sent forth His Son, born of a woman, born under the law, to redeem those who were under the law, that we might receive the adoption as sons." God our Father, the Father of our Lord Jesus Christ works with the fullness of time.*

Recommended Prayer 31 *Thank you Father of my Lord Jesus Christ that whenever I seem to be delayed in the pursuit of an objective, it is because there is greater glory for you - glory you share with me alongside the blessings that accrue to me from maintaining my trust in you. Thank you Father of my Lord Jesus Christ that whenever I do not insist on my own way either because the other way is just as good or because the Holy Spirit asks me not to insist on my better way it is because there is greater glory for you - glory you share with me alongside the blessings that accrue to me from maintaining my* *trust in you. Thank you Father for grace to continue in faith, love, and hope even as I maintain trust in you in Jesus Name. Amen.*

CHAPTER 30

Knowing when to endure affliction

Context: "...And pray for those who...persecute you" - Matthew 5:44.

How is this commandment different from the preceding two commandments in Matthew 5:40-41?

In Matthew 5:40, an evil person wants to take advantage of you then leave. In Matthew 5:41, an evil person is compelling a righteous person to share in his experiences or his burdens. In Matthew 5:44, Jesus is referring to persecution; that is affliction directed at a believer in Jesus Christ because of their faith in Jesus as Lord and Savior.

In the preceding verses, interactions outlined can occur outside of the context of persecution. In fact, since the evil person leaves in Matthew 5:40 and compels a righteous person to share in their experience in Matthew 5:41, there cannot be any persecution implied in either of the two preceding verses. Rather, there only is an attempt at taking advantage of someone else, regardless of whether they believe in Jesus or not. In Matthew 5:44, the context is persecution, and since persecutors do not like to participate in the persecutions they inflict, the context in Matthew 5:44 differs from the context in Matthew 5: 40-41.

Study Outline

1. What did Jesus have to say about persecution? John 15:20

2. Why does God allow us to go through persecution? 2Corinthians 4:17; Colossians 1:24

3. What should be our attitude towards persecution or affliction? 1Peter 5:8-11; Romans 12:14

4. What is God's promise regarding persecution? 2Timothy 3:10-11?

5. What is one specific manner in which believers are instructed to respond to persecution, and did the early believers obey Jesus? Matthew 10:23; Acts 8:1; Acts 13:44-52; Acts 14:4-7; 19-20; 21-28

6. How did Moses respond to persecution? Hebrews 11:24-26

7. What do the answers to the preceding two questions tell us about how to apply the command: "*submit to God and resist the devil*"?

8. How did Paul spend his time while he was imprisoned by the Romans? Colossians 4:16-18; Ephesians 6:14-20

9. What are some of the approaches utilized ultimately by the devil to persecute us? Hebrews 10:34; 2Corinthians 2:5-11

10. What are God's promises in regard of persecution? Romans 8:31-39; Isaiah 53:4-5

Study Notes

Obedience and Forgiveness

When like Moses we reject the fleeting pleasures of sin and choose rather to honor principles of righteousness instituted by God, we are submitting to God and resisting the devil. When we forgive each other, the Holy Spirit makes clear in 2Corinthians 2:5-11 that we are preventing cracks in our relationships that can be exploited by the devil for the destruction of good relationships among God's people. The Holy Spirit further declares that whenever the church disciplines a believer for any good reason, the church must at the same time affirm the repentant believer to ensure the believer does not become discouraged and receptive to the devil's suggestions or influences. The Holy Spirit makes clear we can condemn sin in a believer and affirm love for the same believer at the same time. Whenever the church condemns sin in a believer but cannot find it in itself to affirm the believer, the church is walking in legalism not love. In this regard, Galatians 6:1-2 states,

> *Brothers, if someone is caught in a sin,*
> *you who are spiritual should restore him*

*gently. But watch yourself, or you also
may be tempted. Carry each other's burdens, and in this way you will fulfill the
law of Christ.*

Civil Authority, Relationships, and Persecution

When we submit to God and resist the devil firm in
our faith, we do not allow enemies of the gospel to
mistreat us. Paul fled whenever his life was under
threat, but went back to places where his life had
been under threat much later when he could safely
do so.

*Where, however, did Paul spend most of
his time?*

In Antioch with other believers.

Life Lesson 5 *Like Jesus or Paul, our Father desires we spend most of our time with people who
like us are citizens of the Kingdom of God. We are
not to respond to persecution by engaging so much
with persecutors or self styled enemies, we spend
most of our time with people who do not share our
value system.*

Now we might wonder why Paul says "*God delivered him out of all his afflictions*" given at the time
he was penning these words, he had been imprisoned by the Romans. Well since the Romans represented civil authority, even though they were not
acting justly in imprisoning him, in the absence
of a directive from the Holy Spirit to the contrary,
Paul had to submit to this treatment and trust God
for his salvation.

*Was this attitude on Paul's part any different
from Jesus' attitude?*

No. Jesus allowed himself to be betrayed only when civil authority came into play. Since there does not exist any civil authority that is not implicitly allowed by God, while a believer must not submit to injustice - Philippians 2:23,24 shows Paul attempted to earn back his freedom - unless explicitly directed by God to the contrary, a believer must submit to civil authority.

Why did Jesus not seek His freedom? Because He knew He had come to die for our sins; to seek freedom from the shame of the cross would have been to sin against His Father, our Father, the God of Abraham, Isaac, and Jacob.

Making the most of the time

While imprisoned, Paul spent his time writing to the believers and preaching to fellow prisoners, guards, and the Household of Ceasar. Paul recognized there was a purpose to his imprisonment and made the most of the time for the glory of God.

What it means to *"flee affliction"*

So what have we learnt? To flee affliction or persecution is equivalent to enduring affliction and equivalent to resisting affliction. When we flee affliction, we continue to seek God's glory so He can deliver us out of all our afflictions then "perfect, establish, strengthen, and settle us" - 1Peter 5:10.

Faith in the Name of Jesus and Armed Struggle

There are situations in which given modern day society, fleeing is not a feasible solution to persecution. In the days of Jesus, there were no visas, immigrant or non-immigrant. In today's world, even if a Christian desires to flee persecution, that just may not be feasible.

During the march of the nation of Israel through the wilderness to the land promised by God, the people encountered a situation in which two nations by name Heshbon and Bashan refused them passage through their territory - passage that was essential to continuation of their journey to the promised land. The story can be found in Deuteronomy 2:26-37 and Deuteronomy 3:1-7. Moses sent word to the king of Heshbon to reassure him the people of Israel only sought passage through their territories, would do no harm during their passage, and pay for any food or water that they might need in the course of their journey. The kings of Heshbon and Bashan rejected Moses' offer in spite of evidence that they had kept their word in their passage through the lands of the descendants of Esau and the land of the Moabites, descendants of Lot.

So what did God instruct the people of Israel to do? Well God instructed the people of Israel to fight the people of Heshbon and Bashan so they could continue on their journey to the promised land. The people of Israel fought and won and continued on to their promised land. We see then that when all discussions, negotiations, and appeasement fails, God can instruct His people to resort to armed struggle.

Ensuring armed struggle is of God

Life Lesson 6 *Before believers in the name of Jesus Christ embark on armed struggle, we must be sure we are getting that directive from the Holy Spirit.*

In order to be sure we are guided by the Holy Spirit we should *have explored alternative solutions to the persecution* such as:

✠ where possible or applicable, making efforts to get civil authority to protect our rights (persecution at times is spiritual, financial, or emotional but not physical and as such is difficult to convey to civil authorities)

✠ trying our best to live a quiet life without attempting to call undue or brash attention to our faith; that is, while we must confess that we have overcome the world in Christ Jesus by our faith, and while we should be able to testify of our faith as guided by the Holy Spirit, we should not challenge persecutors

✠ where possible attempting to negotiate with persecutors on matters that are not of primary importance

✠ Asking the Holy Spirit for direction as to whether armed struggle is necessary, and direction as to the timing of commencement of armed struggle

What happens post armed struggle?

At the end of armed struggle with persecutors, which if led by the Holy Spirit we must win, Christians must display a spirit of reconciliation and forgiveness within the context of accountability. Within this context, accountability involves the identification of people who because of their refusal to change during the conflict must not be allowed to derail, via their inclusion, the new civil authority's attempts at moving society towards God's ideals. If people profess change after the change in civil authority, there is no way to ascertain whether they are genuine or false in their professions. There must never be discrimination against those who though they were not with us, did not have power to prevent or influence the persecution that was endured. Those who were not directly with us but helped us should be rewarded as appropriate.

Neither of Nicodemus nor Joseph of Arimathea identified with Jesus while He was alive, yet both had decided to believe in Him as Lord and Savior.

Life Lesson 7 *The devil attempts to persecute us by attacking our (a) families - spouses, children etc.; (b) sources of income; or (c) health; But we must resist Him firm in our faith in Jesus Christ. Jesus' victory is our assurance of victory. In Jesus Name. Amen.*

Summary

In so far as our walk with God is concerned, our response to persecution is to attempt to live at peace with people around us to the extent to which it is in our power. When we flee affliction, we are enduring affliction and at the same time resisting affliction. The Holy Spirit reserves, however, the right to direct us otherwise. Remember, while all other disciples were scattered from Jerusalem, the Apostles remained in the place where believers were being persecuted. So the command from God is: flee affliction where possible; and endure while resisting affliction when fleeing is not possible. We resist as directed by the Holy Spirit.

Recommended Prayer 32 *Thank you Father of my Lord Jesus Christ for your promise that there is no challenge that comes my way for which you have not provided a solution or way of escape. I rejoice in* *your provision knowing any challenge that comes my way is a stepping stone towards actualization of your blessings and character in my life. In Jesus Name. Amen.*

CHAPTER 31

It is okay not to want to bless if...

Context: "...And pray for those who...persecute you" - Matthew 5:44.

In the preceding lesson (Lesson Three) we have seen that Christians are not supposed to respond to persecution passively; that is, are never to accept persecution. Rather, we respond actively by doing things that enable us to flee persecution or essentially live at peace with our persecutors. While armed struggle is not inconsistent with fleeing persecution (many countries the world over earned their independence through armed struggle against various forms of oppression), we must be sure we have heard from God in regards of such resistance before we embark on such an application of "fleeing persecution".

Having established the Christian response to persecution, we now address the command to *"pray for those who...persecute you"*.

If we are honest with ourselves, we know this is one of the most difficult commandments in the scriptures, yet it is beholden on us by our Lord Jesus Christ Himself. The question then is:

"Is it ever okay not to pray for your enemies?"

In this study, I will make a case for a *"Yes""* answer with the caveat that this Yes answer applies only to the Christian who desires to obey Jesus' injunction that believers in the name of Jesus are to pray for their persecutors; that is, pray for people who via their words or actions have characterized themselves as enemies.

Study Outline

1. What is supposed to happen as we fellowship with the Father, Son, and Holy Spirit? 2Peter 3:18

2. What is the source of our growth in Christ? Ephesians 4:15-16

3. Can we be hypocrites in our prayers for those who in their words or actions towards us have characterized themselves as our enemies? See James 3:17; Ephesians 4:26-27, 25; Psalm 94:3-23

Study Notes

If you have been hurt and you are angry feel free to tell God how you feel about your enemies or persecutors, including all of the justice outcomes you desire for them. This is an application of "*speaking the truth in love*" within the context of our relationship with God and application of the *sincerity* characteristic of the wisdom that comes from God. David demonstrated this sincerity in Psalm 94:3-23.

Having demonstrated sincerity in our discussions with our Father, we proceed to:

✠ **Step 1**: Ask for the grace to forgive those who have characterized themselves as our enemies;

✠ **Step 2**: Intercede for grace that will enable them to change to the path of righteousness

✠ **Step 3**: Ask for grace that enables us demonstrate wisdom that is pure, peaceable, gentle, and without hypocrisy in relations with enemies or persecutors

✠ **Step 4**: Ask God for His justice and grace to reign over our interactions with enemies or persecutors with His stated goals of righteousness and peace as the objective - Jeremiah 9:23-24; James 3:17-18

An Important Aside

It is important to note here that forgiveness does not imply continuation in close association with or pursuit of friendship. It merely means *we do not aspire to delight* in hearing that evil has befallen those who have characterized themselves as our enemies. If we hear evil has befallen our enemies

and in spite of lack of aspiration at delight we experience a flutter of delight due to the weakness
of our flesh, we are to put such delight to death
because love does not delight in evil (1Corinthians
13:6). Since love delights in the truth (1Corinthi-
ans 13:6), however, we are to praise God for His
declaration in Jeremiah 9:23-24 that He delights
in lovingkindness, justice, and righteousness. The
Holy Spirit characterizes love's unwillingness to delight in evil in the following words (Philippians 4:7-
8):

> Finally, brothers (and sisters), whatever
> is true, whatever is noble, whatever is
> right, whatever is pure, whatever is lovely,
> whatever is admirable - if anything is
> excellent or praiseworthy - think about
> such things.[1]

When we declare God's character in light of what
we have heard, if the evil that has befallen an enemy is justice from God for the totality of their
actions, we are delighting in justice and as such
are delighting in what is true, noble, right, pure,
lovely, admirable, excellent, and praiseworthy. If
the evil that has befallen an enemy is in of itself
injustice towards that person, our declaration that
God delights in lovingkindness, justice (including
justice for ourselves and that enemy), and righteousness (right actions) means we are calling God into
that situation and our situations to demonstrate
His justice (right outcomes). Again, we are delighting in what is true, noble, right, pure, lovely, admirable, excellent, and praiseworthy. Love seeks
justice not revenge. Whenever love goes in pursuit

---

[1]Words in brackets mine.

of those who have done evil in situations within which civil authority is handicapped or unwilling to pursue justice on love's behalf, the objective of pursuit is justice not revenge.

Life Lesson 8 *When we learn to declare God's attributes of lovingkindness, justice, and righteousness in light of events in the lives of people who characterize themselves as our enemies, we make it impossible for interest in an enemy's life to hold sway over the path of our lives. This is an application of the command to "give thanks to God in all things".*

Back on Track

Step 1 of our healing process from the hurts of an enemy is extremely crucial and requires sincerity in order to be most effective. If we skip Step 1, we ourselves may not heal from the wounds of the enemy even while praying for our enemies. This is not good for our spiritual health. When we have been wounded, the word of God says we are allowed to be angry (Ephesians 4: 26-27), but in order not to sin, we must not remain angry. In 1 Corinthians 13:5, *"love is not...easily provoked"* because *"love covers a multitude of offenses* (Proverbs 17:9; 10:12)".

Life Lesson 9 *Love can get angry; but in order for us not to sin against God, love must not desire to remain angry. Whenever love gets angry, love desires to reposition itself away from anger towards forgiveness at the earliest possible time. Since God is love and we are the righteousness of God in Jesus Christ, we are the "love of God".*

God understands when we vent our frustrations during our fellowship with Him. The word of God says

> "For we do not have a High Priest who cannot sympathize with our weaknesses, but was in all points tempted as we are, yet without sin" - Hebrews 4:15.

So what should our response to Jesus' understanding of our weaknesses?

> "Let us therefore come boldly to the throne of grace, that we may obtain mercy and find grace to help in time of need" - Hebrews 4:16.

In the Garden of Gethsemane, Jesus told His Father how much He loathed having to endure separation via the cross. This was not doubt or unwillingness to complete the mission on Jesus' part. Why? Because Jesus said *"Not my will, but thy will be done"* - Matthew 26: 36-39; Luke 22: 41-44.

In His request, Jesus was asking His Father for divine strength to complete the mission, at which point His Father, our Father sent an angel to give Him strength. If we do not feel comfortable venting to God, we do not yet see Him as a loving Father. While venting, however, we demonstrate our love for and faith in God by asking for the strength or grace that we need in order to do what is right.

> So when are we allowed to not pray for our enemies?

Life Lesson 10 *When we **sincerely** are waiting for strength from our Lord Jesus Christ that enables us obey His command, God understands if we are unable to pray for our enemies.*

So what are we to do while we are still waiting for strength for which we have requested in obedience to God per instructions in Hebrews 4:16? The answers can be found in Romans 6: 12-14; 5:1-2; 8:1; Philippians 1:6 and Colossians 2:10, which state, respectively:

> "Therefore do not let sin reign in your mortal body, that you should obey it in its lusts. And do not present your members as instruments of unrighteousness to sin, but present yourselves to God as being alive from the dead, and your members as instruments of righteousness to God. For sin shall not have dominion over you, for you are not under law but under grace" - Romans 6: 12-14.

Since there has to be sin in order for it to not have dominion over us, this verse is talking about how to overcome sin e.g. the desire to not pray the right kind of prayers for enemies or persecutors. While we are trusting in God for grace to overcome, however, we remain under grace not under law. This principle is the foundation of the command in Hebrews 4:16 and the exhortation in Hebrews 4:15 to not be ashamed of our weaknesses in our interactions with our Lord Jesus Christ.

In order to obey this command, we need to "reckon ourselves". For a discussion of this principle, see Chapter 10.

> "Therefore having being justified by faith, we have peace with God through our Lord Jesus Christ, through whom also we have access by faith into this grace in which we stand, and rejoice in hope of the glory of God" - Romans 5:1-2.

Since hope that is realized can no longer be hope, whenever we have areas in which we are still trusting in God for grace, this hope, which is grounded in our faith in what Jesus has done for us is supposed to produce peace not guilt. Why? Because we are obeying God in seeking for strength to become more like Him. While we are in transition, the righteousness of Christ credited to us keeps us in God's grace so we are never under condemnation.

> *"There is therefore now no condemnation to those who are in Christ Jesus, who do not walk according to the flesh, but according to the Spirit" - Romans 8:1.*

While we are trusting God for grace and playing our part we do not come under condemnation because the request for strength and the waiting for strength conform with walking according to the Spirit. Concerning this the Holy Spirit declares in Isaiah 40:28-31,

> Do you not know? Have you not heard? The LORD is the everlasting God, the Creator of the ends of the earth. He will not grow tired or weary and his understanding no one can fathom. He gives strength to the weary and increases the power of the weak. Even youths grow tired and weary, and young men stumble and fall, but those who hope in the LORD (*NKJV*: those who wait on the LORD; *YLT*: those expecting Jehovah) will renew their strength. They will soar on wings like eagles; they will run and not grow weary, they will walk and not be faint.

Colossians 2:9-10 and Philippians 1:6 read as follows:

*For in Him dwells all the fullness of the
Godhead bodily; and you are complete in
Him, who is the head of all principality
and power - Colossians 2: 9-10*

*Being confident of this very thing, that
He who has begun a good work in you
will complete it until the day of Jesus Christ
- Philippians 1:6*

In Colossians 2: 9-10, we are already complete
in Christ via the crediting of the righteousness of
Christ to our spiritual account. In Philippians 1:6,
we are in the process of becoming complete via
the manifestation of the grace of God in our lives
through the sanctifying work of the Holy Spirit.
Combined, both verses demonstrate we remain under grace while we are being perfected in Christ.
The key of course is that we must desire to be who
God wants us to be in so far as character is concerned.

Summary

God loves us and understands us. He is not looking for weaknesses to punish; rather, He is looking
for weaknesses to correct so we can have better fellowship with Him and with one another. Speaking
of Jesus, Isaiah writes in Isaiah 42:3,16,

"*A bruised reed He will not break*, and
smoking flax He will not quench; He will
bring forth justice for truth. And I will
bring the blind by a way that they knew
not; I will lead them in paths that they
have not known; I will make darkness
light before them, and crooked things

straight. These things will I do unto them,
and not forsake them".

Recommended Prayer 33 *Thank you Father of my
Lord Jesus Christ because you are the God who
stokes the embers of my light rather than using its
flickering flame as an excuse to put it out. Thank
you Father because your are the God who puts me
back in shape when I am bent out of shape. Thank
you Father that you are the God who creates a new
and right way out of nothing so I can continue on
my path to You and continue in prosperity in this
life. Thank you Father because you are the God
who brings light into any darkness in my life and
the God who gives light to those in darkness. Thank
you Father that while I wait for the hope of actualization of righteousness by faith, reckoning myself
dead to sin and alive unto You, I am complete in Jesus Christ. Thank you Father that You bring forth
justice for truth. Blessed be your Holy name Father.
In Jesus Name. Amen.*

CHAPTER 32

Knowing whether it is okay to quit

Context: 1Corinthians 13:7-8 states:

> *"It (love) always protects, always trusts, always hopes, always perseveres. Love never fails."*

If we take these verses at face value, it appears love never gives up on anything that it believes in. It also appears love never fails. Since we are talking about love, these words must have applications in the area of interpersonal relationships. Also, since we can adopt some projects on the basis of love, these verses also can apply to some of the things that we do in this life or perhaps all of the things that we do; after all, we are admonished to *"do all things to the glory of God"*.

Regardless of Gods' promise that *"Love Never Fails"*, the preponderance of suffering, pain, or mean-

335

inglessness in this world in which we live can tempt us into thinking the love of God fails or has failed. So is it the case God gives up on us - at least for a season - or is it the case that we need to understand the spiritual meaning of the phrase, *"Love Never Fails"?* If God gives up on love or objectives of love so can we; after all, 'as *He is so are we in this world*' (1John 4:17). If God never gives up and *Love Never Fails*, we also must never give up on love. In a world within which people who genuinely have faith in Jesus Christ have experienced divorce; endured separation from their biological children; seemingly failed in attempts at converting people to be Christians or attempts at helping people understand better how to be Christians, can we rationally declare that *"Love Never Fails"?* Does love fail (based on the evidence of failures of Christians or perhaps God Himself) or do we need to arrive at a better understanding of the phrase, *"Love Never Fails"?* This is the focus of Lesson 5 of this Bible Study series.

Study Outline

"Has God's love ever failed?"

1. Did Jesus' love for Israel accomplish all He sought to accomplish for Israel while He was here on earth? Matthew 23:37-39

2. Was God's love for "Israel" (the nation that comprised of nine tribes of the sons of Jacob, excluding Levi, Judah, and Simeon) successful in keeping them within His covenant for the descendants of Abraham or Jacob? 2 Kings 17:1-6,18-24

Study Notes

God's love seemingly "*fails*" whenever it is resisted and God has no choice but to honor the choices of the people to whom He has demonstrated His love. God allowed the nation of Israel to go and live among people who worshipped idols after He had for many years provided them with miracles and delivered them from oppression through the hands of Elisha, God's prophet - 2Kings chapters 4 through 6.

Note, however, that God's love failed only in the sense that God's preferable outcome was not accomplished. In both instances outlined in the Bible verses, rejection of God's way resulted in peace:

> Peace for God since He no longer had to expend energy trying to win the people over;

> Peace for the people since they secured the opportunity to live their lives however, they wanted. While they were released from relationship with God, however, they still were responsible to God in so far as the manner in which they treated each other was concerned.

Since the "*wisdom that comes from above is first of all pure and peaceable*" - James 3:16; while God's preferable outcome has not been accomplished whenever people do not choose relationship with Him, love in reality has not failed. Why is this? Because in God's wisdom, the next best thing - *PEACE* - has been accomplished.

Why is peace between man and God or between groups of people the next best thing whenever people do not choose righteousness?

Life Lesson 11 *Love never fails whenever it produces peace between groups of people or between man and God because one of the goals of righteousness is peace.*

In this regard, Romans 5:1-2 states,

> "Therefore having been justified by faith, *we have peace with God through our Lord Jesus Christ*, through whom also we have access by faith into this grace in which we stand, and rejoice in hope of the glory of God".

While the peace that results from people's unwillingness to choose righteousness is a circumstantial peace, however, the peace God gives is an *inner peace that "surpasses understanding".*   In this regard, Philippians 4: 6-7 states,

> "Be anxious for nothing, but in everything by prayer and supplication with thanksgiving let your requests be made known to God, and *the peace of God which passes all understanding* will guard your hearts and minds through Jesus Christ".

Concerning peace as an objective of love, the Holy Spirit declares in Romans 14:17,

> For the kingdom of God is not eating and drinking, but righteousness **and peace** and joy in the Holy Spirit.

God desires relationship with man meaning the goal of love is loving relationships. Whenever God is rejected, the goal of love switches to peace meaning God can and will stay silent for prolonged periods of time whenever He has been fully rejected by man. Whenever God is silent then it is to respect man's choices and for the achievement of peace. Consider the following words from Judges 3:7-11,

> The Israelites did evil in the eyes of the LORD; **they forgot the LORD their God** and served the Baals and the Asherahs (idols). The anger of the LORD burned against Israel so that he sold them into the hands of Cushan-Rishathaim king of Aram Naharaim, to whom the Israelites were subject for eight years. **But when they cried out to the LORD, he raised up for them a deliverer,** Othniel son of Kenaz, Caleb's younger brother who saved them. The Spirit of the LORD came upon him, so that he became Israel's judge and went to war. The LORD gave Cushan-Rishathaim king of Aram into the hands of Othniel, who overpowered him. So the land had peace for forty years, until Othniel son of Kenaz died.

> We may well ask, "*Was this some one-off interaction between God and His people?*"

Consider the following words from the Book of Judges 3:12,14-15,29-30,

> **Once again the Israelites did evil in the eyes of the LORD,** and because they did this evil the LORD gave Eglon king of Moab power over Israel. The Israelites were subject to Eglon king of Moab for eighteen years. **Again the Israelites cried out to the LORD, and he gave**

them a deliverer - Ehud, a left-handed
man, the son of Gera the Benjamite. At
that time they struck down about ten
thousand Moabites, all vigorous and strong;
not a man escaped. That day Moab was
made subject to Israel, and **the land had
peace for eighty years**.

The passages from the Book of Judges show
that whenever the people rejected God, God left
them alone to their own designs; that is ceased
to expend His energies at protecting them, resulting in subjugation to enemies. With rejection then
came peace between God and Israel the object of
His love. When the people cried out to God for
help, in essence recognizing Jehovah as God, God
saved them, delievered them, and gave them rest
for forty or eighty years. With recognition of the
God of Abraham, Isaac, and Jacob then came rest
or peace for forty years. These passages from the
Book of Judges confirm that regardless of rejection or acceptance of God, peace is the objective
of love. Since God withdraws whenever He is fully
rejected, peace is achieved and *Love Does Not Fail*.
When we accept God's love alongside peace or rest
we experience righeteousness and relationship. It
is obvious in this case of course that *Love Does Not
Fail*.

What else does the word of God have to say
about *peace*?

✠ *Peace comes from God: "Grace be to you and
peace from God the Father and our Lord Jesus Christ... " - Galatians 1:3; Ephesians 1:2;
Philippians 1:2; 2 John 1:3; Jude 1:2*

✠ *"Peacemakers who sow in peace raise a har-
vest of righteousness." - James 3:18*

✠ "*Blessed are the peacemakers, for they wll be called sons of God.*" - Matthew 5:9.

✠ "*For God was pleased to have all his fullness dwell in him, and through him to reconcile to himself all things, whether things on earth or things in heaven, **by making peace through his blood**, shed on the cross*" - Colossians 1:20

✠ *Jesus is our peace - Ephesians 2:14*

✠ "For whoever would love life and see good days ... **must turn from evil and do good; he must seek peace and pursue it**" - 1Peter 3:11. Since to seek and pursue peace is to turn from evil and do good, peacemaking is a centerpiece of faith in the name of Jesus Christ.

✠ *We receive grace and peace through our knowledge of God - 2Peter 1:2*

✠ We must endeavor to allow the peace of God reign in our hearts by giving thanks in all things - Colossians 3:15; Ephesians 4:3

Summary

Whenever we are walking in love towards someone or a group of people and they make choices contrary to the righteous goals of love that we are pursuing, love requires we switch our focus to what makes for peace in the relationship. God demonstrated this principle over and over again in His relationship with Judah. When God sent Judah into captivity in Babylon, God essentially told them (I paraphrase)

"I am doing this out of respect for your
choices, but if while you are in Babylon
you lift up your eyes towards Jerusalem
and pray to return, I will bring you back".

In this regard God declares as follows in 2Chron-
icles 7:14,

If my people, who are called by my name,
will humble themselves and pray and seek
my face and **turn from their wicked
ways**, then will I hear from heaven and
will forgive their sin and will heal their
land.

Life Lesson 12 *Love never fails because ultimately
love has peace as its objective and does not insist
on achieving its goals within a specific time frame.
Whenever love is rejected over some prolonged period of time, love honors the decisions of the objects
of its love and undertakes actions that create or
maintain peace between the groups of people concerned.*

Recommended Prayer 34 *Thank you Father of my
Lord Jesus Christ that you love me so much you
magnify the impact of my righteous choices for peace
and rest. Father while I rest in your love, and as a
result do not worry about how perfect I am, I ask
that you eliminate mistakes from out of my life, reveal and enable me remove in the power of the Holy
Spirit actions or attitudes that negate your peace
and rest from my life, and with your grace destroy
the negative consequences of other people's mistakes
or sin from out of my life in Jesus Name. Amen.*

CHAPTER 33

Knowing how to be angry, yet not sin

Context: Mark 3:5-6 states:

> "And when He (Jesus) had looked around at them with anger, being grieved by the hardness of their hearts, He said to the man, 'Stretch out your hand'. And he stretched it out, and his hand was restored as whole as the other. Then the Pharisees went out and immediately plotted with the Herodians against Him, how they might destroy Him."

In Ephesians 4:31, the word of God states,

> "Let all bitterness, wrath, anger, clamor, and evil speaking be put away from you,

with all malice. And be kind to one another, tenderhearted, forgiving one another, even as God in Christ forgave you."

Combined, the two sets of verses above create
a seeming contradiction. That is, while we are
not supposed to indulge in anger (Ephesians 4:31),
there are situations within which anger is justified.
From Jesus' actions in Mark 3:5-6 and the command to be "slow to anger" in 1Corinthians 13:5 we
know anger can be justified. The seeming contradiction between Mark 3:5-6 or 1Corinthians 13:5
and Ephesians 4:31 is amplified by the following
words about Jesus in Hebrews 4:15 which states,

"For we do not have a High Priest who
cannot sympathize with our weaknesses,
but was in all points tempted as we are,
yet without sin."

In light of this verse and Jesus' actions as de-
scribed in Mark 3:5-6, while anger is not a desir-
able character trait, it is possible to exhibit anger,
yet be without sin.
So when is it ever godly to be angry?

Study Outline

1. Does God display anger? Zechariah 10:3; Jonah
   4:2; Nahum 1:3; Joel 2:13; Micah 7: 18-20

2. What is an important characteristic of God's
   anger? Nahum 1:6; Micah 7:9; Hebrews 3:17.

   (a) These verses equate God's anger with God's
       indignation.

(b) In the Merriam-Webster Dictionary, Indignation is defined as: *"Anger aroused by something that is unfair or wrong"*

3. What does it mean to be "Slow to Anger"? Nehemiah 9:17-18; Psalms 103:8-10; Proverbs 16:32; Proverbs 19:11; Joel 2:13; 1 Peter 4:8

4. What is the advice in the new covenant in so far as anger is concerned? Matthew 5:22; Ephesians 4:26-27

5. Did Paul ever exhibit indignation? 2 Corinthians 11:29

Notes

God's anger or indignation always is directed only at those who persist in doing evil (Micah 7:9). An important characteristic of God, however, is that He is "Slow to Anger" - Nehemiah 9:17. 1 Corinthians 13:5 states very clearly that being slow to anger is a characteristic of the love of God. God demonstrates slowness to anger by:

♡ Not rewarding us according to our sins or iniquity; that is, when God judges us there always is mercy mixed with His justice

♡ Relenting from His anger and blessing us when we repent of our sins

♡ Refusing to forsake or abandon us to our sins when we stray away from Him into any form of idolatry, such as loving our spouses or children more than we love God; loving money more than we love God; or loving pleasures such as sex etc. more than we love God

♡ Seeking us out after we have rejected Him.
When God created Samson the Nazirite to deliver Israel from bondage to the Philistines,
the people were not even asking God for help
in the matter (Judges Chapter 13)

In aggregate we conclude that:

Life Lesson 13 *Anger can be righteous. When anger
is righteous, however, we are slow to anger and give
up the anger once it has been demonstrated, com-
municated, or acted upon. While anger is righteous,
the command "not to allow the sun to set on anger"
means we should never assume it is God's will for
us to stay angry.*

The link between anger and indignation enables
us know when anger is righteous, which is,

Life Lesson 14 *Anger is righteous whenever it is a
response to unfairness or either of wrong motives
or actions. From here on, I refer to such anger as*
righteous indignation.

So what happens when you are the target of
unfairness or either of wrong motives or actions?
Well, according to the word of God, you are allowed to exhibit righteous indignation; however,
you must not sin. That is, while righteous indignation means you are allowed to display your displeasure at the way you are treated, you should:

ᔓ Not begin to also treat people who are mistreating you in an unfair manner or relate to
them with wrong motives or actions - "*Do not
be weary in well doing (doing what is right) for
in due season you shall reap if you do not lose
heart* - Galatians 6:9; 2 Thessalonians 3:13"[1]

---

[1] Words in brackets mine.

᧚ Not seek to take matters into your hands because God has said "*Vengeance is mine. I will
repay*" - Romans 12:19; Hebrews 10:30.

So what should you do?

᧚ State your displeasure at the way you are treated
and provide as much evidence as within your
power to back up your view of the state of
things

᧚ Guided by the Holy Spirit, be like God in so
far as what it means to be "slow to anger" is
concerned

᧚ Use the "Sword of the Spirit", which is the
Word of God to declare that God's anger is
roused against all those who delight in doing
evil, particularly those who direct evil at you
- Ephesians 6:14-18

᧚ Use the Word of God to declare that all those
who treat you right will earn a good reward
from God for their love for righteousness or
what is good - Ephesians 6:14-18

᧚ Seek the direction of the Holy Spirit as to what
you are to do in response to the actions of
those who treat you unfairly. The goal of your
actions should not be vengeance but justice
and the outcome of justice, righteousness or
peace. Since God delights in justice, we are
building up God's kingdom and pursuing His
righteousness whenever we demonstrate interest in justice.

So what if your anger is not expressed perfectly
due to your human weakness?

If we confess our sins, He is faithful and just to forgive us our sins and to cleanse us from all unrighteousness - 1 John 1:9

For we do not have a High Priest who cannot sympathize with our weaknesses, but was in all points tempted as we are, yet without sin. Let us therefore come boldly to the throne of grace, that we may obtain mercy and find grace to help in time of need - Hebrews 4:15-16.

Jesus was tempted to exhibit unrighteous indignation while here on earth, so He understands what we pass through. Given He understands, He is not looking to condemn, but to provide the grace and knowledge that we need so we can become just like Him in ability to express righteous indignation that does not leave any room for sin.

This lesson demonstrates it is an important characteristic of a Christian to do something about sin whenever it lies within our power to do so, especially when the Holy Spirit makes us experience righteous indignation about sinful actions around us. The goal of righteous indignation is not necessarily to punish, however (though there are situations within which this may be appropriate), but to bring about a change in behavior and improvements in the welfare of people that are not being treated right.

Summary

While love covers a multitude of offenses, in situations where people that are offending persist in mistreating others, perhaps including ourselves, there comes a time when just like God, a believer has to switch to righteous indignation which involves demonstration of displeasure at wrong actions or motives, and declaration of God's will in so far as those who delight in doing evil and those who delight in righteousness are concerned. Jesus taught His disciples to pray *"Thy Kingdom come. Thy will be done on earth as it is in heaven* - Matthew 6:10". When we experience righteous indignation and express it righteously, we are saying in our words and actions, *"Thy Kingdom come. Thy will be done on earth as it is in heaven"*.

Recommended Prayer 35 *Thank you Father that you are slow to anger towards me, your people, and all of your creation. Thank you Father that you are patient with me as I seek to know you so I can become your righteousness in Jesus Christ. Thank you Father for your lovingkindness, mercy, and graciousness which you promise make me great. Thy Kingdom come Father. Thy will be done on earth as it is in heaven. In Jesus Name. Amen.*

CHAPTER 34

Knowing when to insist on your way

Context: James 3:17 states

> But the wisdom that comes from above
> is first pure, then peaceable, gentle, will-
> ing to yield, full of mercy and good fruits,
> without partiality and without hypocrisy.

Our focus in this study is on the "willing to yield" or "submissive" characteristic of the wisdom that comes from above. Taken by itself, this characteristic implies a Christian always must be willing to yield in so far as any matter is concerned. In order to put this characteristic in perspective, we will first discuss another characteristic that must accompany "willingness to yield" which is purity, the first characteristic of wisdom enumerated in James 3:17.

Study Outline

1. What things are we to spend our time thinking about? Philippians 4:8

2. What sorts of consciences or hearts are we
   supposed to have as Christians? 1Timothy
   1:5; 3:9; 2Timothy 2:22

3. What should our belief in seeing Jesus face to
   face someday induce? 1John 3:1-3

4. So does willingness to yield apply to men or
   to God, the Father of our Lord Jesus Christ?
   Acts 5:28-29

5. If we combine purity and willingness to yield
   what do we obtain? Matthew 6:33

6. How is willingness to yield illustrated in the
   Book of Proverbs? Proverbs 3:5-8

7. How did Samuel illustrate willingness to yield
   in his relationship with God? 1Samuel 16:1-
   13

8. How did Paul illustrate willingness to yield in
   his relationship with God? Acts 16:6-10

9. How did Peter illustrate willingness to yield in
   his relationship with God? Acts 10:17-23

NOTES

A Christian is not to yield or submit when yielding
or submission is contrary to the principles of God's
Kingdom or God's Righteousness.

How can we pray "Thy Kingdom come; Thy will
be done in earth as it is heaven" yet yield in matters that contradict objectives of the Kingdom of

God and His Righteousness? Jesus says in John 10:10,

> "The devil comes to steal, to kill, and to destroy but I (Jesus) have come that you may have life and have it more abundantly".

The Holy Spirit then commands in James 4:7,

> Submit to God, resist the devil and he will flee from you.

Since the devil comes to steal, kill, and destroy, and we are supposed to resist him, the Word of God commands us to resist anything or anyone that wants to steal from us; kill us; or destroy us unless we are explicitly commanded by God otherwise. In the entire New Testament, the only person explicitly commanded otherwise was Paul. But did Paul know this beforehand? *Yes.* At His conversion Jesus told Ananias concerning Paul in Acts 9:15,

> Go, for he is a chosen vessel of Mine to bear My name before Gentiles, kings, and the children of Israel. For I will show him how many things he must suffer for My name's sake.

So could Paul have avoided being arrested? The answer is "*Yes*" because God forewarned Paul's arrest in dreams both to Paul and to other prophets in Acts 21:10-12. In verse 13 of Acts Chapter 21, however, Paul replied,

> "What do you mean by weeping and breaking my heart? For I am ready not only to be bound, but also to die at Jerusalem for the name of the Lord Jesus."

So what did the believers do in Acts 10:14,

> So when he would not be persuaded, we
> ceased, saying, 'The will of the Lord be
> done.'

The fruit borne from Paul's incarceration - all of the Epistles or theological expositions written by Paul subsequent to his arrest that help enunciate and preserve the essence of our faith of Jesus Christ - is evidence of godly fruit from Paul's incarceration.

Note that Apostles like Peter did not write until Paul began writing to the believers (2Peter 3:15). So not only would we not have had Paul's writings, we probably would not have had most of the other books of the Bible as well if Paul had not been arrested and imprisoned, presumably under house arrest given all of the liberties afforded him, which include: (i) writing materials; (ii) time to write; (iii) uncensored writing; (iv) unimpeded visits from people like Luke, Timothy etc., and (v) Paul's declaration that he had had opportunity to preach the gospel to Caesar's entire household.

One thing at least we know for sure is that Paul was not treated like a common criminal while imprisoned at Rome. Why? Because Paul was a Roman citizen and was not tried in Rome for many years; that is, was awaiting trial during all of the time he was writing the Epistles. Tradition holds Paul was beheaded after his trial at a good old age. Since everyone who put Paul to death also died subsequently, including those who actually beheaded him and the Ceasar who sentenced him to death, death is common to man and is not failure of belief in the name of Jesus Christ.

Summary

Jesus Yields

In Matthew 17:24-27, Jesus illustrated the principle embedded in the command to be willing to yield or not insist on our own way. In verses 24-25, Peter is challenged on Jesus' tax compliance to which he responds that Jesus pays taxes. When Peter got to where Jesus was, Jesus asked him whether in his opinion, kings collect taxes from their sons or from others. Peter responds that taxes are not collected from sons but from other citizens of a kingdom. In verse 27, Jesus responds as follows:

"Then we are exempt," Jesus said to him. "*But so that we may not offend them*, go to the lake and throw out your line. Take the first fish you catch; open its moth and you will find a four-drachma coin. Take it and give it to them for my tax and yours."

Jesus Insists

Peter remonstrated with Jesus concerning predictions of His suffering and death in Matthew 16:22, saying,

> "Far be it from You, Lord; this shall not happen to You!"

Jesus replied in verse 23,

> "Get behind Me, Satan!, You are an offense to Me, for you are not mindful

of the things of God, but the things of
men."

Life Lesson 15 *Jesus insisted on His own way in
matters within which He was sure of God's purpose, plan, and direction. Jesus insisted on His own
way in matters of righteousness and good works
towards people around Him such as the decision
to heal on the Sabbath. Jesus is our standard for
yielding or insisting on our own way.*

Life Lesson 16 *When we have sincere faith, pure
hearts, and good consciences it becomes easier to
know when to insist on our own way or yield to others' opinions. Insincere faith, impure hearts, and
evil consciences make us susceptible to the deceptions of the devil and deceptions of evil men who do
not have faith in God. In Paul's day some Christians strayed away from the faith because they did
not cultivate sincere faith in God, pure motives for
their actions, and consciences sensitive to the illu-
mination of the Holy Spirit.*

Prophetic Word 1 *Because you have read this treatise on what it means to have faith in the name of
Jesus, I declare in the name of Jesus Christ that you
will have sincere faith, a pure heart, and a good
conscience in Jesus Name. I declare that you will
know when to insist on your own way and know
when to yield to others' opinions. I declare that
the Father of our Lord Jesus Christ will direct your
steps so you remain on the path of righteousness
that brings the prosperity, peace, and joy promised
to those who seek God with all their hearts in Jesus
Name. Amen.*

Life Lesson 17 *We are to be submissive or willing
to yield to God whenever we discern His will but*

do not understand the path He has chosen for us. We are to be submissive to God and pursue the things that make for righteousness or peace when men would have us do that which is contrary to the building up of God's Kingdom and the enhancement of God's Righteousness in the earth. So if we perceive a brother or a sister as walking in God's will with the testimony of their character and the things on which they spend their time, then if we have a different opinion concerning their path, we must be willing to yield to God and say "The will of the Father of our Lord Jesus Christ be done in Jesus name. Amen."

Recommended Prayer 36 *Thank you Father of my Lord Jesus Christ for capacity to demonstrate brotherly or sisterly love to fellow believers whose ways appear righteous, but whom I dissagree with as to their path. Thank you Father for grace to know when to insist on my own way and grace to know when to accommodate the opinions of others. Thank you Father for your assurance to me that my faith in Jesus Christ enables me reign in life in Jesus Name. Amen.*

CHAPTER 35

The essence of the Christian faith

Context: In 1Timothy 6:12, Paul tells Timothy,

> "Fight the good fight of faith, lay hold on eternal life to which you were also called and have confessed the good confession in the presence of many witnesses".

In 2Timothy 4:7, Paul states,

> "I have fought the good fight, I have finished the race, I have kept the faith. Finally there is laid up for me the crown of righteousness, which the Lord, the righteous Judge will give to me on that Day, and not to me only but also to all who have loved His appearing".

The question is: "What does it mean to fight the good fight of the faith?"

Study Outline 1

1. What must a seeker of God have? Hebrews 11:6; Romans 8:28

2. When we accept Jesus' sacrifice on our behalf, what do we receive from God? Romans 5:1-2

3. What is the link between Romans 5:3-4, and Romans 8:28?

4. What must this faith be most useful for? Galatians 3:13-14

5. What is the most important gift we receive via the Holy Spirit? Romans 5:5

NOTES 1

In order to please God, we must believe that He is and a rewarder of those who diligently seek Him. This implies we are not fazed when we face challenges because we know God will never reward us with evil while we are seeking Him diligently. How do we know this? Ephesians 2:10 states:

> For we are His workmanship, **created in Christ Jesus for good works**, which God prepared beforehand that we should walk in them.

Our understanding that we are created for good works helps us through challenges. When we reject anxiety during times within which we are experiencing challenges, we are choosing to trust God in line with the advice in Philippians 4:6-7, which states,

> Be anxious for nothing, but in every-
> thing **by prayer and supplication with
> thanksgiving** let your requests be made
> known to God, and the peace of God which
> passes all understanding will guard your
> hearts and minds through Jesus Christ.

So the manner in which we receive peace, joy, and righteousness from God is exactly the manner in which we maintain it; that is, by continuing to believe in the goodness of God which He has demonstrated in His willingness to give His only begotten Son to redeem us from sin. This is using our faith as a defense against everything that is contrary to God.

Just as in any fight there must be offensives, the manner in which we launch offensives in the Christian faith is by using our faith to receive the Holy Spirit. Why is this important? Because God says His love cannot fail and His love is received via our relationship with the Holy Spirit.

I have discussed the meaning of the phrase "Love Never Fails" in Chapter 32.

So how do we launch offensives in the good fight of faith? By walking in love that can only be received via faith in Jesus Christ.

Study Outline 2: The good fight of the faith

1. What must we add to faith so we are fruitful in our knowledge of Jesus Christ? 2Peter 5:5, 8-9

2. How would people know Jesus' disciples? John 13:35

3. What is the essence of the Christian life? Galatians 5:6

4. What are some of the weapons of our warfare? 2Corinthians 6: 6-7

5. How does 2Corinthians 6:6-7 relate to Ephesians 6:10-18?

6. When the devil tries to come into our lives what does God do? Isaiah 59:19-21 (*NKJV*)

7. What is the objective of the "good fight of faith"? 2Corinthians 10:4-5

NOTES 2

Walking in love towards people around us is the essence of the Christian life. Given we receive God's love by faith, however, it is impossible to walk in God's love without faith; hence faith that works through love (Galatians 5:6). It is our ability to maintain our walk in love that distinguishes us as Jesus' disciples.

In order to maintain this walk in love we need to put on the whole armor of God - helmet of salvation, shield of faith, equipment of the gospel of peace, the breastplate of righteousness, and the Sword of the Spirit, which is the Word of God. So we primarily destroy the enemy by speaking the Word of God. This is emphasized in Isaiah 59:19-21. Note every component of the armor of God is provided by God; we just have to be willing to put the armor on so we can fight the good fight of faith. While we are doing our part, however, the Holy Spirit is fighting alongside us, so long as we allow Him to do so by walking in purity, knowledge, patience and kindness, in the Holy Spirit, in sincere love, in truth, in the power of God, with the

armor of righteousness on the right and on the left
- 2 Corinthians 6:6-7.

The Word of God states in Ephesians 4:30-31,

> And do not grieve the Holy Spirit of
> God, by whom you were sealed for the
> day of redemption. Let all bitterness,
> wrath, anger, clamor, and evil speaking
> be put away from you, with all malice.
> And be kind to one another, tenderhearted,
> forgiving one another, even as God in
> Christ forgave you.

This verse from the Book of Ephesians makes
clear it is our actions that can grieve the Holy Spirit.
When we indulge in bitterness, anger, clamor, evil
speaking, and malice, we are in danger of grieving
the Holy Spirit. When we are not kind, tenderhearted and forgiving in our interactions, we are
in danger of grieving the Holy Spirit.

How did the Apostles actualize or activate this
concept of fighting alongside of the Holy Spirit in
Acts 4:29-30?

> "Now Lord look on their threats and
> grant to Your servants that with all bold-
> ness they may speak Your word, by stretch-
> ing out Your hand to heal, and that signs
> and wonders may be done through the
> name of your holy Servant Jesus".

As Christians, we need to acknowledge the work
of the Holy Spirit in our lives and acknowledge the
Holy Spirit as a companion who fights alongside us
and in our behalf. So while the fruit of the Spirit
is produced in us, the Holy Spirit also produces
God's victories in our lives by fighting alongside us.

Like the Apostles, however, we must be operating in faith that works through love. The reason why our fight is characterized as the "good fight of faith" is because the goal is to enable obedience to Jesus Christ and actualization of God's purposes in this life as opposed to control over other people.

Study Outline 3

﹖ What are we commanded in Galatians 6:9 and 2Thessalonians 3:13?

Notes 3

The admonition in 2Thessalonians 3:13 enables us view the command in Galatians 6:9 that we are not to be weary in well doing with the right perspective. Galatians 6:9 is at times interpreted to mean a Christian has to keep on doing good to or remain in association with people that are responding to good with evil. 2Thessalonians 3:13 shows, however, this interpretation of Galatians 6:9 is faulty.

What is the right interpretation Galatians 6:9?

A Christian should never get weary to the point where he or she begins to relate to people around him or her outside of the context of "*faith working through love*". So suppose a Christian has done good to *Person A* who has responded with evil. The Word of God is saying that if the Christian distances himself or herself from *Person A* because "two cannot walk together except they be agreed" and begins to interact with *Person B*, he or she should not adopt the attitudes of *Person A* in interactions with *Person B*. That is, the Christian should not abandon the principle of "*faith that works through love*" in interactions with *Person B* because the application of the principle in relations with *Person A* did not yield the desired fruit of a loving response.

We know this is the appropriate application of these two verses because God at some point in time distanced Himself from His own people Judah and allowed them to go to Babylon because they would not walk with Him. So where possible, distancing ourselves from people who do not respond to our love is an appropriate decision or response in interactions with other people.

Jesus instructed His disciples in this manner in Matthew 10:14,

> If anyone will not welcome you or listen
> to your words, shake the dust off your
> feet when you leave that home or town.

In these words by Jesus it is clear we are not to seek to continue to associate with people who do not respect or value our belief system.

In Jeremiah 3:8, God declares as follows concerning the nine tribes of Israel (excluding Judah, Simeon, and Levi),

> I gave faithless Israel her certificate of
> divorce and sent her away because of all
> her adulteries.

Just as divorce is righteous when it is predicated on fornication, so also God declares in His actions that we are not to seek to continue to do good to people who repay our good with evil.

How we demonstrate that we are not weary in well doing is by continuing to walk in faith that operates through love. When we distance ourselves from people that are not responding appropriately

to our love, we are inducing peace in our relationships. Suppose, however, people from whom
we had distanced ourselves repent of their actions
and draw near to us because they need our help;
what are we to do? Well, if it is our power to help,
the Word of God says to do so. We distance ourselves for the attainment of peace, not because we
are filled with hate. As a result, we are capable of
walking in love towards the same people whenever
our love is appreciated and the opportunity to love
arises.

Life Lesson 18 *We do not love people who have
characterized themselves as our enemies by associ-
ating with them; we love them by refusing to give in
to hatred and by being willing to bless them whenever the opportunity to do so presents itself.*

The Holy Spirit summarizes things this way in
Romans 12:17-21,

> Repay no one evil for evil. Have re-
> gard for good things in the sight of all
> men. If it is possible, as much as de-
> pends on you, live peaceably with all men.
> Beloved, do not avenge yourselves, but
> rather give place to wrath; for it is writ-
> ten, "Vengeance is mine, I will repay"
> says the Lord. Therefore:
> If your enemy is hungry, feed him,
> If he is thirsty, give him a drink,
> For in so doing you will heap coals of
> fire on his head.
> Do not be overcome by evil, but over-
> come evil with good.

When we are willing to help our enemies, we
are blessing them as commanded by our Lord Jesus Christ. We cannot, however, pronounce the

blessings of righteousness on people that are doing evil. That is, refusal to do evil to people who
reject our loving actions does not imply that we
do not pray for God's justice to be done on earth.
The Father of our Lord Jesus Christ delights in lovingkindness, justice, and righteousness (Jeremiah
9:23-24), meaning we also must delight in these
virtues. We are to pray that our enemies change
from their evil ways and accept God's grace as offered through our Lord Jesus Christ, as opposed
to offering prayers that imply we do not want them
to receive what is just from God based on their actions.

Recommended Prayer 37 *Thank you Father of my
Lord Jesus Christ for grace that enables me not to
get weary in love even when I have to distance myself from people who respond to my loving actions
with evil directed at me. Thank you Father of my
Lord Jesus Christ for grace to acknowledge the Holy
Spirit so He can fight alongside me and for me according to your word. Thank you Father for grace to
put off unrighteous attitudes or actions, and grace
to bring forth the fruit of the Spirit to the glory of
your holy name. Thank you Father that your Love
Never Fails. In Jesus Name. Amen.*

CHAPTER 36

Concluding Remarks

The contradictions that we sought to resolve at the beginning of this series of lessons revolve around the following main issue:

> While 1Corinthians 13 enables an understanding of what love is, it does nothing to teach us which attributes of love are most appropriate in any given situation. I illustrated this conundrum with the following questions or scenarios:

✠ When is it better to be patient and kind vis-a-vis emphasizing the truth? Why is this important? Because the Word of God says "truth is to be spoken in love" - Ephesians 4:15, meaning rejoicing in the truth (an attribute of love in 1Corinthians 13) is not independent of

patience, kindness, or every other attribute of
love.

✠ Is it ever okay for love not to protect, trust,
hope, or persevere? If a parent turns in a
son or daughter who has never been involved
in evil but whom they think or believe is planning evil to civil authorities, are they not walking in love because they are not protecting,
trusting, hoping, or persevering in beliefs about
the good character of their son or daughter?

✠ When a spouse gives up on a marriage, are
they violating the requirement of perseverance
and hence not walking in love?

Well, the essence of these lessons is to develop
principles that can be applied to determining appropriate courses of actions in different situations.
By applying these principles you will be better able
to determine appropriate courses of action in different situations. Based on these principles, I have
my views on answers to the three questions posed
above, answers that are explicit or implicit in this
treatise on what it means to have faith in the name
of Jesus Christ. I hope you arrive at the same answers based on applications of principles I have
discussed in this treatise. More importantly, I hope
you arrive at the right answers in applications of
these principles in your personal situations.

In summary, the principles we have discussed
in this Epilogue are:

**The overarching principle of submis-
sion to guidance by the Holy Spirit**

and the following specific principles:

1. The principle that you do not hand over your coat to an enemy unless you are assured by God of realizations of joy consequent on that course of action; this was the case for both Job and our Lord Jesus Christ

2. The principle that you should walk two miles instead of one with a friend or enemy whenever walking two miles brings more glory to God, the Father of our Lord Jesus Christ.

3. The principle that our response to persecution is to attempt to live at peace with people around us to the extent to which it is in our power. When we flee affliction, we are enduring affliction and at the same time resisting affliction. But the Holy Spirit reserves the right to direct us otherwise. Remember, while all other disciples were scattered from Jerusalem, the Apostles remained in the place where believers were being persecuted. So flee affliction where possible; and endure while resisting affliction when fleeing is not possible

4. The principle that it is okay to quit without completing an objective when God says to move on to something else; why? Because our metrics for success are at times not God's metrics for success

5. The principle that we are allowed to be angry with and not pray for our enemies while we are still requesting for strength from our Lord Jesus Christ in order to be able to obey His command to love them and not be bitter towards them; the goal is to allow the Holy Spirit heal our hurt so we do not remain angry or bitter, but instead are capable of lov-

ing people with whom we do not associate because they do not agree with us

6. The principle that we should insist on our
   own way when we are in submission to God
   and doing His will as He has directed us

7. The principle that the outcome of righteousness is peace - either peace that comes from
   agreement or peace that results from recognition of and respect for different choices

8. The principle of faith in God's goodness that
   works by love; the principle that the Holy Spirit
   fights alongside us so long as we are walking
   in faith that operates by love

   I pray you will reap the blessings that are ours
in Jesus Christ as we by His grace live in this world
in the power of the Holy Spirit. In Jesus Name.
Amen.

Made in the USA
Monee, IL
14 September 2021